D0386641

03

ALIENS IN AMERICA

Peter Augustine Lawler

ALIENS IN AMERICA

The Strange Truth about Our Souls

ISI BOOKS

Wilmington, Delaware • 2002

Cataloging-in-Publication Data:

Lawler, Peter Augustine
        Aliens in America: the strange truth about our souls / Peter Augustine Lawler.
    —1st ed.—Wilmington, Del. : ISI Books, 2002.

        p. ; cm.

    ISBN 1-882926-71-4
        1. Social change—United States. 2. Social history. 3. United States—Social conditions. I. Title

HN59.2 .L39 2002   2001097015
303.4—dc21   CIP

Published in the United States by:

    ISI Books
    Post Office Box 4431
    Wilmington, DE 19807-0431
    www.isibooks.org

                Interior book design by Claudia L. Henrie
                Manufactured in the United States of America

Contents

This book was completed prior to the unprecedented events of September 11, 2001. In one day, new enemies managed to kill more Americans on our own soil than the Nazis and communists ever did. We must ask what this threat to our "homeland" will do to the American idea of liberty. Will it alter or even reverse the libertarian and therapeutic drifts in American life that I describe here? Certainly there has been an upsurge in patriotism and respect for our government. Americans have been forcefully reminded of their continued dependence on their nation and its political life. But we also seem to have reasonable confidence in our government to contain the terrorist threat with little sacrifice on the part of most citizens. Our leaders assure us that there is no need to reinstitute the draft, and when the president talks of the sacrifice of citizens he has thus far mainly meant only some inconvenience at airports.

The truth is that the evidence is mixed, and we do not know what is going to happen. It might be that the greatest threat to the future of human liberty is not a mixture of modern principles with biotechnology, as I claim in the introductory chapter, but our increasing vulnerability to the use of destructive technology against us by the enemies of modern life. And one long-term lesson of this book might turn out to be that bourgeois bohemian virtue was really a lullaby that kept Americans unprepared for both challenges they were about to face. It might also be, of course, that the terrorist threat seems to us today to be far more formidable than it will really turn out to be, at least for a while. Much depends on the character and timing of the inevitable second attack, which may have occurred before you read these words. So far, we have to note a contradiction: There has been a significant change in American opinion, but very little change in American behavior.

This book developed over a number of years, and I depended on the help of a large number of people. I can mention only a few here. Several Berry College students helped with the proofing, including David Ramsey, Michael Rupert, and Elizabeth Prince. Paul Seaton carefully assessed every word of each chapter and saved me from many errors. Jeremy Beer of ISI Books has been a meticulous, enthusiastic, and imaginative editor. The confidence and encouragement of Mark Henrie and Jeff Nelson are the reasons I chose ISI Books as my publisher. There would have been no book without the hard work and many skills of Diane Land. Her patience and attentiveness to detail are genuinely remarkable.

There would also be no book without the generous support I have received over the years from the Earhart Foundation.

Thanks to Rowman and Littlefield, Lexington Books, William B. Eerdmans Publishing, *Society, Modern Age,* the *Weekly Standard,* and *Perspectives on Political Science* for permission to reprint earlier versions of material found here.

My greatest debts are to Catherine and Rita.

Bobo Virtue
and the Future of Human Liberty

*A*liens in America* is meant to be an enticing title. It calls to mind what may have been a pretty bad—though certainly an incredibly trendy and successful—Broadway show, *Angels in America*. About that show I know little and will say even less, except that I wouldn't mind being trendy and successful too. Aliens also call to mind the American fascination with the possibility of invasion by extraterrestrials in the years immediately following the Cold War. The blockbuster film *Independence Day*, for example, though exhilarating and entertaining, was quite farfetched. There's no evidence that we need fear an invasion of murderous, parasitical extraterrestrials. The more thoughtful *Men in Black*, in fact, was closer to the mark: the aliens are already here, and they are hard to manage. But most of them really aren't such bad guys.

My title really comes from a question Walker Percy had about the great popularizing scientist Carl Sagan: Why did Sagan spend his time searching the cosmos for aliens when beings stranger than any extraterrestrials we could imagine are right here on earth? Percy's view of the human being as essentially an alien is, of course, Christian. As St. Augustine says, we are pilgrims or aliens in this world because our true home is somewhere else. Homelessness is a fundamental human experience, and the best human beings can hope for is to become ambiguously at home in this world by coming to terms with that ineradicable experience.

We are, in fact, aliens. But the goal of modern philosophy and science has been to transform our condition so as to make us completely at home. That is, the philosophers have aimed to bring history to an end, to create a world in which human beings will live in abundance and contentment while having to do very little work. Marxist revolution tried to create that world, and failed. But some say that good government, the free market, and technology have brought it to America. The average American, as the novelist Tom Wolfe observes, now lives the utopia imagined only by the wildest of the nineteenth-century social theorists.

And yet the truth is that Americans may be less happy, may experience themselves as more lonely and displaced, than ever. The needs of the body are met, but at the expense of the needs of the soul. We aliens are stranger and more troubled than ever. The essays in this book both chronicle that strangeness and criticize American views of liberty that deny, in one way or another, that the alien does or must exist. I am especially concerned with the most recent projects to actually change human nature—a sort of alien extermination program. But rather than repeat here the arguments I make in later chapters, I want to provide what amounts to a cultural and political supplement to them. Here is how Americans appear to me now.

Bourgeois Bohemians

David Brooks has named America's new ruling class the bourgeois bohemians. Members of this class are generally too politically apathetic actually to hold political office, but neither they nor we are so naïve as to believe that George W. Bush sets the tone for our nation. The bourgeois bohemian, or Bobo, is now the model American. The model American town is the Bobo's kind of town, what Brooks calls the Latte Town—for example, Burlington, Vermont. Most towns are still not much like Burlington, but most towns now have latte sections, which are deemed the most advanced or *livable* parts of town.

In attempting to understand this new ruling class, I draw upon the excellent recent books to which Brooks himself refers, such as Francis Fukuyama's *The Great Disruption* and Alan Wolfe's *One Nation, After All*. I have also learned from what amounts to a slight updating and revision of Brooks's thesis in a broader context, Dinesh D'Souza's *The Virtue of Prosperity*, and from the most astute and amusing essays collected in Tom Wolfe's *Hooking Up*.[1] But in some measure, I play fast and loose with all these books in the service of my own view of the place of virtue in American life now and in the near future.

The Bobos exist somewhere between the merely middle-class Americans Alan Wolfe describes and the pathbreaking technological entrepreneurs D'Souza describes. It would appear, at first, that our rulers are D'Souza's entrepreneurs. But men like Bill Gates and Steve Jobs (of Apple), D'Souza observes, are too narrowly obsessed with their work and too inarticulate to be American models. Such genuinely extraordinary human beings often believe and even admit that their lives would be meaningless without their work, and the rest of their lives are, in fact, usually messes. The Bobos—existing just below the technological entrepreneurs on the scales of raw brilliance, power, and wealth—are more articulate and admirable. They live more balanced lives, and they work hard, but not at the expense of family, community involvement, and spiritual life. They give voice to the aspirations of our time. According to Alan Wolfe, our expert on the middle class, we are all Bobos now: even secretaries have gurus and personal trainers. Tom Wolfe reports that he has seen working-class Bobos too—air-conditioning mechanics and burglar-alarm repairmen drinking Quibel sparkling water, rejecting with disdain Perrier and San Pellegrino.

The bourgeois virtues Bobos have include personal responsibility, productivity, the willingness to sacrifice for comfortable self-preservation, and aversion to conflict and war. Their bohemian or antiestablishment virtues include the subordination of money to human fulfillment, disdain for conspicuous consumption, refusal to put on airs or lord it over others, and concern with spirituality and human wholeness. The Bobos identify taste with simplicity, and so they use their money for beautiful but subdued bathrooms and vacations to the rain forest, not for pink Cadillacs and power boats. But they do not confuse simple with tacky or cheap; they have made plain but pricey Shaker furniture trendy. The bourgeois cared about money, and the bohemians fulfillment, but the Bobos know that one is not possible without the other. While they subordinate wealth to a humanly worthy life, they know better than to try to live without money.

Bourgeois Aristotelians?

It seems sometimes that the Bobos are Aristotelians. To act virtuously, Aristotle remarks, we need equipment, and money is an evil only if we regard it as an end, not a means. Money is for the practice of virtue, to show one's class or excellence, and the Bobos do spend to show their class. But the beginning of virtue, for Aristotle, is courage, and the Bobos seem to have no opportunity to act courageously. Nor do they long for such opportunities; tales of warriors do not particularly move them. They have an amused contempt for middle America's love of the WWF and the NHL. The members of the WASP ruling class that preceded them, such as George Bush the elder, willingly fought in their nation's wars. The bohemians, such as young Bill Clinton, claimed to have found a certain nobility in evading unjust service. But the Bobos are not called to military service, nor do they think about serving. War and even hunting are not for thinking men and women today.

Aristotle also says that human beings fulfill themselves through political activity, but the Bobos disagree. They do not think of themselves much as citizens, and they only rarely have an interest in entering public service. They have little sense of civic duty, and even less *noblesse oblige*. Because their privileges are based on merit, on brains and hard work, they do not believe they owe others much of anything. John McCain's presidential campaign reminded us that there is some connection between military service and public service, and Bobos were surely attracted, if only weakly, to his call to serve a cause higher than self-interest. But his only specific reform proposal concerned campaign financing, and the implementation of this reform, obviously, would require no virtue from citizens. Nor do the Bobos, despite their perfect political correctness, march in civil rights demonstrations for blacks and gays; injustice is for students of history. The Manhattan Bobos all too obviously had no interest in bringing Giuliani down (even prior to September 11, 2001), and even Florida Bobos didn't feel the need to cancel a few appointments to keep Bush from stealing the election that they believed African-American Floridians had really won for Gore.

Bobos, in fact, have little reason to be interested in genuine political reform. They are, as members of the ruling class, for practical purposes conservative. They are even theoretically conservative. They are not attracted to utopian political fantasies; their utopia is already here. They are less narcissists than they are individualists, in Tocqueville's sense—apolitical beings confined to a narrow circle of family, friends, and professional associates.

Fukuyama, on an uncharacteristically cynical day, said that the real spirit of the 1990s was a combination of crass materialism and other forms of selfish individualism with the constant proclamation of good intentions. He had, of course, Bill Clinton foremost in mind. Good intentions are exhibited through right opinions on race, class, gender, the environment, and so forth, and almost all Americans with even a touch of sophistication are politically correct now. But I must disagree with Fukuyama. The Bobos are, in their way, more idealistic than their president was; they wanted to be and to do good. The problem is that they lack the moral toughness required to feel moved to perform even small and personal deeds by virtue of right opinions. Clinton himself toughed out two terms, which is no mean feat in our time. He also accomplished some significant reforms, the effect of which were to make the world more safe for Bobos. The president's most intelligent opponents—compassionate or cultural conservatives and compassionate or old-fashioned liberals—fear most of all the coming of a world in which the Bobos would feel even more comfortable being politically and socially irresponsible.

Bobo Christians?

Sometimes the Bobos seem to be Christians. They are critics of the militant atheism characteristic of much of the twentieth century, and they admit they crave the comfort and meaning provided by religious ritual and community. It is hard to raise children without the help of something like a church, and it is harder still to live in solitary denial of the spiritual side of the human lot. So the Bobos have returned to church and synagogue. But they want to combine the advantages of communal authority with those of personal liberation. They reject Christian doctrine concerning, say, sexual morality, because it makes them feel uncomfortably restricted and unnecessarily guilty. In general they expect their religious communities to make on them only minimal personal demands. They don't think about personal salvation, sin, divine judgment, or about whether the personal God of the Bible really exists. They don't even think much about the differences between Christian and Buddhist belief. Atheists hold them in contempt. The Bobo view is that to take a stand for or against God is just too hard. Bobos privilege comfort over truth, and they call true whatever makes them comfortable. Yet their lack of concern for the truth, more than anything else, is what impoverishes their spiritual life.

Because the Bobos do not concern themselves with a personal God, they cannot practice Christian virtue. Charity, of course, and not chastity, is a distinctively Christian virtue. But not only are Bobos not animated by *noblesse oblige*, they do nothing out of love for God. The Bobo is not cruel or hateful toward others, but perhaps that is because his or her heart is not easily moved in any direction. The libertarian Bobos believe, without flaunting it, that they deserve what they have, and that what they owe to the unfortunate is nothing more than not to contribute to their degradation. The Clintonized or Boboized Democratic Party has abandoned its special commitment to the poor, and Bobo spirituality is quite distant from the formerly fashionable theology of liberation, with its activist preferential option for the poor. Evangelical and especially Pentecostal churches today genuinely reach out to the poor, but the Bobos prefer the New Agey serenity that comes with inner fulfillment.

Conservatives might applaud the Bobos for their realization that misguided government programs are no substitute for personal charity, and Christians will agree that charitable, activist communities of faith, much more than impersonal government, effectively curb the selfish excesses of bourgeois society. But Bobo houses of worship do not inspire personal charity, and they seem actually to contribute to bourgeois indifference to the plight of others. In this respect, our leading professor of philosophy, Richard Rorty, already seems reactionary and ineffectual. He calls upon rich American bourgeois liberals to use a portion of their great wealth in a fairly painless effort to alleviate the cruel suffering of others. Rorty hopes that leftist intellectuals like him will inspire the new ruling class to restore the old or genuinely liberal-socialist-progressive Democratic Party. But the astutely pro-Bobo intellectual D'Souza laughs and asks, "Rip van Rorty, where have you been?"

For the Bobos do not share the Christian view that the poor are especially favored by God. In today's unprecedented meritocracy, poverty is viewed as less a matter of oppression or bad luck and more as evidence of an individual's quarrelsomeness, laziness, or stupidity. As D'Souza observes, those professions that used to combine poverty with pride or soulful dignity—professors and the clergy—have been left behind in the information age. Poverty today, the techno-Bobos might retort, is, thanks to hard and smart work by people like themselves, far less of a material deprivation than it used to be. Very few Americans today are malnourished or cold, and those called poor often have DVD players and air conditioning. Being poor is more humiliating than ever, however, because it is harder to blame the rich for one's condition, and because it is hard to see virtue in choosing a miserable condition that really might be avoided.

The old bohemians were, in this respect, more Christian than the Bobos. They lived as if there were dignity in poverty. They weren't at all sensible about money; they joined Socrates in irresponsible neglect of themselves and their own. They were antibourgeois in a most unrealistic and often self-destructive way. (We can think here of the alcoholism, drug addiction, and suicide that have plagued great artists, but we should also not forget Tocqueville's extreme example of Pascal, whom he presents as having thought himself to death before he was forty.) Christianity really is, in large measure, antibourgeois. Truth and charity take precedence over comfort, and Christians are called not to get too comfortable or too at home in this world. I am not saying, of course, that the old bohemians were particularly humble or charitable (think Socrates again). Their arrogant claims in the absence of productivity could usually, with good reason, be dismissed as nothing more than a distraction from the real business of life. But their privileging of soulful misery over bodily comfort did point us in the direction of the saints. A world without any poor or any pure bohemians would surely be one without saints. Brooks admits that the Bobos, despite their participation in a spiritual revival of sorts, inhabit a spiritually impoverished world. He does not go as far as Mother Teresa, who said that affluent Americans are poorer in the most important respects than the poorest of Calcutta's poor.

Bobo Marxists?

At history's end, Marx predicts, the division of labor will disappear, economic scarcity will be overcome, and human needs will be met easily. Human beings will be free to do what they please without being determined or limited by any particular activity. I can hunt in the morning, fish in the afternoon, and philosophize in the evening, without becoming a hunter, fisher, or philosopher. Marx seems, at first, to mean that we will choose our activity according to some human purpose. But in the absence of economic necessity, the materialist Marx cannot identify any such purpose. So all he can say is that at the end of history we will be able to do whatever we want whenever we want. All human activities will assume the status of hobbies. To call them more than that calls to mind the necessities of scarcity, and they will have been overcome. I must philosophize without becoming a philosopher (or obsessed with the truth) to show that I am really unalienated.

The Bobos, in what they expect or demand for life, clearly believe that they live at the end of history. They are bourgeois, not revolutionary, Marxists, because they believe that what Marx hoped would be achieved through revolution has been achieved without it. The Bobos believe they can live as if all life were a hobby, but they don't think that a hobby is passing the time to no purpose. Work must be meaningful. It must be performed non-hierarchically so that every individual can regard his activity as a whole. The division of labor is outmoded. It was characteristic of the industrial age, but it does not describe the information age. Lots of money can be made without doing anything we wouldn't have chosen to do anyway, and we can be rich without exploiting others. No necessity compels us to work, but we work because it fulfills us. And so the distinction between job and hobby is obsolete.

The Bobo world is clearly more weighty than Marx's end of history. Every moment of the Bobo's life must be educational, lucrative, purposeful, enjoyable, and beautiful. And so, the Bobo, as Brooks observes, never stops thinking. He calculates about everything. His children are always busy, his vacations educational and edifying, and his mind is never lost in food, drink, or sex. Yet he must always be having fun. The casualness that is real in Marx's vision is largely feigned in the Bobo's. He wants to leave as little as possible to chance. He is too much of a control freak for us really to believe that he is unalienated. The bourgeois view of the hobby is really a moral imperative: it's not that all of life *is* a hobby, but that all of life *should* be.

Many middle-class and most working-class Americans regard work as a harsh necessity, but that necessary misery doesn't travel with them to their homes, neighborhood bars, or churches. One advantage of being an oppressed wage slave is that one is not always a slave. But the Bobo is both always at work and always at play; his life is a whole. Strictly speaking, he has no time off at all. His life is a work of art that must be constantly and consciously cultivated. The eradication of the distinction between leisure and work seems to be a complete victory for work. Neither the Bobo nor his children ever has a moment to sit under a tree, completely immersed in the present, enjoying the sweet sentiment of existence. Unlike a merely middle-class American, he would regard such an indulgence as irresponsible. Bobo life, in this respect, seems tougher than life has ever been, and the unprecedented dimensions of this choice of calculation over immediate enjoyment can rightly be called a very demanding form of bourgeois virtue. Compelled as we are to admire this virtue, we must also allow the passing, Christian suspicion that the Bobos have mistaken hell for paradise. Bobo virtue is the virtue of aliens, not of beings at home in the world. Or is it, as Walker Percy says, the perversity of aliens who cannot, or will not, see themselves for what they are?

Bobo Hobbesians?

Bobo life brings to light the most obvious problem with Marxian theory, which is the view that scarcity is material scarcity. So if human beings have plenty of stuff with little work, they will be unalienated or satisfied. But we now know that the overcoming of material deprivation does not free us from necessity. We still grow old and die, and in fact we might die at any moment. We suffer, as Whit Stillman writes, from decade scarcity; the fundamental scarcity is time. As long as we are conscious beings, the way we exist will be determined to some extent or another by the necessity of death. And the more comfort and security we have—the more we have to lose—the more that necessity haunts us. One way we divert ourselves from that harsh truth is mistakenly to view death as an avoidable accident. We need not die if we live reasonably or safely. That attitude, as Hobbes explains, is in some measure reasonable. We will, with any luck, live longer if we make thinking about safety our first priority. But Marx was clearly wrong that the end of history would bring satisfaction, for at history's end death seems more of a problem than ever before.

The Bobos claim not to be obsessed with death. They display a casual attitude toward work and time, and they have some spiritual solace. They also appear not to think or talk much about their finitude or possible immortality. So convincing is their talk that writers such as Allan Bloom came to believe that human beings are no longer moved by death at all. But what Bloom was really observing were Bobos, or proto-Bobos, following Rorty's advice: those hoping to put death to death by not talking about it. Yet the Bobos soon discovered that Rorty's linguistic solution does not work much better than Marx's economic one. Not talking about death is not enough. A real pragmatist works hard against it. He mouths

Rorty's therapeutic platitudes while on the treadmill and conspicuously and faithfully abstaining from carbohydrates. The Bobo's regimen of exercise is his one activity that he does not even pretend is always fun. Health is no hobby; it's a necessity, and so it must be cultivated in the most scientific and disciplined way.

The Bobos reject the repressive morality of traditional religion; they are libertarians or nonjudgmentalists on almost everything. When it comes to the soul, they are *laissez faire*. But when it comes to the body, to health and safety, they are toughly intolerant moralists. They are pro-choice when it comes to abortion. But when it comes to seat belts and smoking, there ought to be a law. And safe sex ought to be taught in the schools. It is unrealistic, they say, for our young people to practice chastity. But when it comes to drunkenness and obesity they can and should just say no. Getting fat will kill you, but safe sex, had with anyone and in any way, won't. As Brooks reports, Bobos see no reason not to engage in extra-marital sadomasochism, as long as it is in a safe, structured, and consensual environment.

The Bobos believe that life can and should be both safe and spicy. They prefer both designer sex and designer food. They don't stuff their faces like animals. And their safe and productivity-inducing beverage of choice, coffee, gets better and more exotic every day under their watchful eye.

But the absurdity of all "safe sex" is displayed in neon letters with the idea of safe S&M. What do we do to eros when we calculate so much about it? Conservatives thought that the sexual liberation of the 1960s would destroy civilization. But we now know that the real enemy of sexual liberation is eros. Safe S&M is the price to be paid for the moral imperative that all of life ought to be a hobby. Kinkiness is deprived of its properly perverse pleasure, which comes from being both risky business and sinful. But we can't say that there's *nothing* perverse about Bobo sex, for it's certainly not the open and casual sexuality that Marx anticipated we would enjoy under communism. (As Tom Wolfe reports, the word "perversion" has lost its meaning among our sophisticates. But what can we call the man he describes as hopelessly lost in the world of S&M cybersex—maybe the safest and most disconnected, but still far from open and casual, form of sex imaginable?)

Consider what the demand for safe sex implies: The right and duty to engage in the pleasurable activity without the dangers of disease, reproduction, or risky personal or genuinely erotic connection with another human being. We have to sunder the age-old connections between sex and both birth and love, because they both bring death to mind. Our natural desire to procreate, when thought about, is a choice for our replacement and demise. Our choice to separate sex from procreation is an effort to calculate out of existence the goods that constitute distinctively human beings.

Safe sex cannot be open and casual; it requires *planning*. We cannot thoughtlessly give way to our natural instinct, lest we forget to apply what we've learned about dressing up vegetables. Something of our distinctive humanity remains; no other animal uses condoms. But the perfection of safe sex would be the biological alteration of man, woman, or both, so that reproduction would be impossible.

Another way to appreciate the unprecedented premium the Bobos place on health and safety is to compare them with the WASP establishment of the 1950s and early 1960s. Those men were public spirited, willingly fought in wars, drank martinis at both lunch and dinner, rarely exercised unless they enjoyed it, and were hardly ever without a cigarette. And when they fooled around, they really were living rather dangerously. Compared to the Bobos, they spent their lives laughing in the face of death. Because they took their souls or duties more seriously, they were less obsessed with their bodies. They were more aristocratic and less bourgeois than our Bobos.

Thomas Jefferson hoped that a "natural aristocracy" of talent and virtue would come to rule America. The Bobos are a kind of natural aristocracy; they rule on the basis of their brains and hard work, using well what they have been given by nature. In that respect, they are better than their WASP predecessors, who often inherited their privileges and weren't particularly smart or industrious. (From this perspective, President George W. Bush is a pre-Bobo throwback.) But the Bobos have not really united talent and virtue. The WASPs were, in fact, more courageous and charitable, not to mention far more politically responsible.

The Bobo view tends to be that brains, health, fashionable tastes, and politically correct views are the whole of virtue. So we cannot help but wonder how admirable they would be if suddenly they were caught without money or had to fight for their freedom. They are so impressed with their accomplishments that they try not to acknowledge how dependent they are on forces beyond their control. But with Brooks's help, we see how anxious they really are. If status is based on brains and work alone, then it is all too easy to lose, and when you fall you fall hard, with no safety net provided by friends, family, class, or even government. The Bobos' anxiety, which they try to alleviate without much success through their spirituality, is, in fact, a piece of welcome evidence that they experience themselves as aliens in this world.

There is, don't get me wrong, real virtue in being fit and healthy. Those conservatives who have returned to smoking and martinis as acts of rebellion are rather ridiculous. But when morality or virtue is reduced to safety, we have to wonder whether there is any remaining capacity for love and friendship. Social life, as Fukuyama writes, has returned, meaning parental and communal concern. But few seem to have noticed Fukuyama's qualification that it has done so with diminished passion and attenuated commitment. The breaking of the connection between sex and procreation has aided the health and freedom of women, but surely at the expense of love. The mother's natural connection to her children remains strong, but the role of the father, which seems to depend on the mother's love, continues to weaken. Friendship or association with others persists, but Alan Wolfe notices that it, like everything else human, seems more calculated or "instrumental" than ever. Love of God and love of the truth, among the Bobos, are in bigger trouble still, as is love of country and one's fellow citizens.

The Bobos and Biotechnological Progress

With their prudent self-discipline, which has, of course, allowed them to accumulate their wealth, the Bobos have, on average, extended their lives almost a decade. And that's just the beginning! Advances in biotechnology will very soon add a couple of more decades at least, with the not-so-remote possibility of doubling or tripling the typical human lifespan lurking on the horizon. Seemingly sane scientists say that something like immortality—indefinite longevity—is a quite reasonable goal over the next century. Why would the Bobos not welcome this remarkable progress? There are, nonetheless, very good human reasons to choose against it. With the disappearance of death must come the banning of birth. So sex really will come to have nothing at all to do with reproduction. Would human life really be worth living if it were completely free from the hard and joyous responsibilities of birth and parenting? That question still makes sense to many of us, but maybe least of all to our Bobos. And it is easy to see that it may make no sense at all to the Bobos of the future.

Marriage, in the sense of a monogamous, life-long commitment, would no longer make sense in the future our scientists imagine and our Bobos welcome. The remaining heterosexual unions, as Andrew Sullivan predicts, would take on the promiscuous and transitory qualities of most "gay marriages." Already prosperous, articulate, and artistic gays are the most advanced Bobos. Perhaps the process of love's domestication would accelerate almost to the point of love's disappearance. Perhaps our activities really would come to have no more weight than hobbies. Necessity or scarcity of time causes us to rank our activities, to take them seriously, even in the midst of abundance. What would happen if we no longer knew that we faced decade scarcity?

The fear that has existed since Tocqueville wrote is that this sort of progress will lead individuals to surrender the details of their lives to a providential schoolmaster state. As individuals get smaller or less virtuous, the thinking goes, government must get bigger. But we also remember that Marx thought differently: With the overcoming of scarcity and the division of labor, the state will wither away. And libertarians actually agree with Marx that the state is no longer necessary, that human beings are social but not political animals. One reason the Bobos are not political activists is that government now seems more irrelevant than ever to human endeavors. Everyone with any brains is for the free market now, and so for globalization and against nationalism. (Whatever we might want to say about his moral weakness and contempt for virtue, we must admit that Bill Clinton is *the* brainy Democrat.) Those in the know seem to believe the state is withering away.

Libertarians say that biotechnological breakthroughs will not be weapons in the hands of some tyrannical government because they will be made in the private sector and made available to private individuals. They will be like all the other designer features of life. We will be able to choose them or not, as we please.

But for the Bobos, choosing against biotechnological breakthroughs would be like choosing against health. Who wouldn't choose the best available body and brain for his or her child? The brain as much as the body is a mechanism for comfortable self-preservation. Can the law really allow perverse choices against what is best for any of our children? D'Souza, generally a supporter of biotechnological innovation, draws the line at designing our children, calling that tyranny. We can choose for ourselves an indefinitely long and safe life, but apparently not for them. But surely we have the right and duty to choose health for our children if we can, and every biotechnological innovation can be seen as, at least in part, promoting health and safety. We cannot, in some perverse fashion, will that our children be unnecessarily malformed. From this perspective, every choice against biotechnology is irresponsible, uncaring tyranny.

The Bobos are nonjudgmental on every issue but health and fashion, and so they cannot oppose mere self-preservation with some higher principle. They are not well positioned to consider what human beings lose as a result of the scientific overcoming of what used to be regarded as the limits of their natures. The choice against, for example, indefinite longevity would have to be *against* self-preservation and *for* virtue, love, birth, and death. And I don't see the Bobos having the perspective or the guts to make that hard, courageous, and charitable choice. The anticommunist dissidents Aleksandr Solzhenitsyn and Václav Havel said that the defeat of communism, or the lie, was a victory for human nature and the responsibility given to human beings to live well in light of the truth. But now, apparently, human nature can be changed. The human tendency the dissidents criticized, which is too often to prefer comfortable lies to harsh truth, seems again to be winning out. The problem is that among the Bobos both religion and the state do seem to be withering away.

Not so long ago I read an article by the anti-tax activist Grover Norquist which sought to remind us that the Democratic Party is not primarily stupid but "evil." The Democrats, he claimed, are the party of "coercive utopianism." That phrase, of course, was used to describe the totalitarian regimes of the twentieth century. But say what you will about Bill Clinton, he is no coercive utopian! As president, he put his faith far more in the market than in government planning. And communism, as everyone knows, has been discredited everywhere except in the minds of a few professors. Rip van Norquist is even more out of touch than Rorty!

Dare I say that the danger to human liberty now is far more "anticoercive" than "coercive" utopianism? Both the anticoercive (meaning libertarian) and coercive (meaning Marxist) utopians share the goal of the withering away of the state. We now know that withering will certainly not happen via the revolution Marx described. The old libertarians defended human liberty when they favored the restoration of some freer moment in America's past and whined that history was not on their side. They also served liberty with their anticommunism. But now they believe that the progress of history or technology will make their dream a reality, and they call their opponents, as the Marxists used to do, enemies of the future. The designer future our libertarians have in mind, whether they know it or not, will be without the distinctively human passions and responsibilities that constitute human liberty.

Conservatives are now defined, or at least ought to be defined, by their opposition to unfettered libertarianism and technological progress. They insist that technology be subordinated to human purposes, and they realize that the moral and political limitation of technology will require political coercion. When it comes to abortion, euthanasia, cloning, cyberporn, and so forth, conservatives are now statists. They see that libertarianism is culminating in a misanthropic form of compassion, undergirded by the hope that technology can liberate us altogether from human suffering by overcoming what had wrongly been regarded as ineradicable limits to human choice. As President George W. Bush explained in his fine inaugural address, conservatives now are distinguished by their defense of the virtue of beings who can be not only compassionate but also courageous, and who can acknowledge their necessary and beneficial dependence on God.

Tom Wolfe, once again, is on the cutting edge of contemporary social analysis in his assessment of the significance of the change from *nurture* or *social construction* to *nature* or *genetics* in explaining human behavior and destiny at the dawn of the twenty-first century. The view of the Marxists, for example, was that human beings are historical beings, and so they should work to better their historical situation. The capitalists, in their own way, also had that view. The point is not to understand the world, but to change it. The Marxist social constructionists vastly overestimated what change could occur through political revolution, and their frustration caused all sorts of gratuitous and insane violence. But hope in the power of human beings to shape history also produced remarkable exertions by human individuals, and Americans, in particular, really thought they were working in pursuit of happiness.

With all its deficiencies, modern faith in social or historical transformation ennobled Americans, who worked hard to make the world better. They believed, perhaps incoherently, that such change depended on personal virtue, on self-discipline. But the biologists now tell us that such effort cannot overcome our natural fate; even our chances for happiness are mostly genetic. So the transformation we seek has to come from biotechnology, a transformation that will, in fact, obliterate the need for virtue. Given what neuroscience and allied disciplines have taught us, it seems that the choice for virtue now is the choice for illusion and unnecessary misery. That is why the Bobos, who, as Brooks reports, refuse to think about big questions like the nature and destiny of man, have neither the theoretical nor practical point of view that would allow them to choose against the experts and for virtue—even for their own hard work and personal responsibility. They cannot even defend their own way of life, because they would rather be freed from their alienation, from their anxiety. The big question now is who can defend the view that we should live well with what we have been given by nature and God, even if our experts tell us that what we have been given can be changed? Who will defend the greatness and misery of the alien, the distinctively human being?

That defense emphatically does not and will not come from sociobiologists such as Fukuyama. Their view of returning to nature does not include a return to the teaching of classical thinkers such as Plato and Aristotle. For the classical philosophers, human beings are political animals who also long to know the truth about all things, and our sociobiologists certainly do not see either the *polis* or *philosophy* making a come-back. Nor do they even attempt to describe the recovery of eros or love in the classical—or for that matter, polymorphous—sense. Their return to nature is even less a return to the natural law of St. Thomas Aquinas. These experts, in truth, do not see any evidence that nature was created, or that human beings long to know and love their Creator.

Our biological or sociobiological thinkers today understand the re-turn to nature as a return to the idea that human beings are truly at home in nature. This understanding is closer to Rousseau's idea of the return to nature, of the advent of the posthistorical being who is essentially no different from other animals. Our sociobiologists differ from Rousseau in seeing man as really, if rather weakly, naturally social, and in saying that the return to nature will not require the abolition of technology or a return to prescientific stupidity. Rousseau understood human alienation as historical or unnatural, but our scientists know better. They believe that our return to nature will actually be an alteration of nature; it will be the overcoming of natural alienation through biotechnology. But the disagreements between the biotechnologists and Rousseau, finally, are over details. Our biotechnologists aim to alter nature so that we will become productive animals unmoved by love, God, the truth, or death. The Bobos, properly treated, will become clever animals and nothing more. They believe they can achieve Rousseau's vision of natural good-ness by changing our natures to make it so.

One seemingly ineradicable limit to the biotechnological alteration of nature is that we will continue to die. Biotechnology, in the long run, will not be able to satisfy our bourgeois desire for comfortable security. But as Tom Wolfe argues, biotechnology promises not only to preserve and enhance bodies, but to change minds. We need not be moved by our awareness of death; our thoughts and moods are mere chemical responses that can be altered with other chemicals. What we now do quite imper-fectly with Ritalin and Prozac we will soon be able to do more predictably and more easily with better chemicals. But Walker Percy, the novelist, contended that we have a right to our anxiety; it is not a symptom to be eradicated but a sign or gateway to the truth about our purpose as human beings. To be born, to live, according to Percy, is to be alienated, to be lost or displaced in the cosmos.

Peter Kramer, in *Listening to Prozac*, challenged Percy's privileging of bad over good moods. A pill, in truth, can change our very being. Prozac causes us not to be zoned out Nietzschean "last men," but intelligent, reflective, and productive human beings—and always in a good mood. It can take the edge—the virtue—off being a Bobo. If our moods are in our control, what right do we have to choose bad ones? That would be like choosing certain death over indefinite longevity. We might have no more Pascals, Nietzsches, or even Reinhold Niebuhrs (the theologian of the old WASP establishment), but it turns out that they have nothing to teach us anymore anyway. The philosophic or literary propensity—we might say the bohemian propensity—to be miserable in God's absence has nothing but a chemical—not a natural or divine—foundation. The alienated human reality that Christians such as Percy describe need not be real anymore. And it will not be real if the indefinite longevity promised by biotechnology can be supplemented with pharmacotherapy. We must suppress our capacity to be moved by love and death to really achieve the security we desire.

Bobo Virtue and Our Real Counterculture

We shouldn't conclude without remembering the virtues of our Bobo establishment. America today is in some ways a better place to live than ever before. The gains, in terms of justice, are genuine, and a certain kind of natural aristocracy has come to power. More people are rich and more very well off than ever before. And on balance, people may also be nicer or less cruel. The spiritual superficiality and designer tastes of the Bobos are in some ways laughable, but they seem to promote peace of mind and productivity. And the Bobo attempt to reconcile community and autonomy is nothing less than an effort to resolve one of the fundamental problems of modern life. The concern for health and safety can be mocked, but it is also quite sensible. It is certainly better than lax obesity, obsessive drunkenness, and so forth. The hard work the Bobos devote to designing their lives, finally, cries out to be called virtue.

The Bobos also show us that the counterculture of the 1960s was a mirage. Even at its height, it mixed incoherently the spirit of the commune with the moral injunction to "do your own thing." And that incoherence remains at the heart of Bobo life. The real counterculture in America today is revealed religion. Our establishment has almost always been some form of progressive secularism, and it has always been opposed by some form of Christian, creation-based communalism. Many American Christians, of course, have been as bourgeois as our Bobos, but the more "orthodox" of today's Christians (and Jews, and Mormons and so on) have been co-opted far less than the Bobos. There always is a need for a genuine counterculture, because the present establishment is never without flaws; and human beings, as the Christians say, are in this world most deeply—most fundamentally—aliens.

So the cultural trend that is as important as the emergence of the Bobos is the revival of "orthodox" Christianity as a challenge to the way of life now dominant in America. One thing worth noting is that orthodox Christians seem to know where to draw the line when it comes to the libertarian spirit of technology. They are not Luddites or even agrarians. They use the electronic media to spread the word, and they believe that a good and faithful human life can be lived in the suburbs. But, ironically, these Christian aliens recognize their duties as citizens far more readily than the more at-home Bobos. And they dig in on abortion and euthanasia in ways Bobos and other libertarians find fanatical.

D'Souza unwittingly gives the secular argument for why they are right to dig in. He seems to accept the right to abortion while also arguing that we cannot design our children to fit our whims—that would be tyranny. But genetic manipulation will occur in the womb, where the government now says we already have the right to have the child killed. Surely the natural right our children have to liberty or self-determination, and so to think and act against our will, depends on their prior right to life. The fight against understanding abortion as a matter of unconstrained choice is part of the fight against the right to have perfect children, the right to choose children just as we choose furniture or coffee. The pro-choice view that all children should be wanted or chosen, combined with the capacity for genetic enhancement, becomes the view that all children should turn out exactly the way we designed them. When our freedom is unlimited, that of our children more or less completely disappears. They would become no more and no less than what we quite consciously make them. Eventually, indefinite longevity may well lead us not to desire to make children at all.

Bobo indifference to the more admirable virtues, such as courage and charity, comes at the expense of any spirit of resistance to cultural fashion and technocratic expertise. That would not be so worrisome if the present level of technology were to continue indefinitely, because the Bobos, despite their best efforts, continue to exhibit the greatness and misery of alienated human liberty. But the problem remains that the Bobos do not have the spirit to resist the rapidly approaching biotechnological threat to the very existence of human liberty. Their libertarianism will not serve them well if they are—as they may soon be—called upon to choose for love and death against a seemingly carefree form of indefinite and complacent longevity. They do not have what it takes to choose for the human good and against evil. The Bobos have to be displaced as our ruling class, for their own good and ours.

Let the reader beware that this book follows an anti-Bobo strategy in a number of ways. The early chapters are accounts of contemporary anti-alien writers, and they aren't so different in style from this one. But I gradually work my way back to our nation's constitutional, philosophical, and theological foundations. I hope the later chapters illuminate the earlier ones. There is in our time no alternative to rediscovering our natural, political, and divine debts, as well as the genuine meaning of human liberty. The whole book points to the two most thoughtful and noble anti-Bobo alternatives, presented by two men named Percy.

I need to issue the reader one other warning. The early chapters depend on a philosophic distinction between *nature* and *history*. The question of whether that distinction really exists was the basis of a famous dispute between Leo Strauss and Alexandre Kojève, two of the most impressive thinkers of the twentieth century. Kojève defended the view of the philosopher Hegel that human beings are distinctively historical—not natural—beings, and that history has come to an end. The end of history *is*, according to Kojève, the end of distinctively human existence.

My intention is not to show that Kojève was right in his dispute with Strauss but only to make clear all that is implied in the influential and illuminating thought that history has come to an end. I explain as well as I can what history and nature are for Kojève and Hegel. I do not think that the Hegelian distinction between nature and history is that hard to understand, but readers unfamiliar with it might have to stop and think when they encounter it. It may be harder for them to keep in mind as they read on, because it is in important ways contrary to common sense.

CHAPTER ONE

The End of History Today

My purpose in this initial chapter is to present evidence, from the perspective of America in 2002, that history has ended. I am presenting a case as a lawyer would, and so I usually do not call attention to objections, even obvious ones, to the points I am making. But let me begin by saying quite dispassionately that the case deserves to be made. Francis Fukuyama did well to remind us of that fact in *The End of History and the Last Man*, but he also confused us beyond belief.[1] Because just about nobody, as far as I can tell, was persuaded by his argument, he actually reinforced the commonsensical view that it makes no sense to speak of history's end. We human beings are still around and dissatisfied; liberal democracy has not won everywhere and is still quite fragile and less than completely admirable; and we are still making history. But there is actually much to be said for the view that distinctively human or "spiritual" existence is withering away, and that is the fundamental claim of the most consistent argument for the end of history.

Matter vs. Spirit

The argument that history has ended is of great theoretical complexity, and it must be supported, of course, by all sorts of historical evidence. But thanks to the clarity of the foremost account of that argument, the one presented by Alexandre Kojève in his lectures on Hegel's *Phenomenology of Spirit*, the basic factual claims on which that argument depends are not so hard to summarize.[2] There are two kinds of reality—matter and spirit. Nature is merely matter; even animate nature is merely matter in motion. So all natural phenomena obey impersonal, mechanical laws, and animals are guided wholly and unconsciously by instinct.

Human beings, according to Kojève's Hegel, are unique in being free or historical beings. "Spirit" freely negates nature, and by doing so becomes something other than matter. The evidence of the spiritual or historical existence of human beings is their ability to transform nature through their actions, and the record of their success is what we call history. All other claims that human beings possess freedom, except historical ones, are not really worth taking seriously. There is no evidence for them but the imagination. Why human beings alone among the animals are free is impossible to know. History, from nature's perspective, is an accident. It comes into being for no reason, although it can be understood at its completion on its own terms. That is, spirit has its own *logos* that makes sense independently of matter or nature. Understanding this account of distinctively human or historical existence *is* human wisdom, and this understanding is available to the human mind at history's end. Understanding the real or historical evidence of human freedom is the perfection both of human reason and of human freedom.

Human beings make history—or they act against nature—Kojève argues, because they are discontented with their natural existence. Other animals do not know that their existence is temporary; they do not know that they are going to die. In the decisive sense, they are not *temporary* at all. They are not governed by time, and they are not moved by their contingency (their possibility of dying or disappearing at any moment) or their mortality (their inevitable death). So they have no reason to be dissatisfied with their natural limitations. Their satisfaction is like God's, although God differs from the animals in being self-conscious. The human being is like God in being self-conscious and like the other animals in being mortal. This mixture is the cause of his discontent. He alone among the animals has desires that cannot be satisfied naturally. And so, eventually, he satisfies them historically.

The Universal and Homogeneous State

Human beings at a certain point in history, the argument continues, imaginatively created a God who rules in another world. This God satisfied the human desire to be recognized as a free being. This God provided evidence that humans were not determined by nature. But that satisfaction, of course, is not real. At a later point in history, human beings come to believe that this world is the only one, and so they self-consciously pursue satisfaction of their longing for freedom politically or historically. Through political action, through revolution, they create a world in which all human beings are freely and equally recognized as citizens. That world is, in a way, history's end: A better political or historical world cannot really be imagined, and all other political orders are henceforth regarded as illegitimate or reactionary. What Kojève calls the Universal and Homogeneous State is the perfected state. There, all human beings are recognized as free citizens in exactly the same way, and so they are all equally or completely satisfied with their freedom. That state has no place and no need for God; for belief in God signals human dissatisfaction—or, as Marx says, signals that this world is defective.

The state or government at this very late point in history is perfected, and the details of that perfection gradually infuse social life. Distinctions based on race, class, gender, family, ethnicity, and so forth disappear everywhere, as all human relationships are constituted with wisdom available to all. From this perspective, the end of history came in principle with the American Constitution—silent as it is on race, class, gender, and religion—and the so-called history of America is the gradual perfection of all of American life according to the principle of equal freedom. The distinction between the national and state governments withers away over time, and government becomes progressively less limited in its pursuit of justice. All human institutions once regarded as private or non-political, such as the church and the family, are subjected to political judgment. God disappears from more and more of American life. To the extent He remains, He is increasingly employed as a means to inspire Americans to eradicate all social injustice, to perfect the details of history's end.[3]

So the end of history is the premise that informs American progressivism, whether the progressives realize it or not. Friendly critics of America such as Alexis de Tocqueville complain that the modern, and democratic view of progress or perfectibility is less individual than it is social or historical, and so also more indefinite or vague.[4] Today's American Hegelian-pragmatist Richard Rorty, the professor of philosophy who claims to have captured the spirit of our time, actually praises the fuzziness of our utopianism.[5] For Rorty, to have our hopes for the future governed by the limits of experience and reason would needlessly constrain our imaginations. But Kojève rightly points out that historical change can only be called progress if we know the point or purpose of history. That purpose, being itself a product of history, can only be known at history's end. So Hegel could claim he saw the purpose of history because he had seen it all; he thought at history's end. And Marx thought he was close enough to the end to discern what would happen next, what would make sense of it all.

If we know American history is progressive and human beings are essentially historical beings, then Americans must now be situated by history to see the purpose of human or historical existence as such. The pragmatist Rorty's denial that we really have such knowledge makes human life too contingent or arbitrary for us to know what to hope for and what to work toward. He says that there is no such thing as "truth"; we might call anything true that we find useful. But Rorty's claim that the abolition of cruelty and the classless society are goals he has chosen for no reason except personal preference is incredible. If we are provided no guidance by nature and God, as pragmatists say, then surely we are governed by history. Rorty's choices, as he sometimes admits, are determined by his place in history, by his wisdom concerning human contingency and human liberty or self-creation over time.[6]

Political Correctness

The idea of the end of history is also the real foundation of today's academic insistence on political correctness. Education, for many of our professors, has become wholly a matter of race, class, and gender. The truth is that human beings are free and equal citizens, but they have been falsely and unjustly degraded in the past by being oppressed or stigmatized as blacks, poor, or women. We are certain that we now know that racism, sexism, and classism are wrong; we know what justice is. The task of education is no longer to ask what justice is, but to use our wisdom about justice to judge thought and action past and present. We must employ our wisdom to root out residual error embodied in our institutions and individuals, and to judge thinkers of the past as racists, sexists, and aristocrats, that is, as limited by their places in history. By saying that education is only about race, class, and gender, we say that, in the most important respects, there is no more intellectual progress to be made, that we are now all wise. Love of wisdom is replaced by wisdom itself.

Much of the American opposition to political correctness does not contradict the premise that history has ended. The politically correct are accused with dogmatically connecting opposition to racism and sexism, which in itself is surely just, with support for affirmative action. And this dogmatism is meant to suppress discussion about how much affirmative action has succeeded or can succeed in achieving its goal of overcoming the effects of past racism or sexism. Insofar as political correctness makes discussion about practical success impossible, it is opposed to the standard of history. And so some opponents of P. C. often serve better today's goal of implementing the principles of the Universal and Homogeneous State. The justice of affirmative action can only be defended by its results. Considered in itself, as some sort of categorical imperative, it is clearly racist and sexist. (So the Supreme Court has worked its way to the conclusion that affirmative action is contrary to the Constitution's premises concerning individualism and dignity unless it can be *proven* to overcome the effects of racism.) Multiculturalism is also racist, sexist, and otherwise narrowly chauvinistic, if taken seriously as a political principle. If taken as an affection for particular forms and rituals that have now been detached from what was at one time a nonegalitarian way of life (Quebeçois linguistic chauvinism, contemporary Native American spirituality, etc.), it is merely a form of empty snobbery, form without content, and so of no great consequence.

But other opponents of political correctness go further and object to its standards being applied to all of education and to all of human life. For them, the thinkers of the past are not completely discredited because they did not share our wisdom concerning justice. The less politically enlightened of our forebears still have much to teach us about love and death. Political progress is not the same as human or personal progress, and some human problems do not have political solutions. We still have longings that are, at best, imperfectly satisfied in this world, and we still must live well with the truth about our ineradicable alienation and mortality. We still have connections with and responsibilities to others that are hardly exhausted by the idea of justice, however perfect it has become.

Such opponents of political correctness seem vulnerable to Marx's criticism of Hegel: For history to end completely, for it to be human as opposed to merely political emancipation, the universal and homogeneous principles of justice must inform all of human life.[7] Kojève accepts this criticism, which is why he finally rejects the Hegelian principle that the end of history can merely be the free and equal recognition of one citizen by another. Human beings know they are not, most fundamentally, citizens; they know that political recognition is abstract and hence not really satisfying. Political recognition is as much about dependence as it is about freedom; for I am dependent on *your* recognition for *my* freedom. Marx is in some sense correct. The state must wither away for human beings to live free and unalienated lives.

Animals Again

History is the record of distinctively political or uniquely free action. At the end of history, then, there could be no more such action. There would be nothing left to do. Both political or historical life, and the being capable of it, would wither away. At the end of history, human beings would have to become in every respect like the other animals again. Our species would once again live wholly according to nature. Human beings are alienated from or discontented with their merely natural existences. The end of alienation is the overcoming of the inexplicable distinction between nature and history. Comprehensive wisdom, finally, cannot be historical wisdom; the world or the cosmos makes sense only with the end of history.

History had a beginning, and so it must have an end. It is not like matter, which is neither created nor destroyed. The human or historical being is the being with time in him, and so the being defined by his contingency and death. Each human being is temporary, and history as a whole is too. The historical being, from the view of nature, is an error. The error becomes, over time, more conscious of himself as error—or free from the illusion that he is somehow, like God, more than a temporary being. Once the self-conscious mortal becomes completely conscious of himself as a temporary error, then in the name of wisdom and content-ment (only historical beings are discontent) the error disappears. Once the human being completely understands himself as the being who dies, which he can do only when history itself has ended, then he also ceases to die, in the precise sense. For he is no longer aware of, moved by, or de-fined by his mortality. He no longer is discontented, wanting to be more than he really is. And the disappearance of history or human uniqueness, far from being a cosmic catastrophe, actually makes the cosmos a com-prehensible whole again. But there is no one left to wonder at this whole.

At the end of history human desire is no longer different from that of the other animals. Our passions are no longer inflamed by self-con-sciousness, and so the intensely social passions such as love and pride contract. Sexual desire, for example, is no longer mixed up with illusions about the soul or immortality. It becomes, as Rorty observes, open and casual; the cruelty of love and hate fade as we no longer attach undue or spiritual significance to our rutting.[8] We find this casualness about all human activity in Marx's description of communism in his version of the end of history, *The German Ideology*. According to Marx, at the end of history we do whatever we want whenever we want, without being ob-sessed with any particular activity or, by implication, any particular per-son. (It is hard to say why Marx calls the end of history "communism," because his posthistorical humans are not connected or devoted to each other in any strong or communal sense.)

But where Marx goes most wrong, in Kojève's eyes, is in believing that human beings somehow can remain distinctively human or self-conscious at history's end. Like all animals, they will still die, and if they are moved by or are genuinely conscious of that fact, they will remain discontented.

That is, they will still be, in some sense, spiritual beings, even if material or economic scarcity is overcome. The real human scarcity is scarcity of time, and being defined by time is the mark of the temporary or historical being. For human beings to be as easygoing or unobsessed as Marx describes, they must not be distinctively human at all. Human beings must become unconscious—completely governed by natural instinct—at history's end.

Solzhenitsyn's Dissident Observations

The idea that human beings are in the process of surrendering their human uniqueness rightly offends common sense and seems to contradict personal experience. We still claim to fall in love, we are still conscious of being proud and angry, and we are still afraid of death and full of anxiety about nothing in particular. One of the most penetrating critics of the contemporary world, Aleksandr Solzhenitsyn, says that people are now more lonely and death-haunted than ever. What he calls the "howl" of existentialism is the result of longings that we not only cannot satisfy, but about which we seemingly cannot even speak. We live in a time not of self-consciousness and contentment but of self-absorbed confusion and miserable self-denial. If Solzhenitsyn is right, then the destruction of natural human ties that is the result of our doctrine of rights—the result of the principles of justice of the Universal and Homogeneous State—has actually made human life harder than ever, because human beings have deprived themselves of the resources they need to confront life's challenges and their own limitations. They have deprived themselves of the virtues of courage and self-limitation, and of the orientation provided by spiritual life.⁹

But Solzhenitsyn might be understood to provide more evidence for history's end. Our nation was ennobled by the struggle against communism; we understood ourselves as defending truth and liberty against ideological lies and despotism. And the dissidents in the communist nations saw in their own courageous efforts on behalf of truth and responsibility evidence contradicting modern materialism and atheism. But communism collapsed. America was suddenly without ennobling national purpose. The words of the dissidents were suddenly deprived of their weight or connection with noble, life-risking deeds. They could now speak freely, but what they said was met with indifference. The dissident criticism of the modern West seemed to evaporate almost overnight, and the vision of Václav Havel that the alternative *polis* of the dissidents would provide the foundation of a new Czechoslovakia now seems laughably naïve. Solzhenitsyn's prediction that America could not and would not be the model for post-communist Russia now seems quite misguided, at least if interpreted to mean that Russia would develop a morally superior alternative to Americanization.[10] Many of the former dissidents, such as Havel, have for the most part even abandoned their earlier unfashionable critiques.[11] Solzhenitsyn is a noteworthy exception, but he is usually viewed as a relic of the past.[12]

Until communism's unexpected and abrupt collapse, the argument that modern liberalism culminates in totalitarian catastrophe seemed plausible. The best thinkers of the West wrote of the crisis of liberalism under the shadow of totalitarianism's threat.[13] But now with the absence of that threat, that crisis seems to have faded. The evidence that modern thought and practice ends in unprecedented terror and tyranny invigorated the West. The possibility of communism's victory or global destruction in nuclear war made everything modern of questionable value. But as Fukuyama reported in his famous book announcing history's probable end with the end of the Cold War, American liberal democracy has now won everywhere, at least in principle.

This global victory was achieved without bloody revolution and by depriving the world of any prospect of salvation or destruction through political or technological apocalypse. What do we do if the bomb doesn't drop? asked the philosopher-novelist Walker Percy. But he really wasn't that worried. His expectation was that the West would somehow self-destruct—or perhaps that it had already somehow been destroyed, making room for love in the ruins.[14] Now, Percy's novels are more often viewed as reflections of personal neurosis than as profound and prophetic commentaries on the malaise of our time. Only a God can save us now, exclaimed Heidegger. But today most of the Westernized world—that is, virtually the entire world—blinks and says, Save us from what? From unprecedented peace, freedom, and prosperity, from the disappearance of all forms of moralistic chauvinism in exchange for a universal and homogeneous global order? Rorty asks, not without reason and quite in accord with the spirit of the time, why we should care about the personal obsessions of a neurotic German Nazi (namely Heidegger).[15] Rorty would, of course, say something similar about Solzhenitsyn, and he has encouraged Havel to get less serious about outmoded ideas such as God and eternity.[16] And in fact, Havel has.

Perhaps the end of history leaves us lonely and death-haunted and with no hope for political or divine salvation, but surely that interpretation is perversely at odds with any reasonable conception of historical progress. Or perhaps Solzhenitsyn's description is too extreme. Surely a certain amount of loneliness and anxiety is a price worth paying for peace, prosperity, and freedom. People with good government and in fortunate social situations do have a tendency to magnify unreasonably their remaining miseries. Today's American or Western whining, contrary to Hobbes's bourgeois fear and Marx's radical hope, is not about to lead to revolution or civil war.

Tocqueville on Democratic Apathy

Alexis de Tocqueville actually provides a way of connecting Solzhenitsyn's telling observations with history's end. In *Democracy in America* he almost

begins by defending his own version of the end of history: Democracy
has or will triumph everywhere in the world, and it is futile for aristocrats
to imagine any restoration because democracy or popular sovereignty is
the only principle of political legitimacy that remains credible.[17] The
only question is what sort of democracy we will have, and Tocqueville
defends the American propensity to incorporate aristocratic inheritances—such as the family, intermediary association, local government,
religion, and so forth—into our understanding of democracy. These
fortunate inheritances help limit and shape human liberty, and by so
doing make liberty lovable—and so sustainable— in an increasingly democratic time.[18]

The problem with Tocqueville's strategy is his own subtle opposition to democratic progress or history. He knows that the love of equality, an impersonal passion, undermines human love, love of particular
beings or entities as they actually exist. And so he knows that the particular American institutions he defends will be eroded over time by the
democratic understanding of justice. He seems finally quite pessimistic
about the future of human liberty or distinctively human individuality
and greatness. The best Tocqueville can say is that his efforts to direct
democracy are not inevitably futile, because we cannot say for certain that
free human action will not continue to have some conscious influence
over historical change. In some ways Tocqueville both affirms and resists
the end of history, and we must wonder how tenable that combination
can be, even in his most capable hands.[19]

In Tocqueville's eyes, the danger of modern democracy is not, most
fundamentally, totalitarian terror, although as a student of the French
Revolution he certainly knew what that was. Democracy's most enduring
pernicious tendency is toward what Tocqueville calls individualism, an
isolated, apathetic existence without the social passions of love and hate.
Individualism is not only compatible with but seems almost inevitably
to generate a soft or gentle form of despotism, where the individual

surrenders control of the details of his life to some provident, impersonal authority. Individualism, above all, is the judgment that concern
for others, and so love and hate and concern for past and future, is more
trouble than it is worth.[20] The result is the denial or imaginary destruction of almost all of human individuality. Tocqueville agrees with Kojève
that the perfection of democracy would mean the abolition of human
liberty, the disappearance of that singular being capable of acting freely
or historically.

The deepest Tocquevillian observation concerning the psychology
of this surrender might be found in his account of democratic poetry or
idealism. Egalitarian skepticism eventually destroys all illusions human
beings have about gods, heroes, and even the future. All that remains is
the simple truth about the human individual: He exists for a moment
between two abysses and then disappears.[21] Human existence is absolutely contingent because of the individual's consciousness of his own
contingency. From the perspective of nature, consciousness is a mysterious error, one that is bad for both nature and one's own productivity and
happiness. The democratic perception of the truth about the unsupported individual—of not only the democratic individual but also the
human condition as such—is too hard to bear, too hostile to life. The
unadorned truth produces human self-destruction, including the end of
the being capable of perceiving and being moved by the truth.

Tocqueville, like Solzhenitsyn, sometimes presents Americans as
lonely and anxious about death, restless or uneasy in the midst of prosperity. But he also fears that they will eventually not be moved by death,
love, or pride at all. They will be mindlessly engrossed in the present,
gladly surrendering the concerns that constitute their humanity.[22] The
gradual self-surrender Tocqueville dreads and almost predicts may, in
fact, explain much of recent American history. It is hard to tell whether
Americans are becoming more lonely or just more disconnected, more
obsessed with death or just not bothered by it at all. It is certainly plau-

sible to say that today there is a lot more sex but a lot less love, and that the bodily connection has been more completely sundered from love and enduring human relationships and institutions than ever before. That was a provocative conclusion of Allan Bloom's *Closing of the American Mind*. For Bloom, American souls have ceased longing, ceased, properly speaking, being souls at all.[23] How much evidence do we really have in America today for the withering away of the soul?

Laissez Faire *Everywhere*

Bloom's analysis came before the Cold War's end, and the defeat of communism and the accompanying prosperity of America under Reagan merely intensified an already rapid American movement toward individualism. The more common name of that movement is libertarianism. As sociologist Alan Wolfe has observed, middle-class Americans are now applying the principle of *laissez faire* to all areas of human life.[24] The political principle of tolerance—or, more precisely, moral nonjudgmentalism rooted in both fear and respect—has now become a comprehensive social principle. A Marxist might say that our political principle of free and equal liberty has gradually infused all of American life. But a Marxist might also say that what remains of American community is being destroyed, and that the capitalist or Hobbesian spirit of fearful isolation now separates even neighbor from neighbor. Certainly churches and families have been weakened, and most Americans may now understand religion and morality to reflect merely private whims. Furthermore, Americans consciously *use* each other to pursue their private interests more than ever before. Judging, which is sometimes tyrannical and sometimes charitable but always social, has been replaced by using. American associations are now primarily instrumental and far less heart-enlarging than Tocqueville had hoped. The Marxist ambivalence about American progress is resolved by Tocqueville. Marx's description of communism is really the same as the apathetic isolation Tocqueville calls individualism. Under communism, each individual can do whatever he wants whenever he wants. Communism is most deeply libertarian, and not communal.

The 1960s and the 1980s: Two Forms of Moral Destruction

The recent American movement toward the universalization of the *laissez faire* principle has rather definite stages. The first is the 1960s. The various social movements of that decade had political or idealistic dimensions, but their enduring effect was to destroy the credibility of traditional or religiously based personal and familial morality. One fundamental contradiction of the 1960s was embodied in its idea of the *commune*, in which people shared the same way of life in close proximity while doing their own thing. Such communities is not communal enough to last, but what their antimoral morality dissolved seemingly cannot be restored.

The contribution of the 1960s to the perfection of the Universal and Homogeneous State is clear in the cases of blacks, women, gays, and even Jews, and we often forget the place of the 1960s in the destruction of the residues of aristocracy—concern with breeding and lineage—that had taken root in America.[25] But not only unjust political distinctions were discredited; morality as such was discredited as well. The political principle of liberation was promiscuously applied to all of social and personal life. With respect to sexual morality, as Rorty notices, the result was casualness or indifference. Nobody ought to care what you do with your body, and nobody should have an opinion even concerning your soul. The illusory or outmoded mixing of soul with body is a cruel deprivation of bodily pleasure. In this respect especially, Rorty says, *the* enemy of justice and happiness is Platonism, which is the philosophical alternative to Hegelianism.[26]

The political idealism of the 1960s was, in part, a continuation of welfare-state liberalism. America is a national community; each citizen has a duty to provide for the unfortunate among his fellow citizens. The foundation of that duty is care or compassion, which overcomes the selfishness of apathy. That duty is expressed in the redistribution of income through taxation to support various government programs. The destruction of the principle of redistribution was one goal of the 1980s Reagan Revolution. The other was to roll back the moral permissiveness of the 1960s, especially as it found expression in government policy.

The first goal was achieved. The discrediting of the welfare state was assisted mightily by the failure of socialism, not to mention a huge deficit that made new programs impossible. And it is not so hard to convince people of what is, after all, largely true: A free economy is best for everyone, and intelligent personal selfishness is genuine compassion. Public devotion to caring for the poor is counterproductive. Reagan's second, moral goal was not taken so seriously; its pursuit was compromised by the libertarianism within Reagan's own party and even his own soul. Reagan and Bush, despite appointing six of nine members of the Supreme Court, could not even get the pro-choice *Roe v. Wade* decision reversed. The so-called Religious Right or "Moral Majority" got plenty of stirring words from the president, but very few deeds. From our contemporary perspective, the 1960s and 1980s were both victories for freedom, or individualism, over morality. Eighties freedom whipped sixties moralism, and sixties freedom easily fended off eighties moralism.

A second libertarian innovation of the 1980s for which we can thank Reagan is freedom from the duty of military service. The American victory in the Cold War, confirmed later by a crushing victory in the Gulf and another from 15,000 feet in the air against the Serbs (won even though we actually hit very few targets) makes the draft seem almost unimaginable for the foreseeable future. (September 11, of course, has not changed this situation.) Conscription, of course, has been the exception to the rule in American history, because of the nation's history of isolationism. But now our unprecedented technological superiority makes something like global dominance possible with amazingly few men in the field.

We can bemoan the lack of concern today for national greatness, and we can even be drawn for a moment to something like John McCain's exhortation on behalf of virtue, for devotion to something higher than self-interest. We could almost, but not quite, forget that McCain was never able to give that greatness any content. We also notice the decline in the quality of our leaders as we move away from the time of war and compulsory military service. But we do not really long for war. We are, in fact, thrilled at the reach of American power without citizen sacrifice. Our experiments with alternative forms of service, from the Peace Corps to Americorps, remind us that William James was wrong and Hegel was right. There is no moral equivalent to war. (So the newly commenced war against terrorism arguably may do America some good.)

Bill Clinton, Model Libertarian

Sixties personal liberation combined with eighties economic and civic liberation explains in remarkably large measure the presidency of Bill Clinton. His administration is judged by both liberal Democrats and conservative Republicans to have been morally deficient, although for quite different reasons. For liberals, he abandoned their commitment to the poor, and for conservatives he was a poster boy for the personal decadence of our time. He did it all, from dodging the draft to completely sundering sex from love, or even concern for the other. But conservatives, in truth, have little reason to be dissatisfied with his economic policy (shaped in part, of course, by the Republican Congress).

Clinton may have done as much to kill the principle of redistribution as Reagan. He signed the bill that brought the national government's responsibility for welfare to an end. And his secretary of the treasury actually understood the details of "trickle-down economics" and rather faithfully implemented them. The Clinton administration in many ways allied with congressional Republicans to promote free trade against the liberal Democrats' reactionary efforts to protect jobs. The result was an unparalleled period of prosperity and the end of deficit spending. The national consensus on the economy, with plenty of reason, is arguably more libertarian than at any time since before the New Deal. Middle-class entitlements persist (today's American individualist is not a rugged individualist), but the era of the compassionate welfare state is over. Despite Hillary Clinton's loose talk about a national village and the president's own words about feeling our pain, government and citizens became more apathetic or individualistic, in Tocqueville's sense, under her husband's watch.

Most liberal Democrats applaud Clinton's achievements on behalf of pro-choice causes concerning personal morality. The gays and their agenda have been a cherished cause of the former president and his party, and during the Clinton years they made gains both in the military and in the courts. As Harvey Mansfield has observed, the president's defense of his philandering with the help in the White House has made the phrase "consenting adults" more than ever the nation's standard of personal morality, even for chief executives who are married with children.[27] The middle class's toleration of the president's shameless and devious behavior and its acceptance of moral *laissez faire* have driven many religious conservatives to political despair.[28] Many have withdrawn from public involvement into small countercultural communities to protect themselves and their children from amoral America. This withdrawal, of course, leads to personal narrowness and political indifference, and it surrenders public life to an easygoing pro-choice consensus on almost any issue imaginable. It is an admission of defeat; the moral majority that some followers of Reagan hoped would come to guide America is nowhere near a majority anymore.

Bourgeois Bohemians at the End of History

I present the foregoing evidence that we are at the end of history unjudged. Americans, more than ever, treat each other as free and equal individuals. They have never been less willing to judge each other morally, because all such judgment is now regarded as meddlesome and inegalitarian. We may know less about each other than ever before, but we respect each other more as individuals. The libertarian spirit of Marx's end of history is closer than ever to being an accurate account of America. We are relatively content living in freedom and abundance without doing all that much work. And maybe we are less moved by love and death, and so less distorted by cruel, moralistic anger, than people have ever been.

I am not saying that we are no different from the other animals. We are more than clever animals until every detail of our lives has been transformed by history's end. The differences, though, do seem to be fading. As Alan Wolfe shows, American women want to live both as free and equal individuals and as devoted and responsible wives and mothers. Life, for them, is still rather hard, because they do not have enough time to do justice to both of their self-understandings. But usually it does not occur to them not to think of themselves as individuals and not to demand justice. American women will not go back, and so they gradually go forward. They spend less time with their children with every passing year. Getting by with less love, children too become more independent and withdrawn. Perhaps most troubling to social or religious conservatives is that their (in a sense, hopeful) prediction of a social crisis rooted in excessive permissiveness has not come true. The Clinton years have proved that the spirit of the 1960s, purged of its superficial communalism or idealism, is quite compatible with social stability and personal prosperity.

David Brooks has named the new model Americans, the new "establishment," *bourgeois bohemians*.[29] They combine the affectations of cultural radicalism or progressive, egalitarian lifestyles with inconspicuous concern for the acquisition of wealth. The money, they say, is for living a bohemian or nonconformist life. But they would never live in such a way as not to have money. They work hard, but they believe their work must be both creative, or self-fulfilling, and efficient, and that there is no necessary tension between the two. In good end-of-history fashion, they reject all talk of hierarchy and sexual moralism, except, of course, concerning safe sex. They seek spiritual fulfillment, but they are simultaneously convinced that God or the One would make on them no unreasonable or discomforting demands—no demands, properly speaking, at all. They are emphatically not anxious or restless in the absence of God; they look down on obsession with personal salvation as unenlightened and unhealthy.

But morality the bourgeois bohemians still have. They are toughly judgmental when it comes to smoking, alcohol abuse, obesity, and seatbelts. The limits to their radicalism are set by the requirements of health and prosperity. Bohemianism or cultural nonconformism, properly domesticated with fear and greed, can be completely compatible with living according to the natural goal of comfortable self-preservation. Artists and intellectuals no longer abuse their bodies because they no longer have souls. Life can be interesting (American food, coffee, shoes, vacations, and bookstores have become more tasteful and diverse under the guidance of bohemian consumers) and even a bit risky (in the entrepreneurial sense) without being very tough, because we are no longer really moved by the great political or spiritual longings of the past.

So the bourgeois bohemians, David Brooks concludes, have become thoughtless conservatives, unable to imagine a better life than the one they have. He also concludes that Tocqueville's prediction has become true. Their lives are petty, quietly complacent, and free from genuinely human aspiration. We can add that they seem uncannily like the people Marx describes at the end of history: They have come close to reducing

life to an interesting series of hobbies or cultural experiences while refusing to becoming obsessed with any of them.

Alan Wolfe would push Brooks's analysis even further. The aspirations and even the achievements of the bourgeois bohemians are not
limited to the wealthy establishment. The broad middle class, including
managers and secretaries, aim to combine material comfort with the bohemian quest for "higher meaning." Many of them have acquired personal trainers for their bodies as well as personal gurus for their souls.
Wolfe also notices that Evangelicals can be just as therapeutic in their
spirituality as Unitarians. So he presents what amounts to the Hegelian
conclusion that "Boboism . . . *is* American life."[30] Life at the end of history is more clearly than ever the shared goal of all Americans and is
available to more and more of them with every passing day.

The Canadian political thinker Waller R. Newell, for one, wonders
whether this sort of analysis of our time is superficial. Young people are
still full of passion. They still have strong, antinomian desires and ambi-
tions. During the day, they tend to conform to the orderly, unadventur-
ous requirements of the bourgeois bohemian way of life. But there is also
a nightly "Dionysian underworld" of drugs, dance clubs, manic music,
piercing self-mutilation, passionate and beautiful expressions of male
and female sexuality, and even the passionate excess of androgyny (as opposed to the lifeless, bureaucratic suppression of difference). Newell's
hope is that this underworld is evidence that human nature remains
unmanaged, that eros still reigns supreme, if only covertly, in the human
soul.[31] But that world seems to me well under control; the young blow
off steam (admittedly, they still have steam) and gradually their nights
conform to their days. Their eros, uneducated (and so unsublimated) and
without any institutional support, simply fades. The day rules the night,
and everything that goes on at night becomes safely packaged. What used
to be regarded as criminal lust or pederasty is aroused quite predictably
and privately by a Calvin Klein ad.

Biotechnology and the New Ambiguity of Nature

I have not yet mentioned the most powerful weapon at our disposal for eradicating what remains of human distinctiveness, biotechnology. The argument of the dissidents, Solzhenitsyn and Havel, that the fall of communism shows that human nature is capable of resisting all ideological or historical impositions, is powerful. It could certainly be argued that Rorty's pragmatic view that we can somehow talk out of existence intense love and hate, cruel obsessiveness, and death, is weak. People still know that we are more than words; that their being is not completely determined by their language. It is easy to agree with the sociobiologists that certain inegalitarian features of our natures cannot be overcome through political or environmental change. And many cannot help but return to the belief that human beings will remain discontented or homeless in the world in ways that elude social and political reform. Libertarian apathy or contentment is surely only part of our story today. Our easygoing, nonjudgmental words may mask, more than they describe, our genuine experiences.

But what if we can alter our natures in ways that can eradicate natural resistance to the goal of history's end? Walker Percy writes of the significance of our anxiety, depression, and general unhappiness in the midst of a beneficent environment. This depression, he notices, cannot in fact be remedied by environmental improvement or soothing therapeutic language. And it is actually worsened when the impersonal language of scientific expertise does not correspond to our human longings. The more we can explain scientifically, the more the self or what remains uniquely human seems an inexplicable leftover. Our depression and anxiety, Percy concludes, are evidence that we are strangers in this world, aliens by our very natures. The depressed or melancholic, if they reflect on their miserable dislocation, can see through the platitudes of scientific humanism to the truth about our being and even to the possibility that

Christian anthropology and maybe Christian revelation might be true.

According to Percy, we live not at history's end but at the end of the modern world. Our language is exhausted and our cultural inheritance has become incredible. The result is not only loneliness, but also a rare opportunity to see the human being as he truly is. The result is also the possibility of the undeluded love of one self-conscious mortal for another. Percy agrees with Tocqueville that modern democracy, through its destruction of all forms of privilege, shows the human being in all his contingency and dislocation. But he adds that there is also some joy in knowing the truth, which is much more bearable than our experts think. The West may self-destruct, but according to Percy the uniquely human being will continue to exist in one form or another.[32]

But, Peter Kramer, in his very thoughtful *Listening to Prozac,* doubts that Percy's celebration of the wisdom of the depressed or melancholic is much more than delusion. Prozac can so improve a depressed person's life that he experiences a transformation in his very being. He is freed from his miserable experiences in a way that enhances memory and self-understanding and contributes to optimism and personal productivity without any unpleasant side effects. The Prozac taker is not some zoned-out "last man" but an intelligent, reflective, outgoing, risk-taking person in a good mood. Kramer admits that Prozac or some similar drug could have deprived us of the novels of Percy and Dostoyevsky. But now it seems their self-understandings have turned out to be untrue, and so we no longer see any profundity in their brushes with suicide and searches for God. Depression and melancholy are merely biological disorders with a biological remedy; they are not some gateway to the truth about being. A person feels much more at home, because he really is more at home, after taking the capsule.[33] Kramer recommends a new aesthetics of optimism and sanguinity for this new world. Knowing that mood is a function of chemical balance keeps us from privileging bad moods because they are more truthful; we are free to choose the ones that make us productive and happy.[34]

What is possible now through mood-enhancing drugs (the effects of which we can expect will become progressively more safe and predictable) may soon be achieved even more effectively through gene therapy and other forms of biotechnology. We will be more and more able to manipulate our natures. This success would seem to contradict the idea that the end of history can be achieved by merely political means. Perhaps human nature can become like that of the other animals only if it is altered. Political-historical effort by itself cannot eradicate the error that is the free being, because human freedom has a natural, and not only a historical, foundation. But the uses to which we will put biotechnology do seem to be set by the principles of the Universal and Homogeneous State. We will eradicate those aspects of our natures—aggression, anxiety, and so forth—that cause us to remain dissatisfied with it. We will no longer be religious, metaphysical, political, or even polymorphously erotic beings. We may remain, as Fukuyama argues in *The Great Disruption,* social beings, but the circle of our sociality will shrink and simplify.[35]

Perhaps we would have never quite believed the modern, expert propaganda that our "spiritual" experiences are merely illusions. But what if we did not have such experiences anymore? Our secular or merely scientific language would finally seem adequate; we would lose any intimations of deprivation. Our agenda, set by history, would be to perfect what has already been achieved in principle. We would make ourselves different in degree but not in kind from the other animals. We would become clever, reasonably contented, safely gregarious animals—and nothing more.

It must be emphasized that we now lack the moral resources to resist the biotechnological project. Communism, in fact, was much easier to resist. It was clearly rooted in terror and tyranny, and the standpoint of resistance was most clearly human nature. But now not only human nature but nature itself seems an ambiguous and imprecise term. One meaning of nature is what we have been given and cannot change, an ineradicable limit to human effort. But now almost everything natural seems technologically alterable. Even our dependence on this planet, even the idea that we have only so long a life may no longer be necessary. All living beings will still have to die sometime, but we may be able to choose how much we are moved or determined by that fact.

Most uses of biotechnology, even Prozac capsules, seem beneficial. They are used to cure mental and physical illness, to prolong life and alleviate suffering. And the distinction between preserving human life and enhancing it through natural transformation is hard to maintain in particular cases. Even if our government were to implement restrictions, it would still be easy to find the technological therapy we desire elsewhere in our Internet-connected world. The Supreme Court has declared moral regulation of the Internet by our government unconstitutional because such regulation is so obviously futile. Technology, and especially technology combined with universal principle, has made impossible the moral defense of national borders.

We might fear that biotechnology will turn out to be a tool used by new tyrants to impose their wills on the world, to dismantle the Universal and Homogeneous State. It is true that we will end up trusting scientific experts far too much in chemically ordering ourselves and our world, but our own inclination, like the inclination of our experts, will be in the direction of becoming productive, unalienated members of a liberal society. That is, we will be energetic and contented conformists, and our scientists probably won't be much different. We now know that this type of conformism is compatible with economic prosperity and technical innovation. Given that all other forms of rule are regarded as illegitimate by our elites, we can reasonably expect that the universal and homogeneous principles of the Bobos, and not deranged, obsessive individuals, will guide our gradual surrender of the qualities that actually distinguish us as human beings.

CHAPTER TWO

Francis Fukuyama as Teacher of Evil

The aim of conservatives for some time now has been to resist what C. S. Lewis called "the abolition of man." One effort at that abolition was communist ideology; another is the therapeutic pragmatism of Richard Rorty and others.[1] But the most dangerous threat today comes from the science of biology. Denial of human distinctiveness is increasingly rooted in the homogeneous materialism of evolutionary biology. And advances in biotechnology are providing the means to destroy what is qualitatively different about our species.[2] Especially troubling is the uncritical acceptance of biological reductionism by writers often called conservative. In this chapter, I advance the reflections offered in Chapter 1 by using Walker Percy's defense of the goodness and mystery of the human being to expose the misanthropic implications of this reductionism in the influential writing of the "neoconservative" Francis Fukuyama. I present this effort as an example of what conservatives should be doing as the twenty-first century begins.

The philosopher-novelist Walker Percy claims that, contrary to modern reductionism, the human being is by nature an alien.[3] According to Percy, modern science has made great progress in explaining everything but the human self and soul. Scientific experts tell people that they are fundamentally no different from the other animals, and so they should be happy in a world where lives are more free, prosperous, and secure than ever before. Their feelings of homelessness are either basically irrational or merely physiological. They can be cured through a change in environment, soothing therapeutic or ideological platitudes, or the right mix of chemicals.

The experts are evil, Percy contends, because they want to deprive human beings of their distinctive humanity, of their longings that point them beyond the satisfactions of this world and toward each other, the truth, and God. Their efforts may never completely succeed, but allegedly wise experts—from communist tyrants to therapeutic psychotherapists—have destroyed or needlessly diminished a huge number of human beings. The experts claim, in part, to be motivated by compassion. They want to provide the freedom from misery that the Christian God promised but could not produce in this world. But the compassion they claim to feel for others they really feel for themselves. They, too, are aliens, and they want to free themselves from their trouble. They think that by reducing others to comprehensible or simply biological beings they can raise themselves to become something like angels. They seek not to be at home in the world of human beings but in a world that completely transcends the human. And so the world they have conjured into being is increasingly fit for angels and pigs, for theorists and consumers, but not for human beings.

For Percy the best human life is to be at home with one's homelessness or alienation, and so to be free to enjoy the good things of the world while conscious of their limitations. This way of living is easier for Christians, who have an explanation for why human beings feel like aliens in this world. But such a way of life does not necessarily depend on religious belief. It is available to anyone who can tell the truth about himself and live well in accepting it. We are born to trouble, and doomed to failure and death. But we have compensations in the joyful sharing of what we can know with others, and in the love of one human being—one self-conscious mortal—for another. Those human goods are only given to aliens, to the beings with language who can explain everything but themselves. Percy's goal was to restore the Socratic or psyche-iatric tradition and discard psychotherapy. People can be happier as human beings not through platitudes or drugs but through the search for the truth about their extraordinary natures.

Nature of History?

From this perspective, a leading American teacher of evil over the last decade has been Francis Fukuyama. Fukuyama's writing is more insidious than that of the largely discredited socialists and reductionistic scientists, for he claims to be a defender of human liberty and dignity, as well as of the superiority of American liberal democracy to other political orders. Many of his policy recommendations and philosophical preferences seem conservative, and he is quite popular in some neoconservative circles. He has written two very comprehensive and at first glance contradictory best-sellers. The first, *The End of History and the Last Man*, took seriously the possibility that history ended with the end of the Cold War, and that the only credible regime left in the world is liberal democracy.[4] It seemed a lullaby calculated to make Americans, and the rest of the world, content with America's undeniably great victory. His more recent book, *The Great Disruption* (GD), claims to show that nature triumphs over efforts at human or historical transformation.[5] Human beings are social and rational beings by nature, and their natural instincts lead them to replace depleted social capital. This book, too, seems a lullaby, but one calculated to make Americans, and the rest of the world, satisfied that the contemporary view of morality and justice and their longings for community are compatible. Fukuyama's conclusion is that the human longings for love, the truth, and God are not natural at all.

Fukuyama's thoughts on history's end, he acknowledges, are indebted to the great Hegelian Alexandre Kojève, the semi-secret founder of postmodernism.[6] Kojève claims to understand even better than Hegel himself that the end of history would have to be the end of human distinctiveness or liberty. Everything, for Kojève, depends on the distinction between nature and history. Nature is what is determined by impersonal, rational laws. But human beings are distinguished by being free or historical. They alone can act to negate nature and transform themselves over time. They are temporal beings because they are self-conscious mortals. So human wisdom is a complete articulation of all that is implied in being a mortal. Every human life has a beginning and an end. History itself must have a beginning and an end. Only at history's end can one be certain that human existence is essentially historical. That certainty, and the radical atheism it implies, constitutes Kojève's alleged wisdom.

Specifically human desire, Kojève contends, is the desire to be recognized as free by another free being. It is the desire to be definitively free from one's natural dependence or finitude. Human beings act in response to that dissatisfaction, and that action is history. At the end of history, human beings are seen by each other as equally free or equally historical beings. They also see that the free being, the one who can act, must still die. The recognition of human freedom, paradoxically, must be the recognition of human finitude. Kojève implies that political recognition is finally an insufficient compensation for death, and so the misery connected with death overwhelms the satisfaction that comes from being a free and equal citizen. At the end of history, death, or the being who dies, must be put to death. The lesson of history is that history was an error.

Kojève's radical observation is that both liberal and socialist societies recognize the equal freedom of all human beings as citizens, and so are devoted to putting death to death. Freed from illusions about nature and God, and therefore able to understand the historical being as an error, they aim to complete the reanimalization of man they have accepted in principle. No moral resistance to the technological effort to extinguish human liberty and make human beings—like the other animals—completely at home in nature can be effective. The moral principles that might support such resistance have been authoritatively discredited by history.

For Kojève everything depends on whether humans are essentially historical or natural beings. He claims to have evidence that they are historical, and that human liberty has no future. He might be called a teacher of evil insofar as he promotes a life *without* good and evil. Much of his writing was undertaken to show the futility of resistance to the destruction of what may remain of human liberty. But Kojève, at least in his later writing, claims to write in the mode of description, not ethics. He merely chronicles the record of human self-destruction. Human beings cannot choose whether or not to be like the other animals again. At the end of history, the alien or stranger in the cosmos, the historical being, has disappeared. Far from being a cosmic catastrophe, that disappearance is good for nature; the cosmos is really a cosmos once again. The alien is expelled.

Instead of presenting the choice between nature and history plainly, Fukuyama makes the incoherent claim that at the end of history the reigning form of government will be completely satisfying to human nature. He employs the Socratic, tripartite account of the soul to show that liberal democracy satisfies human desire, human spiritedness, and human reason. Human beings may now be satisfied or completely unalienated as human beings. Religion, according to Fukuyama, must wither away under liberalism. There is no need for otherworldly longing if this world is lacking in nothing.

Fukuyama pays lip service to the Nietzschean fear that the world at history's end might be filled with contemptible last men, but he does not really think that contemporary Americans are subhuman beings. With his confusing mixture of human nature and history, Fukuyama is far more pernicious than the openly misanthropic Kojève. The death of God, Kojève rightly says, must be the death of man. But for Fukuyama human beings can continue to be human at history's end, even without God. He gives human beings no reason to resist the idea of history's end.

The Return of Nature

The Great Disruption seems at first glance to choose human nature over history. Fukuyama opens with the famous quote from Horace about the foolishness of human efforts to throw out nature with a pitchfork. Nature "always comes running back," triumphing over history and technology, and not the other way around (*GD,* vii). Fukuyama now seems to believe that he was confused when he considered seriously the possibility that history might end, and he makes no such claim, at least explicitly, in this book.

Fukuyama sees that the distinction between nature and history made by Hegel, Marx, and Kojève really came from Rousseau. For Rousseau the natural human being is asocial, stupid, and wholly determined or unconscious. And so human reason and sociality are nothing but historical constructions. This state-of-nature premise, in truth, is the foundation of all modern individualism, including classical liberalism or libertarianism. The individual has no natural inclination for society, and he cooperates with others only as a means of achieving his individual or natural ends. Fukuyama observes that recent "primatological research is revealing because it shows us that a great deal of social behavior is not learned but is part of the genetic inheritance of both man and his great ape forebears" (*GD,* 167). If historical man evolved from the apes, as Rousseau thought, then we now know that natural man is a social being. Natural sociality, and not free human construction, is the main source of social and political life.

Rousseau wrongly thought that natural man was healthy and content because he was solitary and self-sufficient. At history's end, Kojève concluded on the basis of this Rousseauean foundation, human beings must return to that radically individualistic existence. But all the evidence we now have shows that humans are gregarious by nature, and that isolation or excessive individualism is pathological. The human animal cannot be content alone. All we now know about hunter-gatherer and prehistorical societies, not to mention what we now know about our close evolutionary relatives, the chimps, shows that Rousseau was also wrong to contend that natural man was more peaceful than allegedly late historical beings. Those societies long past were at least as violent as recent human society (GD, 166–67). The aggressiveness and status-orientation of the chimps even suggest that there is no specifically human quality that makes human beings more bellicose than other species. The competition among chimps to be alpha male Fukuyama understands as at least incipiently political, contradicting Kojève's view that the desire for recognition is distinctively human or historical.

Fukuyama sees the breakdown in social life in recent decades to be pathological but temporary. The disruption caused by the technological movement from an industrial to an information-based economy, and especially by the invention of the birth-control pill, is now in the process of being repaired by human reform rooted in the persistence of social human nature. Human beings desire social stability and communal belonging, so they naturally or spontaneously create social rules. The libertarian "spontaneous order" literature, according to Fukuyama, correctly argues that human beings will produce order if left to their own devices, and that order will be small scale and decentralized (GD, 232).

Fukuyama endorses most recent conservative reforms in opposition to those policies implemented in the 1960s that combined permissive individualism with big, centralized government. Yet he opposes, most of all, conservative critics of capitalism or liberalism. "Social capital," he asserts, "is not . . . a rare cultural treasure passed down across the generations—something that, if lost, can never again be regained" (GD, 145). Because it is rooted in nature, "it is not something with a fixed supply that is now being remorselessly depleted by us modern, secular people" (GD, 282). Nature cannot be cast out by misguided human projects, and so modern society does not depend on the premodern inheritances of religion, family, and political community. Each of those institutions has a natural, and not merely historical or traditional, foundation, and so each is bound to reappear in some form or another.

The good news is that we can look to the future without seeking authoritative guidance from the past, and we are free to reject those aspects of the past that seem irrational or unnatural. Rationalism does not lead naturally to individualism or unconstrained permissiveness, because the rational being by nature is also a social one. Reason properly understood is a tool for a human being to fulfill his natural and largely social longings. Fukuyama agrees with Burke that "reason is insufficient to create the moral constraints needed to hold societies together." No rational-choice theorist can ever account for the emotional or social dimension to human choice, and so those theorists misunderstand how human beings employ reason. But Fukuyama also rejects the "relativistic element to Burkean conservatism," which comes from a lack of confidence in natural sociality (GD, 251).

Fukuyama's confidence comes from the life sciences, and so he finds the foundation of human stability in the fact of natural evolution. Human beings are "born with preexisting cognitive structures . . . that lead them naturally into society" (GD, 155). But these "hard-wired" structures did not always exist (GD, 158). The coming-into-existence of all human characteristics, he believes, can be explained by the requirements of the species' adaptation to its environment. Contrary to individualistic philosophers such as Hobbes and Locke, Fukuyama says that evolution can be explained more in terms of species than individual preservation, although both are important motivations of behavior. So humans are partly social and partly self-interested beings, and sociological and economic explanations of human behavior are both partly correct, though not for the reasons social scientists give (*GD*, 148–50, 154–55, 160–62).

Fukuyama notices that the size of the human brain has tripled during the time that the human line of evolution separated from that of the chimpanzees. He admits that the evolutionary explanations for that rapid, unprecedented growth are only speculative, but he seems certain that some such story must be true. He knows that the development of the neocortex gave human beings seemingly unique qualities like complex language, consciousness, religion, and culture, but in his view these institutions and capabilities exist as means for evolutionary or essentially physiological ends (*GD*, 175, 177, 182). He refuses to join Kojève in considering the possibility that the capacities for language and consciousness are inexplicable cosmic accidents that must be accounted for historically, not naturally. Nor does the possibility of an inexplicable discontinuity within nature itself open him to the possibility of the truth of biblical revelation.

Fukuyama dismisses as unrealistic the libertarian dream in which coercive, hierarchical political life will completely wither away, to be replaced by wholly spontaneous and efficient social cooperation. Human beings will remain to some extent political or status-seeking beings. Like chimps, they naturally organize themselves into hierarchies (*GD*, 227–28, 234). And history has shown that political coercion or formal legal authority and war have been required to extend the scope of human cooperation and social order. It is naïve, for example, to believe that American slavery would have evolved out of existence because of its inefficiency (*GD*, 221).

Human beings have gone much further than the other animals in organizing their entire species hierarchically. Their organizations have increased in complexity, from families to tribes to political communities. Human beings have done so, in part, because they naturally desire to rule and receive recognition, and their brains allow them to use reason much more efficiently to satisfy this desire than do the brains of chimps. Here Fukuyama surely, if perhaps accidentally, calls attention to a tension in human desire. Our social natures point in the direction of the communal belonging and selfishness of small, tightly-knit groups (GD, 236–37). But our political natures point to large and finally universal or universalistic states. The mixture of reason and the natural desire for recognition might be understood to disrupt the natural affinity for bonding with family and friends. But that apparently fundamental natural tension is not one of Fukuyama's themes. He does not present the great disruption of our time in terms of contradictory tendencies in human nature, even if he does admit "that the progress of capitalism simultaneously improves and injures moral behavior" (GD, 254).

Moral Universalism

Near the end of his book, Fukuyama actually acknowledges, although not consistently and surely contrary to Horace, that human moral progress is not rooted in nature at all, but in the idea of moral universalism, or the recognition of the capacity of each human being for moral choice. Life scientists, of course, do not explain human thought or behavior that way; at this point Fukuyama's mode of expression suddenly and unexpectedly becomes Kantian or Hegelian. Human beings, it appears, have the freedom to negate nature on behalf of rational idealism. They, alone among the animals, can establish their autonomy or freedom from nature. Human beings, it appears, have rights, Fukuyama strongly suggests, because they are free beings, not because they are natural ones. The "principle of universal recognition" links the Declaration of Independence, Kant, Hegel, "the Universal Declaration of Rights, and the rights enumerated in the laws of virtually all contemporary liberal democracies today" (GD, 280). The elites in these liberal democracies do not understand rights to be rooted in nature. And all human experience, except that of the modern West, is that social beings do not understand themselves as beings with rights.

Fukuyama does make a rather lame effort to reduce moral universalism to a rational tool for self-preservation. He announces that the Enlightenment discovered that all traditional sources of community were irrational because they led to social conflict internally and war with other communities externally. Moral universalism, on the other hand, leads to a peaceful domestic and international order. Fukuyama asserts that "the great moral conflicts of our time have arisen over the tendency of human communities to define themselves narrowly on the basis of religion, ethnicity, or some other arbitrary characteristic, and to fight it out with other, differently defined communities" (GD, 274). That might explain National Socialism to some limited extent, and the conflicts in Northern Ireland and in the former Yugoslavia. It does not account at all for the Cold War, which was a competition between two forms of universalism. Nor does it account for the approximately one hundred million people killed in the name of (morally universalistic) communist ideology during the twentieth century. Religion and ethnicity, all things considered, have not ranked near the top of the most murderous motivations of our time. On the moral evolution from war to peace on the basis of self-preservation or fear of the consequences of high-tech war, Fukuyama shares the naiveté of Kant and his disciple Woodrow Wilson. But they had the excuse of not having the benefit of post-World War I experience.

Fukuyama becomes even more confusing when he observes that moral universalism actually originated with religion and was only later secularized or politicized. He does not explain why, or even if, human

beings are religious beings by nature. Following the lead of the life sciences, he does not think that consciousness or any other human quality is
the source of the longings which point beyond the natural world. He also
seems to accept Kojève's Hegelian or historical view of religion. Human
beings, dissatisfied with their inability to satisfy their desire for recognition in this world, imaginatively create another one where this desire is
satisfied. That imaginary construction becomes a project for historical
or political reform. Fukuyama writes that the Christian principle of the
universality of human dignity was "brought down from the heavens and
turned into a secular doctrine of universal human equality by the Enlightenment" (GD, 279). The political effort of the modern West has been
to achieve in this world what the Christian God achieved only in heaven.
In other words, "the business of building higher-order hierarchies was
taken away from religion and given to the state" (GD, 237). The shared
values of human beings used to be religious; now they are political. At
one time nearly all Americans might have regarded their nation as essentially Christian, but now only a small and suspicious minority do.

The separation of religion from "state power," Fukuyama contends,
was the cause of its "long-term decline" in "the developed world" (GD,
238). This decline is beneficial and irreversible. He dismisses the hope of
some conservatives and the fear of many liberals that "moral decline"
might be stemmed "by a large-scale return to religious orthodoxy, a Western version of Ayatollah Khomenei returning to Iran on an airliner" (GD,
278). His identification of orthodoxy with the fanatical Khomenei rather
than Orthodox Judaism or John Paul II reveals his belief that God is dead.
That is, Fukuyama suggests that sophisticated people now associate orthodox belief with unreasonable moral and political repression, which
apparently is evidence that there is no natural foundation for such hierarchical belief. Fukuyama emphatically does not praise the countercultural
role small orthodox communities have played in filling the moral vacuum
caused by the temporary depletion of social capital. And that is because

"we ... are not so bereft of innate moral resources that we need to wait for a messiah to save us" (*GD*, 278).

No Mere Restoration

The closest Fukuyama comes to praise of religious orthodoxy is his presentation of Louis Farrakhan's Islamic Nationalist Million Man March and the "conservative Christian" Promise Keepers as evidence that "something was amiss in the expectations society had of men, and that men had of themselves." But he soon dismisses those groups as "highly suspect" to liberal, democratic, and morally universalistic Americans (*GD*, 275-76). The subordination of women discredits the Promise Keepers, as anti-Semitism does the Nation of Islam. Treating the two groups as immoral equivalents shows how promiscuous Fukuyama's disdain for orthodoxy and religious hierarchy is. The return to orthodoxy, or, specifically, the idea of the sanctity of marriage, cannot be the way to restore paternal or parental responsibility. That would seem to be especially bad news for fatherhood, and Fukuyama quietly accepts and affirms that troubling conclusion.

Fukuyama notices that the nuclear family is again strengthening in reaction against the social disruption caused by its near collapse. But the end of disruption will be no mere restoration. Fukuyama believes that people will not return to the old, largely religious norms concerning sex, reproduction, and family life. The new technological and economic conditions have made strict "Victorian values" obsolete. After all, "no one is about to propose making birth control illegal or reversing the movement of women into the workplace." And if "unregulated sex" no longer leads to pregnancy, and having a child out of wedlock no longer leads to "destitution," then why have legal or moral sexual rules at all? So "the stability of nuclear families is likely never to recover," and "kinship as a source of social connectedness will probably continue to decline." Parents, mindful of "their children's long-term life chances," will continue to have fewer of them (*GD*, 275–76).

Fukuyama seems to welcome a world full of promiscuous, prosperous, but never lonely single mothers. Technology, contrary to the general thrust of Fukuyama's pitchfork argument, has changed the nature of women by dissociating sex from reproduction, and so has also altered the more culturally created role of the man as father. The life scientists regard the relationship between mother and child as strongly natural, but that of father and child as only very weakly so. In this sociobiological view, men are so naturally promiscuous that women have had to trick them into being faithful husbands and fathers.

Such trickery is no longer worth the trouble. Fathers are free to live naturally or promiscuously without guilt, legal responsibility, or social stigma. Fukuyama criticizes the therapeutic platitude that children grow up just as well in a single-parent than in a two-parent family, but he also makes clear that we better hope that the therapists are not all that wrong (*GD*, 273–74). The new family in the new society will be nothing like the one traditionally supported by hierarchical religion.

Yet religion has not quite withered away. Fukuyama notices a return to "primitive," decentralized, and merely instrumental religion. No religion has ever until now understood itself as merely instrumental, but that has changed. Religion has become merely a "convenient" and "rational" support for our desires for social belonging and social rules. This new religion is not some *civil* theology, because the thoroughly secularized moral universalism of the political realm is quite able to stand alone. It is merely a *social* theology, generated by various forms of spontaneous order (*GD*, 238).

Fukuyama suggests that today's "benign" religion assists in repairing the damage done to social life by orthodox religion (*GD*, 238). But from a merely natural perspective, how orthodox religion came to oppose spontaneous, decentralized order with moral universalism remains a mystery.

People today are more enlightened because they are conscious that religion should serve their natural inclinations. Free from hierarchical, orthodox fanaticism, they feel more at home as natural beings. But religion could not have achieved the goal of moral universalism had it been viewed as merely instrumental. Our knowledge of ourselves as merely natural, social beings must have been a product of historical development, and it has brought the morality-altering and historically transformative role of religion to an end. In a loose way, Fukuyama is in greater agreement with Kojève in *The Great Disruption* than he was in *The End of History*. He points to the conclusion that history has come to an end, and the result is that humans are merely natural beings again.

Fukuyama also seems to agree with Richard Rorty, who says that Americans have come to prefer comfort to truth, because they now know they are not, by nature, inclined to know the truth. People, Fukuyama explains, "will repeat the ancient prayers and reenact age-old rituals not because they were handed down by God, but because they want their children to have proper values and want to enjoy the comfort of ritual and the sense of shared experience it brings" (GD, 279). Ignoring for now the question of whether proper values can really include unregulated sex, we must wonder whether genuine comfort and sharing is available to human beings who have no concern for God and truth.

The return of religion without hierarchy or God is part of a package for social restoration that, according to Fukuyama, includes the celebration of the national independence day, "dress[ing] up in traditional ethnic garb," and "read[ing] the classics of [one's] own cultural tradition" (GD, 279). Today's priests, rabbis, and ministers, to recall an old joke, are all dressed up with nowhere to go. The form, not the content, is for Fukuyama what binds us to the past and to each other. Kojève said at one point that posthistorical beings can still remain snobs; likewise, our ability to perpetuate the meaningless forms of the past for their own sake might still separate us from the other animals. Perhaps Jewish and Chris-

tian sacred services have become no different from Japanese tea cer-
emonies. But Fukuyama's instrumental traditionalists are not snobs,
a term that sounds too proud and hierarchical and not comforting
enough.

I am not going to dwell on the fact that the principles of the American Declaration of Independence claim not to be traditional but true,
and that Fukuyama's affirmation of moral universalism is in some way an
affirmation of their truth. Yet I must mention that the most successful
effort to revive the reading of the classic texts of the Western tradition in
our time, the one inaugurated by Leo Strauss, was inspired by the pursuit
of truth, not comfort, as Fukuyama well knows. I must add that those
religious sects which claim to speak truthfully and with authority about
a living, loving God are the ones that are flourishing, and that those that
believe in the authentic sanctity of marriage and the family are the ones
with the best value-laden programs for children. Those that consciously
claim to provide nothing but a comfortable, communal experience tend
to languish.

Fukuyama has confused us about whether human beings crave hierarchical authority by nature, or whether that chimp-like quality has been
eroded almost beyond recognition by free, historical progress. But it is
another thing altogether to say that human beings do not long to know
the truth about God and the fate of their souls, that they are not, in their
self-conscious perception of their incompleteness and their mortality, in
some way open to the divine. And it is another thing still to say that love
and anything resembling marriage are compatible with unregulated sex.
But Fukuyama is not particularly concerned with the intimate, personal
union between man and woman, the love of one human being for another, but only with properly providing for the rearing of children.

Percy versus Fukuyama

The key difference between Percy and Fukuyama on evolution is that Percy holds that the development of the neocortex made human beings qualitatively distinct from the other animals. They became self-conscious beings who are defined by love—including love of each other, God, and the truth—and death. Percy understood what we know about evolution in light of the long Western tradition that human beings are tormented by nature by a longing for immortality, and that they have excellences, perversities, and a capacity for both good and evil not given to the other animals. There are responsibilities given by nature to human beings that are shared neither by angels nor by chimps.

Part of Fukuyama's lullaby—the dominant view of evolutionary biology—is that species survival, not personal survival, is the major source of our longings. In this view, we are only moved, unconsciously, by instincts no different in kind from those of the other animals. As Fukuyama explains, "throughout the natural [including human] world, order is created by the blind, irrational processes of natural selection" (*GD,* 146). One of Fukuyama's teachers, Allan Bloom, like Percy said that human beings are defined by love and death, and that the capacity to be moved by them is fading in sophisticated America today. So Fukuyama ought to know what is conspicuous by its absence in his analysis of human nature. He says virtually nothing about the experience of self-consciousness and the love of one conscious being for another. For Fukuyama human eros appears not to be polymorphous, nor does human perversity. He may believe, though it is unclear, that the homogeneous, reductionistic explanations of evolutionary biology become more completely true as human self-consciousness or history recedes.

But Fukuyama's suggestion that love and death might disappear, or almost disappear, is more perplexing than Kojève's. Consciousness of death, the intractable natural limitation, would seem, on Fukuyama's account, to be natural. What Kojève and Rousseau regard as historical acquisitions, Fukuyama views as the product of human nature. So somehow he must contend that human beings are not always shaped or moved much by what they really know by nature. Human perversity, Fukuyama suggests, is about to evolve out of existence, because the human being no longer wrongly understands himself as an alien, as more than a natural being. In this respect, Kojève would have observed, Fukuyama writes as a pragmatist, one who vulgarly or fearfully refuses to speak the truth of existentialism—that the human is a being who is dissatisfied because he knows he will die.

Fukuyama's most coherent but still quite questionable claim is that history progresses but nature is cyclical (GD, 282). His most fundamental criticism of Kojève is that human beings cannot return to being stupid, asocial animals because that is not what they are like by nature. They have social (but not spiritual and only minimally political) needs that must be satisfied. So political life, the family, and religion can be reconstituted in ways compatible with our historical achievement of moral universalism. On this point, Fukuyama is also more realistic than his fellow pragmatist Rorty. Rorty writes as if all human experience is the product of description and redescription. For Rorty, everything human is a linguistic creation; people are not limited or directed by nature at all. Rorty writes as if religion, the family, and perhaps even the state could just be talked out of existence, and he views all social life as merely an instrument for the enjoyment of private fantasies. Rorty also says that human beings are coming to define themselves, in Darwinian fashion, as clever animals and nothing more. They have decided to surrender their cruelty-producing illusions concerning theology and metaphysics. On this point, Rorty seems more realistic, more honest than Fukuyama. They both define man as merely a clever (social) animal, but Fukuyama does not present that definition, as Rorty does, as morally inspired propaganda.

The social beings of the great restoration of human nature will have no point of view by which to resist or be alienated from social and political life. They will long for community and social stability, but they will not have any moral or religious principles by which to criticize their ersatz communities. Such a principled point of view, coming from the natural openness of human beings to a morally relevant order of Being, allowed the dissidents Solzhenitsyn and Havel to resist communist tyranny, but perhaps in Fukuyama's and Rorty's views the need for such resistance has become obsolete. Hierarchical narrowness and conflict, Fukuyama believes, has little future. Evil, either having no natural foundation or having been overcome by history or both, has disappeared from the world. Human nature is basically good, and there is every reason to believe that it will perpetuate itself.

The End of Human Nature

In an article in *The National Interest* presenting his "Second Thoughts" on history's end, published almost simultaneously with *The Great Disruption*, Fukuyama announces that human nature "definitely" has no future (26).[7] He also says that he was wrong to say that history could end, because, in his mind, that end implies a natural standard by which we can say human beings are satisfied. Socialism was defeated by human nature. But what if human beings can consciously and fundamentally alter their natures technologically? What if they can decide—not through political action or linguistic propaganda, but through scientific manipulation—to become something else? Today, Fukuyama's analysis of human nature in his books remains mostly relevant. But as for tomorrow? "To the extent that nature is something given to us not by God or by our evolutionary inheritance, but by human artifice, then we enter into God's own realm with all of the frightening powers for good and evil that such an entry implies" ("Second Thoughts," 31).

In *The Great Disruption* Fukuyama reduced human beings to clever, social animals, but in "Second Thoughts" he says they are on the way to becoming gods. The twenty-first century, he predicts, will be the century of biology (28). His *Great Disruption* aspires to be the definitive biological or sociobiological treatise of that century's beginning. There he celebrates nature's victory over human manipulation. Now (and this is an amazing contradiction) he says that we are on the verge of a biology-based conquest of nature that makes all previous human efforts look like nothing. Biologists are about to bring the genetics of aging under human control, and soon human beings will live for hundreds of years, with no certain limit on life expectancy. More importantly, biotechnology will soon be able to alter the functioning of human beings in ways that affect not only the treated individual, but "all subsequent descendants of that individual." What the communists and Nazis failed to do politically the scientists may soon accomplish technologically: They will create "a new type of human being," one not at all determined by natural inclinations beyond human control ("Second Thoughts," 28).

The first efforts at genetic manipulation will be to eliminate disease and obvious physiological disorders, and it will be difficult to quarrel with the results. But soon the efforts will extend to the eradication of dwarfism, and then mere shortness. And then scientists will address human personality characteristics deemed undesirable, if not exactly unhealthy. Men are more violent and aggressive than women, and their genes as much as their environment point them in the direction of prison. So why not eliminate these distinctively male qualities? Fukuyama himself had gone a long way in *The Great Disruption* toward the conclusion that such quantities have become superfluous. A well-ordered person is one with no propensity for violence, no desire to strike out against others or his community. Biotechnology will bring cruelty to an end. Fukuyama cautions that there must be discussion about "what constitutes health," but he gives no argument for the goodness of the male spirit of resistance ("Second Thoughts," 29). Perhaps science can correct certain residual aberrations of evolution in the general spirit of evolution's intent.

The prelude to the biotechnological determination of the future is the successes of neuropharmacology, or drug therapy. Ritalin and Prozac are powerful, widely used drugs that have fundamentally changed human behavior. They have helped those who are severely disruptive or depressed. But Ritalin is also routinely given to boys "characterized simply as high spirits." And Prozac calms nervous women through chemically produced feelings of high self-esteem. By taking the edge off being either a man or a woman, the drugs "move us imperceptibly toward the kind of androgynous human being that has been the egalitarian goal of contemporary sexual politics" ("Second Thoughts," 30–31).

If Fukuyama is correct everyone will come to have the same, well-ordered personality, according to our egalitarian ideal. Biotechnology can do a better job than nature herself in making us perfectly social beings at home in the world. The distinction between male and female has always been alienating and confusing. What could be wrong with doing away with it? Fukuyama "wonders what the careers of tormented geniuses like Blaise Pascal or Nietzsche himself would have looked like had they been born to American parents and had Ritalin and Prozac available to them at an early age" ("Second Thoughts," 31). They would have been untormented! True, their torment was intertwined with their ability to know much of the truth about Being and human beings, and to be haunted and deepened spiritually by God's hiddenness or death. But according to evolutionary biology, human beings are not fitted by nature to know the truth, and the fanatical pursuit of truth by tormented geniuses has not been good for the species. Fukuyama's suggestion in *The Great Disruption* is that the world is better off without such men, who preferred truth to the comfort of social belonging, who had with special intensity the disquieting experience of being aliens. He observes that the alleviation of depression by psychoanalysis, or telling the truth to oneself about oneself with the help of another, has been replaced by psychotherapy, the chemical management of symptoms. The latter method, of course, works much better.

Fukuyama has little hope that human beings will be able to resist biotechnology on behalf of God, nature, or just manliness or womanliness. There are two global revolutions going on, one in information technology and one in biotechnology. According to Fukuyama, the information revolution has had leveling, libertarian, and beneficial effects. There is an attempt by nonscientists to regulate biotechnology morally, but soon the "libertarian mindset" of the market-defined and morally universalized world will brush such moral concerns aside as "uninformed prejudice" ("Second Thoughts," 32).

He cannot help but conclude that "within the next couple of generations we will have the knowledge and technologies that will allow us to accomplish what the social engineers of the past failed to do. At that point, we will have definitively finished Human History because we will have abolished human beings as such. And then, a new, posthuman history will begin" ("Second Thoughts," 33). But posthuman history is qualitatively different from human history. And so Fukuyama, in spite of himself, finally explains how human history will end. Human beings will drug out of existence everything that makes them miserable—love, death, anxiety, spiritedness, depression. They will live for hundreds of years, but they will not care all that much about the lengthening lifespan. Death will mean little or nothing to them. It goes without saying that science cannot actually eradicate the fact of death, but perhaps it can keep death from distorting or defining what otherwise would be healthy human life. Human beings will become fundamentally no different, except perhaps less spirited or aggressive and so less gregarious, than other gregarious animals.

The Teacher of Evil

Contrary to his liberal intentions, Fukuyama is a teacher of evil because if the account of human nature he gives in *The Great Disruption* is correct, then we have no motivation, no reason to resist the impending evil he describes in "Second Thoughts," an evil potentially far worse than the Holocaust or the Gulag. Those who prefer comfort to truth and are rationally or skeptically distrustful of all hierarchies will swallow pills and submit to operations for their obvious social and survival values. Fukuyama is a teacher of evil because he has not really asked the questions Percy does in *The Thanatos Syndrome*, a novel just a bit ahead of its time about a scientific project with political support to use chemicals to suppress human self-consciousness: Why is the surrender of self-consciousness bad for human beings? Why does it diminish them? Why does it enslave them to experts, that is, self-proclaimed gods, who exempt themselves from the treatment they impose on others? Why does the effort to eliminate all human disorder and suffering in the name of health lead to projects for the extermination of large numbers of human beings? Why is it better to be a dislocated or alienated human being than a contented chimp? And finally, why, in the end, are the attempts to alter nature and to replace God doomed to failure?

CHAPTER THREE

Aliens Are Us?

*F*rom the beginning of the West, morally sensitive and politically astute writers have criticized the moral and political effects of the self-forgetfulness characteristic of natural scientists. Aristophanes, in the *Clouds*, ridicules the practical obtuseness of the natural scientist Socrates, who understands everything that exists except himself and his fellow human beings. For Aristophanes, Socrates was dangerously indifferent to morality because he abstracted theoretically from the distinctiveness of human nature, from human fears, passions, and longings. Plato, accepting that criticism, presents a different Socrates, one who remains philosophical but is attentive to the human difference, to the natural foundation of moral, political, and religious longings. Walker Percy, in his instructive mocking of the natural scientist Carl Sagan, is the Aristophanes of our time. But his comedy, like Plato's, is in the service of philosophy rightly understood. Percy, a strange combination of novelist, philosopher, scientist, and Catholic, may show us bet-

ter than anyone else how to correct our natural scientists' self-forgetfulness without abandoning science or philosophy. Percy, in my view, is a
sort of Catholic Socratic, if by Socrates we mean the one portrayed by
Plato, not the one criticized so well by Aristophanes.[1]

Sagan and Percy both wrote prose and fiction that are wrongly la-
beled as popularizing. They connected scientific knowledge to the fundamental questions of human life, and so no question was alien to either
of them. Percy wrote his *Lost in the Cosmos: The Last Self-Help Book*, a hilari-
ous and profound mixture of literary forms that includes a two-part
space odyssey, partly to correct Sagan's elegant *Cosmos*, a huge best-seller
as a book and equally successful as a television series. Sagan's *Pale Blue Dot*
(*PBD*), containing his thoughts on the human condition, intelligent extraterrestrial life, stars, planets, comets, and a possible human future in
space, was written after Percy's death, but it is the fullest and most inspirational version of Sagan's literary project.[2]

Sagan and Percy agree that human beings are naturally wanderers and
wonderers, but they disagree on why human beings wander and wonder.
So they also disagree on both the likely benefits of space travel and on the
nature of aliens, if such exist. Although they were both prolific writers, I
will, for the most part, limit my comparison of the two to their arguments in *Pale Blue Dot* and *Lost in the Cosmos*. Though my analysis of Sagan
will come first, it is driven by my desire to see why Percy found Sagan so
curious, and why Percy, rather than Sagan, better understands why human beings wonder and wander.

Sagan on the Wanderer

Sagan knows that the attractiveness of vast expenditures for space travel
faded with the end of the Cold War. Mere curiosity or wonder is rarely
enough to animate people or their political leaders. So Sagan's first words
are "We were wanderers from the beginning" (*PBD*, xi). And according to

Sagan we humans have been wanderers, hunters, and foragers until quite recently. We altered our way of life because we found better ways to satisfy our material needs, but "the sedentary life has left us edgy, unfulfilled" (*PBD,* xii). Despite our material success, we tend to believe that human greatness is past, that the best human efforts in literature, art, music, even science, are behind us. We even speculate, says Sagan, "that political life on Earth is about to settle into some rock-stable liberal democratic world government, identified, after Hegel, as 'the end of history.'" We are edgy because there is nothing new to do, and no point in wandering. But our nature, our biological desire for fulfillment, somehow still prods us to wander (*PBD,* 384–85, 390).

Sagan arouses a little nostalgia through an appeal to anthropology: "Judging from some of the last surviving hunter-gatherers just before they were engulfed by the present global civilization, we may have been relatively happy" (*PBD,* 390). We can make that judgment because we know we are relatively unhappy now. But there is no going back. We have forgotten how to be hunter-gatherers, and even if we had not, that way of life could not support the number of people now on the planet. But most of all, Sagan contends, as hunter-gatherers "we would be helpless before the impact catastrophe that inexorably will come" (*PBD,* 383–84).

Sagan believes that just as the original hunter-gatherers roamed in the pursuit of survival, we need to wander again for the same reason. This is because we now know that "the chance is almost one in a thousand that much of the human population will be killed by an [asteroid] impact in the next century" (*PBD,* 320). And if not in the next century, the impact will surely come eventually. The only way our species can perpetuate itself indefinitely is for some of us to abandon this planet. From another planet, we may be able to develop and use the technology required to reliably deflect asteroids from earth. And even if that technology fails and life is destroyed on earth, the species will survive because it will have dispersed. "The eventual choice" of all intelligent, planet-dependent species is "spaceflight or extinction"(*PBD*, 327). And space travel must eventually be more than just planet-hopping. We should not be deceived by how "reliable" the sun has been so far (*PBD*, 387).

So Sagan contends that we need to begin to wander through the planets and eventually solar systems and galaxies to give our species "a jolt of productive vitality" (*PBD*, 284) and with the purpose of making the species as safe as possible. Our era is extraordinary because of the unprecedented danger of self-destruction (through nuclear war) and the unprecedented opportunity for indefinitely postponing destruction, both the result of the present state of technological development (*PBD*, 373–74). Sagan cites Bertrand Russell's idea that space travel might "show to even the most adventurous of the young that a world without war need not be a world without adventurous and hazardous glory" (*PBD*, 284). Purposeful, species-unifying adventure without war is just what we need today. Space travel will save us from both asteroids and each other.

We may wonder whether Sagan's analysis of wandering is too simply biological. But he does say that without the "escape hatch" of space travel, "we may have been locked and bolted into a prison of the self," and that we need to get our minds off ourselves and on to "something vastly larger" (*PBD*, 405). And saying we cannot help but wander is of great help in explaining our dissatisfaction. Sagan disagrees with those who hold that we are homesick for our roots, for some stable and particular social order. He writes, in part, to make us at home with our homelessness. The strongest human longings, properly understood, do not hold us to any particular community, planet, or solar system.

Wondering About Cosmic Magnificence
and Human Insignificance

Sagan says that human beings are passionate and inquisitive, or wonderers, by nature (*PBD*, 36). They rightly wonder about the human place in the cosmos, about the vast, awesome, and magnificent universe considered as a whole, and about the possibility of intelligent extraterrestrial life elsewhere in the cosmos (*PBD*, 54–56). Human beings "experience a stirring of wonder" when they first discover the simple truth that we are cosmic accidents and that the universe was not made for us (*PBD*, 12). Sagan quotes Tolstoy, who wrote, "The meaningless absurdity of life is the only incontestable knowledge available to man" (*PBD*, 53). But our pretensions are as natural as our curiosity and wonder; "our natural way of viewing the world" comes from the primates, who proudly privilege their own group. We are naturally given to "a kind of ethnocentrism" (*PBD*, 47).

We both do (because of wonder) and do not (because of pride) want to view ourselves as modern science does—as accidents. Human beings want to believe in a providential God or nature, that they are cared for and are the highest part of existence. But the progress of science has been the "Great Demotion" of man to a tiny, insignificant being who is in no qualitative way different from the other animals. Efforts, borne of pride or religion or both, to resist scientific truth "betray a failure of nerve before the Universe—its grandeur and magnificence but especially its indifference." The truth discovered by science is rational and impersonal, and it is this: there are no grand and magnificent persons (*PBD*, 50–51). According to Sagan, our wonder eventually overwhelmed our prideful and religious delusions: "As we began to indulge our curiosity, though, to explore, to learn how the universe really is, we expelled ourselves from Eden" (*PBD*, 56).

Sagan refuses to agree with the argument of some contemporary physicists that our ability to understand how the universe really is, its order and design, is evidence that the human mind, at least, is somehow at home in the cosmos; human existence could not simply be accidental or insignificant. We may be specks of dust on a pale blue dot, but we can also crack the "cosmic code." Wondering about the cosmos or the whole of nature and our knowledge of that whole have no obvious survival value, and they are hard or impossible to explain in terms of some accidental process of evolution.[3] But Sagan skeptically—if also dogmatically—refuses to say that our purpose is to know the cosmos, although he does say that we cannot help but wander and wonder. The scientists, Sagan contends, who adhere to some kind of anthropic principle, the view that life had an inherent tendency to evolve in the direction of consciousness, are infected by "residual pride" (PBD, 38).

Sagan on the Sacred

Modern science, in Sagan's eyes, seems in some respects to demonstrate the truth of existentialism. Science shows us that human life is absurd and insignificant, and human beings must have the courage to admit that there is no providential God and that nature views their existence with indifference. Sagan says that "knowledge is preferable to ignorance," but not because it is enjoyable or comforting. "Better to embrace a hard truth," he asserts, "than a reassuring fable" (PBD, 57). For Sagan, courage, and so pride, more even than wonder or wisdom, sometime seem to be the qualities that lead us to the truth.

But existentialism is not Sagan's final word. He admits that "we crave some cosmic purpose" and apparently cannot be cured of it. Human beings were left without a "telos" when the advance of science finally eroded tradition and religious belief. But humans still need "a sacred project," "a sanctified notion of humanity's potential" (PBD, 403). And so, Sagan says, "let us find ourselves a worthy goal" (PBD, 57), and call that "long-term goal . . . a sacred project" (PBD, 405). A worthy goal, for Sagan, is one that integrates our natural or biological inclinations to wander, wonder, and preserve the species. Space travel aims to satisfy all three longings simultaneously. In order to begin to wander effectively, "we [must] vastly increase our knowledge of the Solar System," or make discoveries that flow from our wonder (*PBD*, 377). And of course our wandering will open our minds as never before to the magnificence of the universe, for Sagan the most awesome source of wonder.

Our wandering and wondering, Sagan declares, are rooted in the responsibility to survive given to the species by nature. The "longing for safety," most fundamentally, is what leads us to wander, and if human beings were ever to become content with the species' duration, the wandering would end. But then our species would have evolved into something else (*PBD*, 400). For now, meaning probably for millions of years, we can make species-safety our sacred cause. It is the one most solidly rooted in nature, and it is relatively free of proud delusion (*PBD*, 399). Here we must note Sagan's innovation. Liberal or bourgeois thinkers, following Christian psychology, connected human wandering or restlessness to the *individual*'s longing for safety, and the existentialists share that focus on the individual's, not the species', fate.

There are at least two reasons for Sagan's correction of the individualism of liberalism and existentialism: Obsessing about one's own fate leads to a narrow fearfulness incompatible with courage and openness to wonder. And the individual, of course, cannot really do much to fend off his impending death. In the name of virtue and success, our attention must turn from the individual to the species. But are self-conscious beings—those who wander and wonder—really motivated all that much by their species' fate? Or can they be made to be so in the future? Concern for the species may be more solid or scientific than concern with God, but can devotion to the species really replace my love of a God who cares for me in particular? Human beings really are individuals, each concerned with his or her own mortality. One of the ways Sagan tries to turn the focus away from the uniqueness of human self-consciousness is to say that chimps are self-conscious too (*PBD*, 31). But Sagan, the celebrant of wandering and wondering, does not really want us to revert to the consciousness of chimps, much less become unconscious.

Sagan searches for "myths of encouragement" to support our choice of "many worlds" over none. He notices that "many religions, from Hinduism to Gnostic Christianity to Mormon doctrine, teach that—as impious as it sounds—it is the goal of human beings to become Gods."

Sagan says for the record that he worries "about people who aspire to be 'god-like,'" but for purposes of encouragement he is willing to let that thought pass. He asks us to "consider the story in the Jewish Talmud left out of the book of Genesis," in which "God tells Eve and Adam that He intentionally left the Universe unfinished." The responsibility of our species "over countless generations" is to complete creation. Perhaps in the name of survival we can "rise to this supreme challenge" and eventually become gods (*PBD*, 382). Or will we? For in the religions Sagan mentions each god is immortal, not the species of gods.

Despite these pieties, Sagan's final word on religion is that "science has far surpassed religion in delivering awe." Because we have focused our thoughts on ourselves and not on the universe, we have come up with a puny God who mirrors our own insignificance. If religion would turn its attention to the universe in its grandeur, elegance, and subtlety, God himself would seem much greater, if quite indifferent to us in particular. Sagan's prediction is that "a religion, old or new, that stressed the magnificence of the Universe as revealed by modern science might be able to draw forth reserves of reverence and awe hardly tapped by the conventional faiths. Sooner or later, such a religion will emerge" (*PBD*, 52). That is, if we would not only turn our attention from the individual, but also from the species, we would finally find something worthy of our devotion.

Extraterrestrials and Intellectual Progress

Sagan wonders both about space travel and the possibility of extraterrestrial intelligence (ETI). Of course, the discovery of ETI need have nothing to do with space travel. The best method, in fact, according to Sagan, is radio contact, and Sagan encouraged the American government to pour resources into both the space program and signaling ETI. He was distressed by the American government's lack of interest in pursing such fundamental knowledge, observing that "every civilization in human history has devoted some of its resources to investigating deep questions about the Universe, and it is hard to think of a deeper one than whether we are alone."[4] Much of his writing is conducted in support of that search.

Sagan is distressed that extraterrestrials are so often portrayed as aliens, as beings fundamentally different from and threatening to us. If they find us, the thinking goes, "they will come here and eat us," making both space travel and sending out radio signals foolish (*PBD*, 353). To counter this, Sagan reports, he convinced Steven Spielberg to make his two hugely successful films about benign ETs (*PBD*, 355). Sagan himself, with his wife, wrote a strikingly similar film script, based on their best-selling novel *Contact*. The film, more than the book, is an encouraging myth, a story with a vaguely but insistently religious dimension. It begins with a brilliant and lonely girl who becomes a scientist and spends her life searching through the world with a shortwave and later through the cosmos for contact. She finally discovers comforting, paternalistic, advanced beings, who have been watching over us and gradually and benevolently intervening in our affairs. Through this initial contact, otherwise unknowable secrets about the nature of the cosmos are revealed to a human being. This discovery or revelation mysteriously brings inspiration to people searching for meaning to replace discredited biblical religion.[5] But in *Pale Blue Dot*, Sagan mocks all such pictures of fatherly providence as they have appeared throughout history.

Sagan too obviously manipulates the image of the biblical, paternal God to promote his allegedly more scientific view that ETI would likely be benign. Our fears about extraterrestrial intelligence, he says, are evidence of our "guilty conscience" about human history. They make no sense in terms of understanding a society more advanced than ours.[6] Given our obvious isolation in a particular part of the universe, Sagan can add: "The vast distances that separate the stars are providential. Beings and worlds are quarantined from one another. The quarantine is lifted only for those with sufficient self-knowledge and judgment to have traveled from star to star" (PBD, 398). But from a scientific view, even this claim, because it invokes providence, is suspicious.

Yet even the skeptical, scientific Sagan cannot help but often really see something rather providential: that technology and morality clearly evolve. Sagan writes that human conflict and violence are rooted in "the deep, ancient reptilian part of the brain." Human history is the movement away from violent, reptilian behavior and toward living scientifically and cooperatively, from pure body to pure mind.[7] With time, all intelligent life becomes less passionate and violent, or more benignly godlike. So even the biological desire to wander, he muses, might eventually fade away. The only glitch in this process is that moral evolution sometimes lags behind technological development, as is the case now on earth, raising the prospect of technological self-destruction. Extraterrestrials, Sagan says, may aid us in moral evolution, saving us from ourselves. If they appear at this crucial moment, especially when the government is dragging its heels on space travel, it must be regarded as providential.

But in musings buried in a footnote, Sagan makes clear that he knows that the Spielberg-Sagan picture of benign ETs is not necessarily true. There are, in truth, several imaginable ways that an advanced extraterrestrial civilization might view our species. It might, in Contact fashion, seek us out, offering the good news that a high-tech society can "avoid self-annihilation." Or, having escaped self-inflicted catastrophe in its own development, such a civilization might fear discovery, might consider contact with other civilizations dangerous. But it might also be "aggrandizing . . . looking for Lebensraum," or just aiming "to put down the potential competition"(PBD, 372).

One way of speculating on which of these possibilities is most likely is to consider Sagan's view of our species' extraterrestrial future. Sagan believes that we will abandon earth, which cannot support life forever. We will wander from planet to planet and solar system to solar system, consuming resources as we go. But the planets most useful to sustaining human life will be the ones already most likely to possess life, and Sagan admits that homesickness for earth will make those substantial and well-lit planets particularly attractive. We might find potential conflict well worth risking (*PBD*, 391).

Does Sagan want us to become planet-hopping, parasitical, life-destructive, resource-consuming aliens like the ones portrayed in the film *Independence Day*? When it comes to the survival of the species he is "an unapologetic human chauvinist," and our exploration of our solar system will, unfortunately but necessarily, be a danger to any other life that may exist there (*PBD*, 376). He even adds, "A less sympathetic observer might describe" such cosmic wandering "as sucking dry the resources of little world after little world." His rejoinder is simply to observe that "there are a million little worlds in the Oort Comet Cloud," which will just be the beginning of our journey. For all practical purposes there is an infinite amount of sucking to do (*PBD*, 387). By thinking about ourselves, we can see that we have no particular reason to believe that extraterrestrials we contact will be good to us. A civilization must minimize internal conflict to wander the cosmos, but it might do so, like a band of pirates, to prey on others.

We are inclined to conclude that Sagan is too hopeful about extraterrestrial benevolence, because he hopes that intellectual development can save beings from their personal troubles. In his view, scientists are less screwed up than ordinary people, and that view gives rise to his hopeful imagining about beings more advanced and intelligent than our best scientists. But Sagan is less hopeful than he wants us to be. In encouraging the quest for contact, he is promoting a noble risk. His curiosity about ETI is greater than his concern for banal human troubles, and he actually expects that the fulfillment of his hope for the discovery of other intelligent beings will be the culmination of the beneficial lesson science has taught us. The discovery of ETI will show us that even our intelligence is nothing special in the cosmos. It will show beyond doubt, in Sagan's mind, the untruth of our anthropocentric biblical religion.

Although he is confident that we will eventually establish contact with any number of forms of intelligent life throughout the cosmos, Sagan nevertheless admits the small possibility that despite our best efforts we will never hear from anyone. Yet even that failure would be most instructive: "It would speak eloquently of how rare the living things of our planet are, and would underscore, as nothing else in human history has, the individual worth of every human being" (*PBD*, 72–73). But this is strange: The last thing Sagan wants to do is to focus on individual worth. For his hope is that if the search for ETI succeeds, it will underscore the worthlessness of every human individual and show how ridiculous our individual self-obsession is. Our devotion will then turn to the magnificence of the cosmos.

Sagan believes that human beings must both discover and become intelligent extraterrestrials to fully come to terms with the truth about their existence as insignificant cosmic accidents, with no purpose except species survival. Both of these projects turn us away from the ineradicable truth of individual contingency and finitude by submerging us in some more enduring natural whole. Perhaps Sagan's deepest teaching is that the incontestable truth affirmed by Tolstoy is too hard for him or us really to bear. Sagan, finally, does not make us at home with our homelessness, but diverts us from what he believes to be the truth about how homeless we really are.

Percy's Self-Help Book

Walker Percy's *Lost in the Cosmos: The Last Self-Help Book* (*LC*), rightly views Sagan's *Cosmos* as fundamentally a failed attempt at a self-help book, and we can see that *Pale Blue Dot* is too. Sagan analyzes the plight of the wonderer and wanderer and offers a solution, and Percy does the same. But their understandings of our predicament and what we might do about it are quite different.

The core of Percy's self-help book is his explanation of "why it is that man is the only alien creature, so far as we know, in the entire Cosmos" (*LC*, 2). The human being, Percy shows, is the being with the capacity by nature for language. Because of that capacity, he can come to understand pretty well everything in the cosmos except himself. The self, or the being that can know the cosmos, is always a leftover in any account of the cosmos. So as modern science explains more and more about the cosmos, the human being experiences himself as more and more an alien. Modern science also tends to deprive that being of the language to articulate and come to terms with that growing experience of alienation. Percy disagrees with Sagan that that experience of human uniqueness is a proud delusion, with the Marxist that it can be remedied by economic transformation, and with the behaviorist that it can be cured through behavioral or environmental change. He also disagrees with Sagan that the remedy is wandering through space.

In Percy's first published novel, *The Moviegoer*, the protagonist Binx Bolling calls himself a wonderer and a wanderer. He begins as a self-forgetting scientist, a spectator or moviegoer, wondering about everything but himself. And his search barely diverts him from his despair. But soon he begins to wonder about himself, the searcher or wanderer. He discovers the true relationship between wondering and wandering.[8] The human being is a wanderer *because* he is a wonderer. The being who wonders cannot really account for or locate himself in the reality he can describe. He does not wander because he must hunt and gather, but because of his capacity for self-consciousness.

For Percy, the capacity for language, and therefore consciousness, is natural, but it introduces a fundamental discontinuity into nature that cannot be accounted for by the species' adaptation to its environment. "Neo-Darwinian theory has trouble accounting for the strange, sudden, and belated appearance of man, the conscious self which speaks, lies, deceives itself, and also tells the truth" (LC, 161). Percy imagines a conversation between two scientists in a stalled elevator in the Rockefeller Foundation building. The one who challenges the "post-Darwinian" asks, "How do you account for the fact that with the appearance of man . . . almost immediately thereafter [follows] a train of disasters and triumphs which seem to have very little to do with adapting to an environment," from suicide through heroism to "child abuse and loving care for the genetically malformed" (LC, 197)? Modern science, exemplified in Sagan, is unable to acknowledge this discontinuity, and is thus unable to acknowledge the source of the unique joys, miseries, and perversities of human nature. Our species obviously exists for more than self-preservation, for we are the only animals capable of consciously and perversely acting against self-preservation. We can commit suicide and murder, not to mention heroically risk our lives, for no natural reason. Language is a natural human capacity, and so consciousness, wondering, and wandering are natural too. But they cannot be explained in terms of the generally correct homogeneous theory of evolution. Human beings are by nature qualitatively different from the other animals.

Percy introduces this "thought experiment" to show that Sagan's dogma prevents him, most of all, from understanding himself:

> Imagine that you are the scientist who has at last succeeded in puncturing the last of man's inflated claims to uniqueness in the Cosmos. Now man is proved beyond doubt to be an organism among other organisms, a species in continuity with other species, a creature ex-

isting in interaction with an immanent Cosmos like all other creatures, like all elements, molecules, gaseous clouds, novas, galaxies.

Now, having placed man as an object of study in the Cosmos in
however an insignificant place, how do *you*, the scientist, the self
which hit upon this theory, how do you propose to reenter this very
Cosmos where you have so firmly placed the species to which you
belong? Who are you who has explained the Cosmos and how do you
fit into the Cosmos you have explained? (*LC,* 170)

Carl Sagan cannot locate Carl Sagan in the cosmos he describes: he
has no place even in his own species. Percy understands and even sometimes shares the scientist's motivation to transcend absolutely the dreariness of ordinary life, and he knows the feeling of the scientist or philosopher or artist that his activity is the most pleasurable for human beings,
so much so that all other human activities "are spoiled by contrast" (*LC,*
143). But the trouble is that such transcendence cannot define a whole
human life. Sagan cannot, in fact, become more than human by scientifically reducing all other human beings to beings just like the other animals. He remains a self or soul, born to trouble, and his science cannot
tell him how to reenter the world of his own kind.

It is not surprising that Percy goes on to ask, "Why is Carl Sagan so
lonely" (*LC,* 173)? Sagan, with as much single-mindedness as the heroine
of *Contact,* searches the cosmos for other intelligent life because he, having transcended or reduced to mere animal impulses the troubles and
concerns of his fellow human beings, has "no one left to talk to other
than the transcending intelligences of other worlds" (*LC,* 173). But a truly
transcendent intelligence would have no need for others, no experience
of loneliness, and no longing to love. Sagan denies human uniqueness,
but what member of what other species has undertaken the search he
has? Sagan's own curious behavior provides plenty of evidence for what he
denies. Because Sagan has not really wondered about Sagan, he does not
know anything fundamental about either aliens or himself. There are, in
fact, no chimp scientists or theorists, and the theory of the Great De-

motion cannot explain why there are human beings such as himself.

The first page of the two-part space odyssey that concludes *Lost in the Cosmos* includes a note where Percy acknowledges his debt to Sagan in writing it. He says that reading Sagan gives him great pleasure, and that he agrees with his choice for the rigorous, self-correcting scientific method over superstition, including the various forms that seem to "engage the Western mind now more than ever." But Percy adds that he finds reading Sagan more "diverting" than anything else, because everything he writes is infused with the "ignorance" of "unmalicious, even innocent, scientism." Scientism is the ideology which holds that all that exists can be explained in the same, reductionistic way; and a diversion, according to Pascal, is something we use to get our minds off what we really know about the greatness and misery of the human condition (*LC,* 201–2).

Sagan, Percy complains, is not realistic at all; he does not give an account of what human beings, including the lonely, troubled Sagan, really experience and know. And Percy is amazed that Sagan can account for the whole history of science, from the ancient Ionians to the present, without acknowledging any contribution at all from Christianity (*LC,* 201–2). Christians, such as Pascal, understand better than their Ionian or Greek predecessors why it is that human beings wander, and the relationship between wandering and wondering. Christian realism, or the philosophy of St. Thomas Aquinas, is more scientific than Sagan's modern science, which is as much a diversion from as an expression of the truth. Human beings wander because they cannot, as wonderers, experience themselves as being at home in this natural world.[9]

The first part of Percy's space odyssey concerns an earth starship's discovery of ETI, and the highlight is the conversation between the earthship and the extraterrestrials. The extraterrestrials describe themselves as possessing "the joy of consciousness and the discovery of the Cosmos through the mediation of symbols and the cooperation of others and the preservation of this joy against the incursions of boredom, fear, anger, despair, shame, and the love of war and death and the secret desire for the misfortune of others" (*LC*, 209). They enjoy both consciousness and scientific discovery without the characteristic perversities of being human. They are Percy's version of the benign ETIs of *Contact*.

These extraterrestrials are anxious to determine the nature of our species' consciousness before allowing the earthship to land on their planet. They have discovered that "in some evolving civilizations, for reasons which we don't entirely understand, the evolution of consciousness is attended by a disaster of some sort. . . . It has something to do with the discovery of the self and the incapacity to deal with it" (*LC*, 210). The typical result is various forms of self-denial, "playing roles, being phony, lying, cheating, stealing, and killing. To say nothing of exotic disordering of the reproductive apparatus of sexual creatures" (*LC*, 210). These disorders produce beings who are cruel because they are sentimental (the teary compassion they claim to have for others they really have for their own disorders), and the ETIs are afraid of such civilizations. Beings with our kind of consciousness may be the only thing that can scare them. We are bound to be big trouble (*LC*, 211–12).

The extraterrestrial civilization has been free from this trouble because it became "aware of its predicament, sought help, and received it" (*LC*, 212). What this help is Percy leaves unclear, though we immediately think of God's grace. But it is clear in Percy's account that the predicament of the self cannot be cured by the self, and it does not evolve out of existence as intelligence increases. And it is equally clear that those on the earthship, despite the fact that their civilization on earth has self-destructed, are unaware of either their troubled predicament or their need for help. So the extraterrestrials decide quickly and forcefully to order the earthship out of their planet's orbit, wanting to "get them out of here" immediately (*LC*, 216). Their advice to what remains of our species is to "take your chances" with another screwed up civilization on another planet (*LC*, 216–17).

Percy's thought on extraterrestrials is that they quite likely would be as "curious" and "murderous" as we are. A civilization that had transcended the mixture of joy and misery of self-consciousness would have done so only with help beyond scientific understanding (*LC*, 216), and we have no reason to believe we would ever encounter such a civilization. By imagining the character Sagan explaining to the ETIs that "we still have aggressive traits, but these can be explained by our residual reptilian brain" (*LC*, 217), Percy allows us to see how a genuinely advanced civilization would see that explanation as an instance of ridiculous self-denial. It is equally ridiculous to think that the help we need will come from a superior extraterrestrial civilization. A civilization that did not suffer from troubles like ours would have nothing to do with us, and a civilization like ours would surely only be more trouble for us. But Sagan's search might still be viewed as more than a diversion. It is an acknowledgment, however misguided and incomplete, that even the scientist needs help he cannot provide for himself.

New Ionia vs. Lost Cove

Percy's second space odyssey concerns a starship that was sent to follow up on what was thought to be a promising lead on extraterrestrial intelligence.[10] The mission failed to make contact, and the theme of this part of the odyssey is "what can happen if there is no one out there" (*LC*, 2). The focus of Percy's tale is the ship's captain, Marcus Aurelius Schuyler, a man with the same "dark" understanding of the human condition as the philosopher-emperor after whom he was named. He views human beings as more full of mischief and hatred than love. They are almost surely destined for self-destruction. But unlike the captain, the passengers on this starship understand none of this, and their strongest motivations are unconscious. The captain's view is darker than the Christian's, but they are alike in being free from the diversion of scientific optimism or progressivism. "He was like a Christian," Percy writes, "who has lost faith in everything but the Fall of man." His view is that of the pre-Christian or Stoic philosopher (*LC,* 228–29).

But Marcus is also "sardonic"; his dark view also has its pleasure. He enjoys being fully conscious of "playing the unflappable captain." He takes pleasure in living well with the strange contingency of human existence, and in not losing his bearings by "sticking with his decisions," even as they probably lead to failure. He also takes pleasure in the fact that, after leaving behind all his worldly possessions, including his woman, he feels no compulsion to look back. His sardonic role-playing is a form of pleasurable transcendence based on self-confident self-knowledge. It is evidence to himself that he can exempt himself from the consequences of the Fall (*LC,* 228–29).

The mission returns to an earth devastated by nuclear war. Landing in Utah, they find the astronomer Aristarchus Jones, who is as devoted to science as his Ionian namesake, three (two black and one Jewish) Benedictine monks, and about a dozen genetically malformed and misbegotten children. Aristarchus, named after the founder of science (according to Sagan's *Cosmos),* and Abbot Liebowitz offer the captain two incompatible plans.

Aristarchus, like Sagan, thinks about scientific truth and the perpetuation of the species, and he believes his plan to wander from earth is in the name of wondering. Life on earth is finished, but might be reestablished on a firmly scientific foundation on a satellite of Jupiter. He is excited by the possibility of a "New Ionia," where people will live free from the "superstitions and repressions of religion," free from the contentious mystifications of the Bible and Plato. They will live in peace, self-knowledge, and sexual freedom, and the arts and sciences will flourish uninhibited. In the name of science, or the species' perfection, the genetically malformed must be left behind. Nothing will be malformed in New Ionia (*LC,* 245–46).

The abbot says they must proceed to Lost Cove, Tennessee, where the effects of radiation may well be minimal and life sustainable. The abbot, siding with Plato and the Church against Ionian or apolitical science, tells the captain and his passengers to repopulate the cave. But this cave is "lost." It is for the lost, for beings who, as the Church says, will never feel completely at home in this world.

The abbot's task is to perpetuate the Church. For him the children born on the starship are potential priests. He gives an elegant, theological version of Percy's science, the one that incorporates the languaged being or "ensoulment." In fact he criticizes the Church, as a Catholic Jew, for not loving science and art more. He hopes to repopulate the University of Notre Dame with Jewish scientists. He realistically tells the captain and his party that they cannot escape the predicament of the soul or self merely by escaping planet earth; Aristarchus (Sagan) is wrong that planet-hopping can cure what troubles us as wanderers. The Church—not science, the earth, or some new physical location in the cosmos—points to the home they are seeking (*LC,* 247–51).

Percy does not have the captain make one choice or another. He does suggest that if he chooses Lost Cove it will be because of the influence of the woman he has unexpectedly come to love (who sees how religion protects marriage, the family, human community, and the mystery that is at the foundation of the love of one human being for another). The choice is left for the reader. But as an aid to choice, Percy imagines for us the consequences of each choice for the captain.

New Ionia's founding principles are freedom without God and self-knowledge through absolute honesty. Honesty is secured through "group self-criticism," which aims to abolish secrecy and lying. More generally, New Ionia is based on "the principles of Skinner's Walden II, modified by Jungian self-analysis, with suitable rewards for friendly social behavior and punishment, even exile, for aggressive, jealous, solitary, mystical, or other antisocial behavior." The principles are derived from Sagan's characteristically modern, scientific view that human behavior is not qualitatively different from that of the other animals. But New Ionia's aim is actually to suppress distinctively human qualities; a behaviorist utopia is a social order which works to *make* the Great Demotion true. In the name of self-knowledge, manifestations of human experiences of self are to be eradicated. In the name of honesty, antisocial or personal experiences are punished. But in truth, only the being ironic enough to lie and keep secrets can tell the truth to himself about himself. And there are no real experiences of the goodness of human life in New Ionia. The substitute supplied to make life bearable is the "euphoria" caused by a drug. So much for self-knowledge.

The captain remains "somewhat ironical" about the group exercises, viewing them as a new sort of AA meeting. He finds no pleasure in his irony. It has become a reaction against human beings who have been or are just about free from the consequences of the Fall, thanks to behavior modification and drugs. His only pleasures are liquor and sex with any well-formed body or bodies (and so not with his old wife, who sulks, showing that she still has a self), and Shakespeare and Mozart, who remind him of his species' human, troubled past (*LC,* 256–57).

It might seem unfair to identify New Ionia with Sagan, or even Sagan with the behaviorist Skinner. Sagan holds that human beings will remain wonderers and wanderers as they leave this planet, but the problem is that this thought contradicts his denial of human uniqueness. Skinner explains, more clearly than Sagan, the culmination of the way of thinking of modern science. Human beings like the other animals are or will be completely determined by stimulus and response.

The most important lesson Sagan should have learned from Percy is that it is impossible to see how the sciences and arts could flourish in New Ionia. For in New Ionia there are no restless selves—those who wander because they wonder—longing for the truth and seeking absolute transcendence from the dreariness of ordinary life. More precisely, there are just two miserable, superfluous selves—the captain and his wife. And if Sagan were there, he would join them in their misery. New Ionia has solved every human problem, it seems, but that of the self or soul of the scientist and philosopher.

In Lost Cove, we find the captain "watch[ing] ironically yet not without affection" two black priests saying Mass in the cave. The community is flourishing with all sorts of human beings, including the most malformed and misbegotten, and the love and hatred of political life ("us against them") is returning, along with racism, feminism, war, and religious fanaticism. Wherever there is love of particular troubled selves for others, there is hatred too. The captain's thought is "Jesus Christ, here we go again," and he laughs.

Marcus sits "above the cave" (where you'd expect to find a philosopher) with a community of "good friends," a variety of dissidents and unbelievers known as the "heathen." When his wife asks him to come to Mass, Marcus responds, "My cathedral is the blue sky. My communion is with my good friends." And she counters, "Bull." The tension between the two somehow does justice to both reason and revelation, because each is, with some good reason, ironic about the limitations of the other.

The captain now enjoys his friends, the love and affection of others. He is happy with his wife, satisfied with being monogamous. He also likes liquor and pork and just being alive. He still does not believe; he remains somewhat detached or ironic, a wanderer and wonderer. But now ordinary life is more than bearable. He knows why he has affection for the priests and their Church. He knows, as he did not before, the limits of his independence. His freedom depends on the cave; his skepticism depends upon belief; and his pleasurable experiences of the goodness of life, even the theoretical ones, depend upon his love of others. He knows he is more alike than different from other human beings. He lives well with all sorts of misbegotten selves, because he knows that he is one too, and not free from trouble or disorder. What the captain now knows is the true foundation of human wandering and wondering. He knows what Sagan did not: why it is that human beings can be scientists or philosophers, or restlessly in pursuit of the truth (*LC,* 258–62).

The Preposterousness of Wondering and Wandering

Percy also presents, as an aid to making the choice between New Ionia and Lost Cove, a thought experiment on "the relative preposterousness" of "Judaeo-Christianity" and the modern scientific consciousness of Aristarchus Jones. He begins by observing that "we are all Aristarchus Jones," that is, "rational, intelligent, well-educated, objective-minded denizens of the twentieth century, reasonably well versed in the sciences and arts" (*LC,* 252). Sagan merely expresses the pervasive scientism of our time. And Percy does not deny that Judaeo-Christianity is preposterous from the view of scientism. So in the name of truth and courage, we characteristically refuse, like Sagan or even Marcus, to choose religious illusion over scientific fact.

But Percy adds a "new perspective," from which "the objective consciousness of our age is also preposterous." Consider that "the earth-self observing the Cosmos and trying to understand the Cosmos by scientific principles from which the self is excluded is, beyond doubt, the strangest phenomenon in all of the Cosmos." And that strangeness is evidence that "the self . . . is in fact, the only alien in the entire Cosmos" (*LC,* 253). What is most preposterous, finally, is that we are sometimes so far from self-understanding that we do not acknowledge the very existence of the self. Scientism attempts to dispense with human mystery and human uniqueness. But actually doing so would create a world not only without religion but without science. The Christian or Judaeo-Christian explanation of our alien condition is surely not the only one, but it is one that understands and makes possible both wandering and wondering better than Sagan's scientism.

And who would deny that, after seeing the results of each choice, Sagan himself would choose Lost Cove over New Ionia, because he, like Marcus, could wonder and wander better there? Percy's self-help is not merely showing us that each choice is equally preposterous, and that we must choose. The choice for Judaeo-Christianity, or at least the Judaeo-Christian anthropology, is actually the choice for scientists, and so science. The choice is not only for the truth or possible truth of biblical revelation but for what we really know about nature, including our own natures.

The preposterousness of Judaeo-Christianity may be a reflection of the preposterousness of our being lost in the cosmos, but only such lost souls or selves could come to know the cosmos, or be theorists or scientists. A world perfectly understood theoretically or scientifically would have no one to understand it, and both the self or soul and the political community must remain disordered, like Marcus and his friends and Lost Cove, for human freedom to have a future. In this sense the Church actually protects the mystery that makes science possible. Knowing that alone should make us at home with our homelessness, or "ambiguously at home" (*LC,* 139). We do somehow experience our true home as somewhere else, but that does not mean some other planet or star. Sagan surely has misunderstood his deepest longing.

CHAPTER FOUR

Richard Rorty's America

R ichard Rorty, who has already made several appearances in this book, is America's most influential professor of philosophy. That is partly because he is an exceptionally clear and perceptive commentator on most of the intellectual currents of his time. But it is mostly because he is the best of our pragmatists, and pragmatism—the identification of the truth with what works—is America's most characteristic way of thinking.

Rorty's *Achieving Our Country: Leftist Thought in Twentieth-Century America* (*AOC*) is a tough but friendly criticism of the American Left, which today exists primarily in universities. The criticism is written as a pragmatic or political defense of the United States, and so against both Marxian and "cultural" anti-Americanism. It is also written as a defense of the idea that our country should be viewed as part of the Western project to reduce cruelty and achieve indefinite progress toward a fully classless society. Rorty cleverly aims to revive the American perception, first described by Tocqueville, that pragmatism is the genuinely democratic way of thinking.

Marxism

The pragmatist Rorty agrees with Marx that the point of philosophy is to change the world, not to understand it (*AOC*, 27). But Rorty believes that Marx and Marxists erred by not going far enough in the pragmatic direction. Marx connected changing and understanding. By working toward history's end and comprehending the results of historical struggle theoretically, Marx aimed both to end the misery of the oppressed and to make himself wise. For Marx, his own intellectual satisfaction was at least as important as freeing the proletariat from its misery.

Rorty lumps together Marx, Leo Strauss, Adorno, Nietzsche, Heidegger, Foucault, Lenin, and Mao as antibourgeois and illiberal thinkers. The real enemy of these thinkers has been what Heidegger called the "wasteland" and Nietzsche the "last man," the unselfconscious, enjoyment-oriented culmination of bourgeois culture. This thoughtlessly vulgar culture, Rorty writes in *Truth and Progress* (*TP*), "is the contemporary counterpart of the culture that put Socrates to death" (230). Antibourgeois or pro-Socratic ire is what Rorty says produced "Nietzsche's occasional antidemocratic frothings, Heidegger's attempt to climb on Hitler's bandwagon, Sartre's period of mindless allegiance to Stalin, and Foucault's quasi-anarchism," all versions of intellectual justification of cruel tyranny. And liberals, such as Rorty, "think that cruelty is the worst thing we do."[1]

Due to Marxism's influence, Rorty observes, "the term 'bourgeois culture' has become a way of lumping together anything and everything intellectuals despise," mainly the happy indifference of the "many" to their claims for wisdom (*TP*, 230). Marxism has also kept intellectuals from facing up to their antidemocratic contempt. The Marxist-Leninist imagines that the revolutionary destruction of "the present, degenerate bourgeois many will be replaced by a new sort of many—the emancipated working class" (*TP*, 230–31). This new class will somehow be both perfectly content and self-conscious or Socratic. So Marxist intellectuals claim not to have to choose between their own happiness and the happiness of the many.

But the experience of communist tyranny—Rorty actually echoes Reagan by calling the Soviet Union an "evil empire" (*AOC*, 66)—and the successful revolution against it in 1989 make it impossible for anyone to find Leninist hope credible anymore. So intellectuals now cannot avoid asking whether "we are more interested in alleviating misery or in creating a world fit for Socrates, and thus for ourselves." Rorty argues that we now know that antibourgeois thought cannot be democratic. Intellectuals are saddled with the melancholy conclusion that "we, the people who value self-consciousness, may be irrelevant to the fate of humanity. That Plato, Marx, and we ourselves may just be parasitical eccentrics" (*TP*, 231). The pragmatist acknowledges that the pursuit of wisdom is an idiosyncratic, unachievable whim. The philosophers have no right to rule others on their own behalf, and they can no longer "hold on to the Platonic insistence that the principal duty of human beings is to know" (*TP*, 184). If intellectuals are to be judged useful and unparasitic, they must contribute to the alleviation of cruelty and other forms of human misery. Rorty calls this new kind of philosophy "liberal irony," the result of the philosopher applying Socrates' method to Socrates' activity.[2]

The Pragmatic View of Truth

Rorty repeatedly acknowledges that the alleviation of misery is, in truth, as arbitrary a goal as any other. So he shamelessly appeals to American chauvinism to defend it. Reflecting on Nietzsche, Heidegger, Strauss, and the rest, he contrasts the German with the Anglo-American intellectual world. The former is "dominated by the 'German' longing for some destiny higher than . . . last men" (*TP*, 324). That longing comes not from nature or God but from the contingent idiosyncrasies of German culture or socialization. The Anglo-American intellectual world, by contrast, is dominated merely "by the desire to avoid the infliction of unnecessary pain and humiliation" (*TP*, 324). That reduction or simplification of desire is also a social or cultural product. To support his argument, Rorty quotes Nietzsche: "Man does not live for pleasure, only Englishmen do that."[3] But Nietzsche should have added, "Man does not long for something higher than pleasure, only Germans do that." And surely Americans do not long to be Germans. By showing that Nietzsche's contempt for democracy is nothing but German chauvinism, Rorty hopes to purge our intellectual world of antidemocratic infiltration.

So the Anglo-American Rorty, uninfected by German longings and the cruel illusions they generate, has no trouble subordinating truth to utility or comfort and pleasure. Human beings should call true whatever makes them happy. There is no "objective" or nonarbitrary standard of truth by which human beings can criticize what works in alleviating human misery. In fact, the view that God or nature provides no standard by which human beings might be judged turns out to be the most comfortable view of the truth. Without it, conscience or "sin" might impede enjoyment (*AOC*, 32). Belief in external standards produces unnecessary suffering. By choosing the most easygoing version of the most minimalist view of truth, Rorty shows how philosophy might be unparasitical.

If self-consciousness produces misery, the philosopher Rorty asserts, then it should go. He contributes to that by saying that there is no true self about which one might be conscious anyway. So Rorty does not really mean to include himself among those intellectuals who value self-consciousness. We may wonder whether Rorty really regards his doctrine concerning the self as a true or a useful one; but the pragmatist denies the truth—the utility—of that distinction.

Most useful to Rorty is his fundamental insight that human existence is radically contingent, or radically historical. So all human experience is a linguistic or social creation. This antiessentialism implies a con-
comitant "antiauthoritarianism." Opposition to authoritarianism, Rorty
reports, is what finally and correctly motivated Dewey's opposition to all
forms of thought that are Platonic, or "otherworldly," or are premised on
the existence of a soul or external reality (*AOC*, 29). Dewey and Rorty
refuse to privilege any view of the truth that does not improve the condition of beings with bodies. Rorty adds that Dewey and Nietzsche agree
that we should "abandon the idea that one can say how things really are,
as opposed to how they might best be described to meet some particular
human need" (*AOC*, 32). That is, Rorty does not really think his choice
against cruelty or misery is arbitrary at all. Given Dewey and Nietzsche's
antifoundational agreement, the Anglo-American choice deserves to be
the universal choice, and Rorty hopes it eventually will be.

Rorty does not hesitate to add that the cruelty produced by selfishness and sadism, especially that produced by the metaphysical longings
and other psychosexual obsessions of philosophers (*AOC*, 76), is most
inhumane; pragmatism is therefore the true humanism. The pragmatist
hopes, in love or charity, to free human beings from any residual longings
they may have for the truth about God and nature. The pragmatist will
help them forget about eternity—and so any form of immortality—for
their own good. What Rorty hopes to achieve through linguistic therapy,
others hope to achieve through pharmacology.

Unlike the existentialist, the pragmatist does not teach the radical
contingency of human existence to encourage existential courage in the
face of the "abyss" (*AOC*, 32). But Rorty is not above striking a Socratic or
Epicurean pose to shame intellectuals into becoming pragmatists. He
says in one place that he hopes that human beings can overcome "the
infantile need for security, the childish hope of escaping from time and
chance" (*AOC*, 17). He also accuses intellectuals who cultivate religious

longings at the expense of happiness of a "lack of intellectual courage" or "a failure of nerve" (*AOC*, 34, 37). By not facing up to the truth about the finitude of all that is human, they remain Platonists, inspired primarily by what is eternal or inhuman (*AOC*, 135–36).

But Rorty's more common and consistently pragmatic view is that a secure, risk-free existence is indispensable for overcoming cruelty. People have to be "relatively safe and secure" before it is possible for thinkers, poets, and so forth to manipulate their sentiments effectively in the direction of universal niceness (*TP*, 178). The end of cruelty depends on universalizing material prosperity, but it requires more. People must actually experience themselves as secure. Living well with the prospect of one's own death depends on not being strongly moved by it, on not experiencing the abyss as an abyss. Because "Dewey is as convinced as Foucault that the subject is a social construction, that discursive practices go all the way down to the bottom of our minds and hearts," our minds and hearts can be deconstructed or reconstructed discursively in any way we find useful (*AOC*, 31).

Because there are no necessary limits to the human imagination, there are no limits to human experience. We can even talk death to death. At this point we wonder why the Leninist dream of a misery-free, Socratic existence could not be talked into existence. Rorty's belief that we must choose to be either cruel or unselfconscious contradicts the nerve of the pragmatic doctrine concerning our minds and hearts. That is, Rorty's criticism of Marxism implies some intractable limit to human manipulation, which is exactly what his philosophy denies.

Rorty's own long-term goal, in any case, is to universalize "an agreeable cultural cosmopolitanism" (*AOC*, 85), the easygoing, sentimental, "nice" culture of sophisticated Anglo-Americans (*TP*, 167–85). His hope is that the nation, and probably political life as such, will wither away. But that apolitical future depends on political activity now.

The American Cultural Left

Rorty criticizes today's American Left for putting knowledge before hope and truth before effectiveness—for claiming to know too much to embrace a pragmatic vision for American political reform. Our professorial leftists view America as a "farce," as "Disneyland" and nothing more; they take the perspective of a "detached cosmopolitan spectator," a Socratic perspective. Their descriptions of America are full of disgusted self-mockery. They have been taught by European thinkers such as Foucault and Heidegger that the American wasteland is the culmination of the technological devastation of human thought and imagination wrought by the Enlightenment (*AOC*, 4, 7, 95–96, 99).

Cultural leftists pride themselves in being a "saving remnant" in an "inhumanly corrupt country," one that is beyond help but not beyond understanding. They distinguish themselves from other Americans by the "insight" that allows them "to see through nationalistic rhetoric to the ghastly reality" that is America (*AOC*, 7–8). By writing as detached theorists rather than as engaged citizens, they leave their fellow citizens paralyzed as political agents. Their dark, sardonic teaching becomes a self-fulfilling prophecy, a sort of negative pragmatism. The nation is left to nonhuman and humanly unworthy forces, and the caricature of America that they, the cultural leftists, present consequently comes closer to becoming the real America (*AOC*, 9).

Rorty notices that the detached despair of the cultural Left goes deeper. He asserts that "Foucault's refusal to indulge in utopian thinking" is not the product of his "sagacity" but "of his unfortunate inability to believe in the possibility of human happiness" (*AOC*, 139). Heidegger, Foucault, and their followers create the impression that human happiness is both impossible for—and unworthy of—the wise. They dismiss all reformist pursuit of happiness as "discredited" or naïve "humanism" (*AOC*, 37). Those with insight know that human desire is "inherently unsatisfiable" and that political life will always be distorted by power and oppression. They claim to write against sadistic cruelty, but there is something sadistic in their view of the inevitability of human cruelty. So the cultural Left denies the goodness and possibility of all that really matters to pragmatists or liberals such as Rorty.

Too much matters to cultural leftists, in Rorty's view. They have succumbed to their German longings. Their theorizing aims to "satisfy the urges that theology used to satisfy" (AOC, 38). Their thought is marked by a form of religious otherworldliness in the longing for the ineffable or what must remain beyond human experience. In this sense, the cultural Left is authoritarian, aiming to perpetuate cruel or useless longings that might be described out of existence. The Left gives voice to those "urges which Dewey hoped Americans might cease to feel" (AOC, 38). Their longings are antibourgeois impediments to political reform in the service of human happiness.

The pragmatist deconstructs the theoretical pretensions of the cultural Left with stock Marxian-Nietzschean—which are also pragmatic and democratic—epistemological assertions. First, the pragmatist contends that the perspective of the detached spectator does not exist. That is, all human thought is socially or linguistically or historically determined, and therefore all human thought or imagination must be judged by its practical effects, not its so-called truth. All human conflicts over truth and justice can only be resolved politically: "Disengagement from political practice," Rorty writes, "produces theoretical hallucinations" (AOC, 94). In his view, then, cultural leftism is not only practically pernicious but theoretically groundless.

For Rorty, we must distinguish between "cultural politics"—the whining despair of intellectuals—and "real politics"—the political activity of those who really try to improve the world. Hence, cultural leftism, in truth, is an oxymoron. The founder of American cultural politics, Rorty astutely notes, was the reactionary Henry Adams, who parted from his statesmen-ancestors by mocking "real politics" rather than devoting himself to it (*AOC*, 36).

From Rorty's perspective, Allan Bloom's *The Closing of the American Mind*, with its preference for Socratic wisdom over justice, or knowledge over hope, is part of the fashionable, professorial, antibourgeois hopelessness of our time.[4] For Rorty, all "spectatorial and retrospective" thinking, all Platonizing and hopeless theory, belongs on the Right (*AOC*, 15). He does not state this conclusion so bluntly in *Achieving Our Country*, but only for pragmatic reasons. He hopes to reform the cultural Left with a political appeal and so build a new leftist political coalition.

Rorty portrays the American Right, from its beginning until today, as ignorantly and incorrigibly selfish and sadistic (*AOC*, 45). That obvious caricature is meant to inspire cultural leftists to enter the political fray. Rorty uses fighting words to restore the notion that the virtuous, cooperative, and progressive American Left must engage in a political struggle against the vicious, greedy, and reactionary Right. He observes that when American political competition is determined by that division, the Left wins (*AOC*, 14). Rorty's outlandish demonization of the Right is also meant to mask the extent to which he shares contemporary conservative criticisms of the Left. He calls Pat Buchanan a "scurrilous" demagogue, for example, while agreeing with his pro-union economic nationalism and his criticism of the apolitical emptiness and indifference to social justice of contemporary cosmopolitanism (*AOC*, 83–86, 149n).

National Pride

A characteristic pretension of Socratic and cultural types, Rorty observes, is that patriotism or nationalism is nothing but "simple-minded militaristic chauvinism" (*AOC*, 4). It is a prejudice to be overcome through the cosmopolitanizing tendency of knowledge. But Rorty begins his book with a discussion of "national pride," making it clear how indispensable it is today for human improvement (*AOC,* 3). National pride is the political equivalent of self-respect. Too much pride breeds complacency, but too little produces a paralyzing self-disgust. Without a national pride that outweighs national shame, "imaginative and productive" deliberation among citizens is impossible (*AOC,* 3). American political reform requires human beings proud enough to act as citizens and thus emotionally involved enough with their nation not to find "vigorous participation in electoral politics pointless" (*AOC,* 7).

National pride is an imaginative creation. So all vigorous nations, Rorty observes, rely on "artists and intellectuals to create images of, and tell stories about, the nation's past" (*AOC,* 3–4). The pragmatic or only true purpose of those stories is always "competition for political leadership" (*AOC,* 3–4). In America, the long-standing competition between the politically active Right and Left is largely over the "nation's self-identity, and between differing symbols of greatness" (*AOC,* 3–4). So national history and the symbol of America are best viewed as tools, generated by intellectual elites, to gain power and achieve reform. These stories that our nation tells about itself must be convincing to, and hence effective in moving, a majority (*AOC,* 101).

It is for this reason that those who tell such inspirational, historical stories, Rorty explains, do not aim "at accurate representation," or telling the whole, objective truth about the past. Their descriptions are "attempts to form a moral identity" (*AOC,* 13). But such stories should not be called mythological or ideological as if there were a true story with which they should or could be compared. For the hypothetical "objective" story would be "of little relevance when one is deciding what sort of person or nation to be" (*AOC,* 11). For Rorty, objective history is impossible because it is not useful; likewise, the story that moves the nation in the desired direction is true.

One pragmatic criticism of Rorty might be that he makes it too obvious that his story is not true. Rorty cannot completely obliterate the "objective" distinction between historical truth and falsity. He is limited by the standard of plausibility. He has to give credible versions of events that actually happened and persons who actually lived. He does not claim or want the Orwellian freedom to make history out of nothing, to make the past simply his plaything. He shies away from what he knows about the malleability of all things human to accept pragmatically the constraints of free political and democratic competition under the Constitution. His pragmatic view of the uses and disadvantages of history for the nation's life is Nietzschean: Living well, in hope, toward the future depends on having neither too much nor too little knowledge about the past. Henry Adams and the cultural leftists both perversely insist on telling a story based on too much knowledge, and of the wrong kind.

Rorty presents a statesman's view of the American intellectual's responsibility to form the nation's imagination. His elitism is political, not cultural. So he claims to be both a "thoroughgoing" secularist (*AOC*, 15, 30) and an unreserved proponent of "civic religion." The academic Left sees civic religion as an example of "narrow-minded and obsolete nationalism" (*AOC*, 15). But Rorty wants national devotion properly understood to become the whole of human devotion in America. Following his inspirational American heroes Dewey and Whitman, he wants reform toward "the utopian America to replace God as the unconditional object of desire." So "the struggle for social justice" should become "the country's animating principle, the nation's soul" (*AOC*, 17). Human longing in our country should be for nothing more nor less than "a classless and casteless America" (*AOC*, 30).

Rorty implies that a thoroughgoing secularist would not speak of the nation's soul. He himself, however, does not mean to dispense with the religious "impulse to stand in awe of something greater than oneself" (*AOC*, 17). But, that impulse is not permanent or natural. It is a social or linguistic construction and might be destroyed in the same way. But a thoroughgoing secularist would be an apathetic, detached individual without hope. He might be a person, like Socrates, who preferred knowledge or self-knowledge to doing what is possible to alleviate human misery. Without a hopeful awe for the nation's future, Americans will not act as citizens. So a pragmatist cannot work to end religious devotion now, because that would be the end of pragmatism. The pragmatist's encouragement of civic religion is part of his "easygoing atheism," which is kinder, gentler, and more effective than the Marxist's cruelly "aggressive atheism" (AOC, 142n).

With startling candor, Rorty admits that civic religion is merely useful for achieving political goals. Note that he does not say that human beings need to live in awe of something greater than themselves in order to live well. Nor does he say that political action is some sort of human need or perfection. Rorty believes that we should hope that nations—and therefore civic religion—will eventually wither away. National pride is required today in the effort to create a cruelty-free and nationless world tomorrow; at some point we will need to take pride in the effort of our nation to evolve itself out of existence.

Rorty can be too easily accused of using the nation and the devoted individual to achieve a world in which both will be obsolete. That accusation, for Rorty, employs knowledge at the expense of hope. Yet, in the absence of some external standard—God, nature, some duty or virtue that is evidence of proud human freedom—civic devotion does not make sense from an individual's perspective. That is one reason, Rorty observes, why the eighteenth-century rhetoric of individual liberty was abandoned by twentieth-century leftists as no longer useful (AOC, 50). (And he adds, of course, that there is no such thing as a "self" from which an individual could have a perspective.)

But such rhetorical denials do not seem particularly effective in answering the libertarian criticism that devotion to political reform requires the manipulative authoritarianism of an intellectual elite. They also do not do well with the Christian and Socratic criticism that civic religion is rooted in personal self-deception. Civic religion seems as anti-bourgeois or anti-individualistic as cultural elitism. Civic religion replaces "individual freedom" with "social justice as our country's principal goal" (*AOC*, 101).

Still, Rorty's version of civic religion, compared to others, is honest. He asserts that American devotion should be free from "obedience to any authority—even the authority of God." There are, in fact, "no standards . . . against which the decisions of a free people can be measured." A free people does not submit, even in speech, to "anything which claims authority over America" (*AOC*, 15).

Rorty's Whitmanesque American religion depends on the hope that there is "no need" for Americans even to be "curious about God" (*AOC*, 17). Their longings can be limited to American political choices alone. Anything can be described in and out of existence and be made to look either good or bad, even God. Because God was the justification for much cruelty and is no longer useful in the pursuit of social justice, and there is no evidence at all of his existence, the pragmatist is freer in dispensing with him than with historical truth. Americans, Whitman thought, are even free to "redefine God as our future selves," making God an act of self-creation (*AOC*, 22).

By denying that there is an external standard by which American political decisions can be judged, Rorty seems to endorse the most extreme American chauvinism. But Rorty does judge American choices from the perspectives of alleviating cruelty and achieving the classless society. And he employs "the Hegelian idea of 'progressive evolution'" as the most useful way of viewing the West and America (*AOC*, 24).

Hegel

Rorty judges all political activity by how well it promotes progress toward a world in which all American citizens, and then all human beings, are equally free from misery and humiliation. Despite his Anglo-American chauvinism, he admits that the most inspiring Americans, Whitman and Dewey, were in turn inspired by the German philosopher Hegel. For Rorty, Hegel is to be praised for focusing all human hope on the historical goal of a classless society. He is to be blamed for seeming to put theory over practice, or for making historical progress appear inevitable (*AOC*, 27).

Rorty writes that Whitman thought it "obvious . . . that Hegel had written a prelude to the America saga" (*AOC*, 3–4), and in Whitman's Hegelian eyes, "the American Declaration of Independence had been an Easter dawn." America "would be the place where the promise of the ages would first be realized" (*AOC*, 21–22). The realization of this promise would depend on the success of the difficult task of "forgetting about eternity" (*AOC*, 19). Hegel's denial of the reality of eternity through his assertion that "time and finitude"—or history—are all that there is flows from his inspirational choice of pragmatic hope over knowledge (*AOC*, 19). And his antiauthoritarian denial of all reality but history helped Americans choose the classless society as their history's end.

The Hegelian idea of progressive evolution, Rorty explains, shows that the American story cannot include multiculturalism. What is anti-American or anti-Hegelian about multiculturalism is its easygoing relativism, its "morality of live and let live," its "politics of side-by-side development in which members of distinct cultures preserve their own culture against the incursions of other cultures" (*AOC*, 24). The Hegelian, unlike the relativist, has a standard with which to judge cultural and political development and to oppose the preservation of anything unjust or cruel.

The Hegelian wants a dialectical or political contest between "alternative forms of human life," with the hoped-for result being a "synthesis" superior to either of the competing parts. Rorty's example here is the American Civil War. He calls attention to the identification of the nation with egalitarian reform in the Gettysburg Address (*AOC*, 9); the synthesis on his mind must be the moral nationalization of the Fourteenth Amendment. Rorty is usually for nonviolent and piecemeal reform of existing law, but the Hegelian must affirm the results of the "necessary" Civil War (*AOC,* 24).

Generally, Rorty's American story praises the growth of the egalitarian reach of the national government, with its leftist, redistributive vision, its courts, and its expertise. Local government tends to be dominated by unsophisticated populations uninspired by the nation's civic religion; it tends therefore to be racist, sexist, homophobic, nativist, and sadistic (*AOC,* 52). The pragmatist does not favor an active citizenry for its own sake, but only when it is imaginatively directed by thinkers and artists toward a classless society. The constitutionalist political correction that Rorty makes of Dewey's pragmatism concerns Dewey's naïve connection of virtue with participatory democracy. Rorty prudently recognizes that good government, whatever its form, requires technocratic expertise (*AOC,* 103–4). The Hegelian uses nationalist constitutionalism against reactionary, localist populism in the service of democracy properly understood. So Rorty praises court decisions such as *Brown v. Board of Education* and *Romer v. Evans* (*AOC,* 53). They are useful in extending the reach of the national government and thus have helped to eradicate the cruel humiliation connected with popular racism and heterosexism.

Rorty reminds us that the Hegelian Whitman identified the progress of civilization with the end of the cruel repression of sexual eros and the growth of "the kind of casual, friendly copulation which is insouciant about the homosexual-heterosexual distinction" (*AOC,* 25–26). Whitman's vision began to become social and political reality in America with the "youth culture" of the 1960s. Prosperous young people became erotically and morally casual enough not to privilege one form of sexual activity over another and began to abandon their humiliation of homosexuals in particular (*AOC,* 25–26). In truth, Stonewall, the revolutionary uprising of New York homosexuals against the police, deserves to be presented as a key event in American history (AOC, 51).

The American Right wrongly believes that civilization was devastated by the sixties because it connects civilization with the perpetuation of arbitrary standards of personal virtue (AOC, 34). But the Left regards that connection as a failure of the imagination, coming from the illusion that human experience is shaped or limited by "sin," some ineradicable, cruel flaw (AOC, 32). For Rorty, all moral restraint is repressive cruelty unless it contributes to progress toward social justice.

Although a Deweyan pragmatist might be resistant to innovative forms of liberation from cruelty, he must admit that sex, drugs, and even rock 'n' roll contribute to the realization of a fully classless society. So Rorty agrees with Socratic cultural critic Allan Bloom that sexual promiscuity, recreational drugs, and music with the beat of rutting animals are signs that today's students have become nicer and more devoted to the American idea of justice and less moved by love and death. Bloom and Rorty both emphasize that a nice society is a classless one, and Rorty rejects Bloom's Socratic objection to its unselfconscious contentment. Rorty goes so far as to say that universalizing the experience of the sophisticated students whom he and Bloom taught differently but described in much the same way is "all that is needed to achieve an Enlightenment utopia" (TP, 179).

The Hegelians recognize no limits to the reach of government in contributing to such reform, and so they praise as progress the indefinite growth of the welfare state (AOC, 105). And Rorty identifies political correctness as the one achievement of contemporary cultural leftists. Leftist professors—and the educational, governmental, and corporate bureaucracies formed by their influence—insisted, Rorty claims, that American language be purged of humiliating and degrading references to African Americans, women, gays, and so forth (AOC, 76). This cultural reform through political means was easily accepted by sophisticated students at leading universities; these correctly formed college graduates then imposed it on unsophisticated or cruel Americans. The result was a progressive reform of ordinary language. With a change in language, human experience changed too, resulting in a reduction of the amount of inegalitarian humiliation in America (*AOC*, 81–83). Political correctness reduced the influence of know-nothing American populism, "the religious fundamentalist, the smirking rapist, or the swaggering skinhead" (*TP*, 179).

In Rorty's Hegelian eyes, political correctness should also be viewed as a way of removing barriers to the common pursuit of social justice. The "cultural," including religious, experiences that separate one American from another can be talked out of existence. And the key American fact then becomes the imaginative recognition of citizens as citizens. Rorty sees that the function of civic religion in America has always been to oppose cultural diversity with pride in being an American citizen (*AOC*, 100). In an America freed by Hegel from nature and God, it is possible to imagine the complete political destruction of serious human differences. Rorty's optimism concerning the linguistic or historical eradication of the experience of "otherness" separates him, of course, from the pessimism of the cultural Left's multiculturalism, which he connects with the "otherworldly" Christian view that sinful human beings are always resident aliens in this world (*AOC*, 95–96). Success is not certain. If the Left does not once again become nationalist and political, it may leave the American future to the demagogic Buchanans. But there is no necessary limit to the extent to which cruel otherness might be eradicated from human language and so from human imagination and experience.

Rorty's Rationalism?

I have said only enough about Rorty's story of American achievement to show its Hegelian character. Nothing in my account explains why a Hegelian, anti-multicultural vision of a classless society is not, finally, an extreme form of Western rationalism. Rorty agrees with Marx against the cultural leftists that human desire might be transformed to achieve complete historical satisfaction and that there is nothing necessarily mysterious or elusive about human existence. There will be nothing irrational—or cruelly, perversely contrary to human happiness—in the agreeably cosmopolitan life that the pragmatist hopes will eventually be possible for all human beings. But Rorty persists in asserting that the leftist America he is trying to construct "is neither more natural nor more rational than the cruel societies" of the past (AOC, 30).

That assertion, I think, is Rorty's answer to Nietzsche's "insinuation that the end of religion and metaphysics should be the end of our attempts not to be cruel."[5] Morality defined as an egalitarian alleviation of cruelty, Nietzsche contended, is biblical, and its goodness depends on the biblical God's existence. If that God is dead, that morality should be abandoned, because it is not self-evident or rational.

Nietzsche's standard for that conclusion was "intellectual probity," or a truthful confrontation with the human condition.[6] But Rorty rejects what amounts to Nietzsche's rationalism. For Rorty, there is no reason why human beings should not secularize Christian morality and achieve for themselves what God allegedly promised.

As long as human beings remain self-conscious—or moved by the intractable limitations of their finite, death-defined existences—the Christian promise of a world without cruelty cannot become true. Rorty talks away Nietzsche's objection to linguistic self-deception by saying that Nietzsche confused the Christian, existentialist self—the one miserably agonized by its awareness of the abyss that surrounds contingent human existence—with the true self. But there is no true self, as Nietzsche himself said in opposition to Socrates, and so no reason not to create a less miserable self.

In Rorty's hoped-for and worked-for future, human beings will be agreeable, reasonable, and predictably tranquil because they will be largely unselfconscious, unmoved by the limits of their individual existences. Socratics and Nietzscheans affirm the perpetuation of cruel and unreasonable inegalitarian political oppression as the precondition for the existence of rational (meaning self-conscious) individuals. Both the "last man" and Socrates live reasonably, each in his own way.

Rorty chooses the classless society by denying the possibility of self-consciousness. But that pragmatic denial is not very convincing. He lectures Marx and Marxists for imagining that a classless society could also be a Socratic one. He presents that impossibility as the only limit that reason or reality can place on the pragmatic imagination. The choice between Socratic (or individual) and historical (or social) rationalism has to be made, and neither is clearly more rational than the other. In that sense, Rorty cannot call his hopeful choice rational.

It seems to me that Rorty remains too charmed by the fundamentally undemocratic Socratic, rationalist tradition by presenting his choice in that way. The Socratics and pragmatists seem to agree that most people cannot live well in light of the truth about death. And so the ironic philosophers or intellectuals humanely give ordinary people linguistic therapy. Both Socratic and pragmatic thinkers and poets provide lies to talk away the truth in view of its cruelty, and they both use ordinary people to achieve their not wholly rational ends through civic religion.[7]

Rorty is in one way more democratic than the philosopher by refusing to privilege the experience of Socrates. But in another way he is more elitist because his political or rhetorical struggle against the common perception of eternity, and so against the limits of human effort, is more extreme. The Socratics, by perpetuating the distinction between man and God, mean to keep some intimation of the truth in human imagination, but Rorty claims that distinction was a failure of the imagination that Americans have overcome. So for Rorty there are no limits to what political reform might achieve, and there are no human limits to the reach of a government inspired by therapeutic intellectuals.

Although much of Rorty's political criticism of the cultural Left is sensible, finally nothing is less rational than pragmatism. The fundamental, ineradicable human experience, as the American Thomist Flannery O'Connor said, really is consciousness of limitation. And it is beyond the capacity of thinkers and poets to make human beings unselfconscious.

The lesson Rorty should learn from the experience of the failure of Marxist communism is that Being and man, as the Czech dissident Václav Havel said, invariably resist manipulation. From the Russian Aleksandr Solzhenitsyn, Rorty should consider the reasonable observation that if human beings were born only to be happy, they would not be born to die. It is both degrading and impossible for a human being to forget his or her relationship to eternity through total immersion in the thoughtless materialism of everyday life. Death cannot be talked to death. More matters, in truth, than human happiness, and only by attending to the human responsibility of living morally in light of the truth can we be happy as human beings. It is only by renouncing the right to be happy that human beings can become happy. For that reason, it is misanthropic simply to identify God and morality with repressive cruelty.[8]

We can be somewhat grateful to Rorty for reminding us that even a more humanly adequate version of the story of American greatness would have to include a place for liberalism's humane aversion to cruelty, as well as justice defined as the eradication of authoritarian privilege. But we must also recall that what Rorty will surely fail to achieve linguistically, others may achieve through the chemical transformation of human nature. And Rorty will be cheering them on.

Chapter Five

American Political Science

*R*ichard Rorty defends America, his country, as an open act of pragmatic chauvinism. For him, the question of whether our country is "really" a good one makes no sense. But some American students of the remarkable political philosopher Leo Strauss say we cannot help but remember the distinction between what is merely our own and what is truly good. And so they attempt to defend our country because of its goodness, because of its true understanding and effective defense of human liberty. Perhaps the most nuanced and rhetorically sensitive of these American Straussians is James W. Ceaser. He attempts to articulate an American political science that is much weightier than Rorty's mixture of leftist historical propaganda and unabashed nationalism.

Ceaser's understanding of what political science is, and his understanding of its American purpose—defending liberal democracy as a distinctive and humanly worthy regime—comes from his teacher, Harvey C. Mansfield. And both Mansfield and Ceaser are indebted, as they readily and often acknowledge, to Strauss. Ceaser's work does not have the depth or incredible range of Mansfield's. Nor does he have Mansfield's reputation as a contentious public intellectual, an unfashionably sensible critic of the sixties, feminism, and gay liberation.[1] But Ceaser has been more willing to write in a way that his fellow political scientists can understand and appreciate. His work on political parties and the presidency,[2] for example, has been more influential among political scientists than Mansfield's pathbreaking but most difficult study of executive power.[3] And Ceaser's book on liberal democracy and political science was a fairly successful effort to educate and elevate a rather unphilosophic and apolitical discipline.[4]

Ceaser has earned but not received much gratitude from his fellow political scientists. The reason is that he has been branded a conservative and therefore lacking in compassion and insight. He is a Republican, an admirer of Ronald Reagan, and he was a supporter of the effort to remove President Clinton from office. He is also a bit of a moralist, or at least a moral constitutionalist, and he was a resolute anticommunist. But Ceaser is no traditionalist, and he does not write as a religious believer. He is a proud liberal rationalist, although one who realistically acknowledges the limits of rationalism. And we live in a time when all realists are called conservatives. Ceaser's attachment to the principles of liberal democracy is not a mere preference or a case of American chauvinism, but primarily a rational choice based on a genuinely scientific understanding of the limits and possibilities of political life.

Ceaser's writing is witty and urbane and conversant with the latest intellectual currents. (He usually dresses in black, like a New York or Paris intellectual.) Compared to Ceaser, the other political scientists studying American politics are sentimental rubes. But he is more devoted to America than almost any of them. He shows that patriotism is compatible with, and in fact ennobled by, the highest kind of intellectual sophistication.

Reconstructing America, Ceaser's newest book, is meant to save America from various forms of deconstruction.[5] The European deconstructionists' theoretical dismantling of American pretensions began not with the multiculturalists and Heideggerian postmodernists but with the natural historians of the eighteenth century. Americans have been viewed as inferior and degenerate almost from the beginning, and from perspectives that deny the real existence of political liberty. American theorists from Jefferson onward, of course, have often fallen victim to the view that European thought must be on the cutting edge, so they have absorbed various extreme and pernicious doctrines, from racist materialism to Heidegger's concern with Being at the expense of moral and political beings. Today's pompous postmodern caricature of America as a technological wasteland or subhuman end of history is not so different from the eighteenth-century natural historians' equally ignorant view that everyone in America is small, stupid, and unerotic. But Ceaser does not defend the manly vigor, eloquence, and genius of Americans today as Jefferson did for Americans in his time in *Notes on Virginia.* In fact, it is unclear how much Ceaser's reconstruction of America depends on a defense of the quality of contemporary American political life.

American Political Science

The America that Ceaser wants to reconstruct is that of the statesmen, guided by political science or political philosophy, who wrote the *Federalist.* America, for him, is the liberal and democratic political life made possible by the Constitution. And it may be only a slight overstatement to say that, for Ceaser, America *is* political science rightly understood. The best political scientific defense of America in our century came from Ceaser's own favorite European, Leo Strauss, who eventually, although

not completely by choice, became an American. Strauss pointed Ceaser
to another European, Alexis de Tocqueville, who only visited America.
Ceaser's reading of the *Federalist* as a proud and rational defense of the
moral and political nature of human beings is conducted largely through
the European eyes of Strauss and Tocqueville.

Ceaser's political science remains distinctively American only in part.
He defends the capacity of all human beings for self-government, not
just those of a particular time, culture, or race. Yet that capacity must be
exercised, as Tocqueville said, in the context of the traditions and circum-
stances of a particular political community. In the modern world, the
form of that community is the nation. Thus a defense of America in
particular is compatible with a defense of the liberty that we know, from
science or philosophy, to be shared by all human beings.

Instead of being reviled by the whole world, as Heidegger and his
literary disciples have recommended, the American regime, Ceaser argues,
should be admired by all as the best, most scientific, and most successful
form of liberal constitutional government. The greatness of America is
political, and America, like every other regime, should be held account-
able for how it has shaped its destiny through political thought and
action. As bases for accountability the perspectives of culture or Being are
too abstract and too high; as a result, the standards they generate are both
unfair and pernicious. They inspire projects that are too aggressive—such
as the one supported by the early Heidegger—or they promote a cowardly,
inhuman fatalism—such as that of the later Heidegger. Criticisms based
on such abstractions arouse in human beings longings that cannot be
satisfied politically. Literary or philosophic criticism, if taken as political
criticism, undermines, Ceaser concludes, the conditions for free and de-
cent political life.

The political, Ceaser repeatedly says, must be understood on its own
terms, not in terms of what is above or below it. He agrees with Tocqueville, Strauss, and even Heidegger that what is best called the aristo-

cratic criticism of the mediocrity of American intellectual, religious, and artistic life has merit.[6] But all human goods cannot come together in the same place; mediocrity is the price to be paid for a regime in which everyone has the right to exercise political liberty. Political science might even be defined as the science of mediocrity, or the science of the being in the middle—the articulation of the life distinctive to the being who is fundamentally different from the other animals and from God. The lesson to be learned from our apolitical European critics was taught best by Pascal: Those who aspire to divinity end by brutalizing themselves and others. Or, as Tocqueville put it, modern theorists, by reducing their fellow human beings in theory to brutes, proudly believe that they have acquired the knowledge and power of God. From Aristotle to Ceaser, political science properly understood has been a lesson on the natural foundation of the greatness appropriate to the human being, and so it has also been a lesson in proud moderation.

Straussian Political Science

Ceaser agrees with Richard Rorty that most Heideggerian or postmodern criticism is really a form of Socratic elitism. The political life shared by all cannot be subordinated to the questionable obsessions of the (allegedly) spiritually deep or radically liberated few. The Straussian Ceaser, unlike the pragmatist Rorty, knows that the philosophers know much that is really true, and even that political science depends on political philosophy. But the political philosopher Strauss refused to separate his political defense of philosophy from his philosophic defense of politics, and so he may have come closer than any other philosopher to understanding the political on its own terms. Strauss and Ceaser do not go so far as to assert, as Rorty does, the priority of democracy over philosophy.[7] Nonetheless the question remains: Is the purpose of liberal democracy to produce a free and democratic political life or a regime especially safe for—even covertly ruled by—philosophers?

It is fair to say that Straussians, in general, see the need to protect what Ceaser, with greater precision, calls "the relative autonomy" of political life from "overbearing theorizing,"[8] if only because if political life were to disappear altogether, so would philosophy. But Straussians themselves are often more than a bit overbearing in their subordination of the thoughts and deeds of citizens and statesmen—not to mention religious believers—to those of philosophers. Ceaser is one of the least overbearing of Straussians, avoiding the extremes of apolitical detachment and the politicization or Americanization of all theoretical issues.

Ceaser learned from Strauss that political science and political life cannot be detached from philosophical inquiry because the political good must be considered in light of the human good. And "the practice of philosophy itself is clearly among the highest of human activities." Philosophy clearly stands at the top, but it is not alone. We can know through the practice of philosophy that there are a number of worthy human activities, among them philosophical inquiry and political life. Philosophers who degrade political life as being "merely . . . a laboratory for the sake of philosophy" are bad philosophers. Because they have abstracted from the distinctive excellence of political accomplishment they do not fully understand either themselves or the "whole."[9] So Ceaser, at least as much as Strauss, stresses both the theoretical and the practical interdependence of philosophy and politics. Neither exists only for the sake of the other, but each can be understood to benefit the other.

Ceaser learned from Mansfield, Strauss, and Aristotle that the political philosopher is neither a political partisan—a member of a political faction or party—nor a spectator. He is an umpire, judging partisan claims according to a standard that does justice to the mixture of truth and error in each. That standard is the "best regime" in light of which all other regimes and political opinions are ranked by the political philosopher, and that philosophic ranking is what guides political science, properly understood.[10] The sports analogy takes us only so far, however. We do not find baseball umpires who claim to have discovered the foundation of the game's rules and so a sure knowledge of how to interpret them or even when to make exceptions in particular situations.

Ceaser holds that "if philosophy is to descend into the chaotic and shadowy world of politics, it should do so modestly,"[11] and he does very well in following his own advice. But to players, umpires rarely seem modest; nor do they seem to care about the outcome of the game. As Rorty complains, Straussians, unlike pragmatists, do not seem to feel the pain of the oppressed, and so they do not cleverly manipulate the rules to help the underdog.[12] The umpire Ceaser cries foul by exposing the demagogic misuse of compassion by contemporary pragmatic liberals.[13] But pragmatists ignore the call; they know that nobody likes umpires, and only the unusually fair-minded respect them. That may be why the umpire Ceaser usually presents himself as playing on the team of America or the Constitution: He would deliberately compromise his immediate effectiveness by saying that he plays on the philosophers' team.

The Postmodern Ceaser?

As a political scientist focusing on the relative autonomy of political life, Ceaser acknowledges and criticizes, but generally downplays, the Straussian view that liberal democracy can be understood as the philosophers' creation of a world that would be especially beneficial for them. So he seems not to do justice to the democratic or populist criticism that the success of that apolitical, amoral impulse deprives human life of its moral and political content. That criticism is associated with Heidegger, but it is also found in the criticism of America by the anticommunist dissidents Aleksandr Solzhenitsyn and Václav Havel. They say that the atheism and materialism implicit in anthropocentric or modern humanism make it finally not a humanism at all. In their view, communism was only a form of modern extremism. The irresponsible apathy that comes with succumbing to ideological lies can be found to a lesser but real extent in America.[14]

Havel and especially Solzhenitsyn see further than the *Federalist*, which holds that the primary threat to liberty, or good government, is an aroused majority. They agree with Tocqueville that from the beginning liberal democracy contained an individualistic tendency with the power to consume all of human life, replacing a passionate liberty rooted in love and pride with the despotism of asocial apathy. What I call postmodernism rightly understood takes a similar view: America, as a modern regime, is more individualistic than political or social, and the political and social dimensions of the founding were premodern residues that have eroded over time.[15] In attempting to discredit such a view by associating it with Heidegger—a pro-Nazi instead of an anticommunist thinker—Ceaser employs American chauvinism too easily. And he certainly does not emphasize the proto-postmodern features of Tocqueville's friendly but tough criticism of America's founding principles. But Ceaser is more postmodern than he seems.

Ceaser chooses to correct the individualistic excesses of American political development through an unusually political understanding of America's fundamental principles. As a result, he must remain virtually silent on the apolitical basis of the founders' "scientific" doctrine of rights. He does not begin with Locke's pre-political or individualistic "state of nature." He affirms Jefferson's Declaration of Independence, but only in passing and seemingly only for its freedom from racist natural history.[16] By not understanding rights as primarily instruments for pursuing private or individual goals, Ceaser reminds us of Tocqueville, who calls rights beautiful, not useful. But Tocqueville is more extreme than Ceaser; he is completely silent on the Declaration. Ceaser and Tocqueville do agree that the view that America embodies Locke's doctrine of natural rights is a caricature that must not be allowed to become completely real. And Ceaser follows Tocqueville in distinguishing between America as we find her and the logic of modern or democratic thought. He admits that Heidegger's criticism of modern thought is perhaps largely correct, but he distinguishes modern thought from the principles of American political science. Ceaser's defense of that distinction depends more on creativity or ironic selectivity than he usually makes clear. But his defense is only partly postmodern in the usual sense, because it really does rely on a scientific understanding of the way people are. Ceaser does not commit the postmodern error of reducing political science to rhetoric, but he is a very rhetorical political scientist. His realistic—or partly scientific and partly rhetorical—political science is close to postmodernism rightly understood. Only an ironic political science can defend a future full of human beings with the capability and reason to be ironic.[17] A world full of contented animals—or, as Ceaser puts it, "soulless automata exercising in jogging suits"—has no place for the ironist.[18]

Postmodern Anti-Americanism

Heidegger, as Ceaser says, presented a caricature of Americans as beings totally determined by technological calculation, living in a pragmatic wasteland closed to the truth about death and Being. And Heidegger's caricature is repeated by the great European Hegelian Alexandre Kojève, who claimed that Americans live at the end of history, that is, that Americans are no longer historical or free beings but content animals completely unmoved by love or death. Heidegger preferred Nazism to an Americanized world, and Kojève, we know now, was not just a theoretical Stalinist but actually a Soviet spy. Their contempt for America, it seems, caused them to embrace the worst forms of tyranny and to be blind to the human significance of the political differences between America and its totalitarian enemies. Postmodernism as it is usually understood—from Sartre and Merleau-Ponty to Derrida and Baudrillard—is some combination of Heidegger and Kojève, and Kojève himself is a Heideggerization or spiritualization of Marx and Hegel. Ceaser does well in showing us the stunning stupidity and irresponsibility of postmodernist anti-American-ism in general.

The genealogy of postmodernism reveals that its anti-Americanism is powerful enough to overcome the distinction between Left and Right. It combines criticisms of American liberal democracy from both sides and embraces both European snobbery about America's lack of an aristo-cratic tradition and European envy of America's military and ideological success. Even the most intelligent anti-Heideggerian and anticommunist European thinker today, Pierre Manent, shares those qualities in a muted and nuanced way: Manent admits, with unusual candor and magnanim-ity, that America, with minimal European help and considerable Euro-pean resistance, won the Cold War, but he fears that America will now swallow the human contents of what remains of Europe's aristocratic tradition.[19] And through Manent, an admirer of Solzhenitsyn and an authority on Tocqueville, we see what all our thoughtful European crit-ics have in common. When Tocqueville, Solzhenitsyn, and Manent agree, we Americans need to listen, keeping in mind Ceaser's caution that they probably don't know us as well as they think they do.

Heidegger and Kojève are, in truth, only ambiguously critics of America. For Heidegger, to live in the thrall of technology is the fate of our time, and after his failed Nazi flirtation he saw the futility of political resistance to the technological determination of human beings. In his view the Soviet Union and America, metaphysically identical, are our fate. History has spoken, and we can only prepare the way through thought for what might come next. Kojève thought that America and the Soviet Union were two different forms of history's end, and that history would judge which works better in meeting the needs of the posthistorical ani-mal. Had Kojève been alive in 1989 he would have taken America's side, in the name of the truth. Kojève and especially Heidegger arouse nostalgia for the European past, but neither is a reactionary or deluded about the possibility of going back. America, they acknowledge, has won, but they still give Americans plenty of reason to be offended. They maintain that what has been lost in the American victory is the human openness to Being—to the truth—and so our distinctively human qualities. Heidegger and Kojève write as the last Europeans, the last beings able to speak the truth that our species has become Americanized—that is, has become no different than the other animals.

Pragmatism

Richard Rorty, as we saw in the previous chapter, thinks that Heidegger and Kojève more or less teach the truth about our country, and soon the whole world. But Rorty encourages Americans to cherish what Heidegger loathed. The so-called wasteland is really a cruelty-free, classless society. Rorty contends that we are in the process of being freed from love and death through a linguistic manipulation of our sentiments that began with the Enlightenment, and that we are better off as a result. Rorty encourages us not to take seriously Heidegger's perverse obsession with Being and even Socrates' pursuit of the truth. There is no truth to discover, and those who claim privileges on its behalf are parasites. Philosophers who aim to be just, not parasitical, should subordinate truth to comfort, and we can be perfectly comfortable only when we are no longer moved by Being, death, God, and love.

The most famous version of the American appropriation of Kojève is more confused. As we saw in Chapter 2, for Francis Fukuyama the American victory in the Cold War may have signalled the end of history. Liberal democracy stands unchallenged in the world as the only legitimate regime, and it represents the historical satisfaction of human desires for reason, recognition, and material prosperity. No better regime is imaginable. Fukuyama imagines that human beings can remain human at history's end, free from nature and God. But if to be human is to be historical, as Kojève says, then the end of history must be the end of all that is distinctively human. Fukuyama considers the possibility that human qualities will now wither away, but he leaves us with the impression that this is not necessary.[20]

But just a decade after *The End of History* appeared, Fukuyama wrote an article updating his reflections on history's end in which he is virtually certain that the end of human distinctiveness is at hand. It will arrive not through political revolution nor through Rorty's linguistic therapy. Both those methods fail, Fukuyama correctly says, because they cannot alter human nature (he makes clear in his most recent book that human nature can successfully resist even the most misguided efforts at political reform).[21] But biotechnology, Fukuyama reports, now has the power to alter human nature, to allow us to live much longer lives and to be unmoved by death. Today's widespread use of Prozac and Ritalin, drugs that in different ways take the edge off being human, gives us a sign of what is to come. Today's pervasive "libertarian mindset," Fukuyama is convinced, is strong enough that we will cast aside as reactionary prejudices the moral and political objections to biotechnological remedies for the misery of being human.[22] Fukuyama is now convinced, in other words, that Heidegger is fundamentally right. As pragmatists we are about to be totally determined, or reduced to a subhuman condition, by technology.

Political Science vs. Pernicious Theory

Ceaser criticizes Fukuyama for not subordinating his view of the truth to utility. Fukuyama's view of history's end may or may not be accurate, but it is certainly pernicious. If we believe that history or human liberty is finished and there is nothing more to do, then we will do nothing. That theoretical fatalism, Ceaser learned from Tocqueville, is the pervasive temptation of democracy. We democrats skeptically deny a place for extraordinary human activity as a cause of social and political change, and so we surrender the stage to impersonal technological, historical, or material forces that we believe are beyond our control. By contrast, Ceaser's defense of political life, though perhaps only probably true, is certainly salutary. That is, the intellectual defense of choice in large measure is what makes choice possible. For Ceaser, "The decisive choice between freedom and despotism is largely determined by the doctrines and ideas that guide people's thought."[23] The main task of political science is to defend and champion doctrines and ideas that support political life and to discredit with polemic, irony, and of course facts those that don't. Kojève admitted that at least part of the time his writing was propaganda in the service of his theory of history; Ceaser admits that his writing is to some extent propaganda against such theory. To repeat, Ceaser's is a rhetorical political science. And what gives his effort nobility is that, with Tocqueville, he doesn't know with certainty that history has—or will soon—come to an end.

According to Ceaser, Strauss wrote to save Americans from Kojève. But it is unlikely that many Americans would have known of Kojève without Strauss's efforts. Fukuyama learned of Kojève—and learned to be open to his seduction—from a Straussian, Allan Bloom. And Bloom, the most famous of Straussians, describes sophisticated Americans in his *Closing of the American Mind* as flat-souled, polite, apathetic, competent specialists and little more. For Bloom, Americans' eros has become one-dimensional because they are no longer moved by love and death. Their relativism is really a subordination of truth to comfort; they are incapable of taking seriously ways of life other than their own. Bloom writes as if liberal democracy had become therapeutic democracy, as if the great project of that regime were to finish the pragmatist's work of putting death to death. He comes very close, at least, to describing our best students as Kojève's posthistorical animals.[24]

On the level of description, the analysis of Bloom and Rorty seem virtually identical. And we cannot help wondering whether Bloom sees Americans through the lens of Kojève's theory. Strauss, after all, had sent Bloom to France to study with Kojève, and Bloom was dazzled by Kojève's brilliance. But in Rorty's mind, Bloom and Heidegger are in the same camp: self-obsessed, "over-philosophized," reactionary defenders of truth. Rorty claims that for the most part they both correctly describe and wrongly disparage the achievement of America.[25] Strauss, Heidegger, the Francophile Bloom, and even the ironic Kojève, in Rorty's view, are the Europeans who wrongly hold us in contempt. (He writes wonderfully of Kojève's "snobby preference for samurai over salespeople, and for Stalin over Eisenhower.")[26] In effect Rorty adds Strauss and Straussians to Ceaser's list of thinkers with misanthropic disdain for our country.

Rorty's reconstruction of America is, in part, a deconstruction of Strauss, because Strauss makes European antidemocrats too fascinating to us. Ceaser and Rorty agree that Heidegger and Kojève are pernicious, but they disagree on Strauss. Rorty thinks Heidegger and Kojève are right, and Ceaser thinks they are wrong, in their description of American democracy today. Ceaser also thinks the Straussian Bloom is wrong; he believes that America and Americans still have a soul, if only, as Mansfield says, a constitutional soul. But Ceaser defends Strauss himself, saying that what Strauss teaches is both true and salutary for America.

Strauss wrote to save us from Kojève, but he is also responsible for our recent fascination with him. Strauss thought Kojève was a philosopher, a great, liberated thinker.[27] His greatness lies in expressing with rigorous consistency the goal and possible outcome of distinctively modern thought. There is a straight line from the state-of-nature teaching of Hobbes and Locke, with its view that human beings move, in freedom, indefinitely away from nature, to the Kojèvian conclusion that that movement—history—has revealed human freedom to be a miserable error that must come to an end. So if America is a Lockean regime, grounded in the teachings of the Declaration of Independence on nature and inalienable rights, then Kojève explains where America is headed. With help from Strauss and Kojève, Ceaser sees American pragmatism, from Croly and Dewey through Rorty, as a militant form of atheism. The pragmatists think that their project is a criticism of American individualism or Lockeanism, but their criticism is really a radicalization of the Lockean-Jeffersonian hostility to human dependence on either nature or God.[28] If the founders viewed human beings as self-constituting, as the Straussian-Lockean Michael Zuckert claims, then it is a short step from their view of self-constitution to Rorty's view of self-description and redescription.[29]

Strauss turned our attention to Kojève to show us how America might deconstruct or self-destruct. American political life should not be regarded as merely ministerial to the individual's private interests; it exists partly for itself. And so Ceaser's refutation of Kojève, Rorty, Bloom, Heidegger, and their ilk must begin by showing that there is still political life in America. That refutation should properly begin with Ceaser's Reaganism, with a celebration of our great victory in the Cold War—a victory somewhat unanticipated and certainly insufficiently acknowledged even by Solzhenitsyn. (Bloom, we must add, wrote in the mid-eighties as if the Reagan revival and even the Cold War did not exist.) And Ceaser must continue with a defense of the present functioning of our Constitution and our nation. So he tells us that the good news about the failed effort to remove President Clinton from office is that it was conducted scrupulously according to constitutional forms, and that he knows that our great nation will continue to be invigorated by political challenges. Ceaser believes that he sides today with the party of constitutionalism, the mean between the antipolitical elitism of intellectuals and an irresponsible and potentially dangerous populism.[30] His ironic polemic against our European critics is designed, above all, to help us regain confidence in the continuing truth of our fundamental political principles.

Reconstructing America

The political evidence introduced by Ceaser, I think, is insufficient to reconstruct America. Strauss's position is that human beings are fundamentally natural, not historical, beings; human nature is not an oxymoron. Strauss denies the distinction between nature and history that would allow us to think of history's end. But he also makes Kojève's position seem a plausible or philosophic account of the facts, and so he makes it possible for Bloom to write as if history had ended, as if human beings no longer had the longings or social passions connected with love and death. Strauss and Bloom make it clear that the pragmatists are pernicious, but not clear enough that they are wrong. Kojève and Bloom, I think, are far from being close to being right about Americans today, and without the assistance of biotechnology at least, there is little chance that history will come to an end or that the human world will become a wasteland populated by "last men." Ceaser needs to make clear, or more clear, that he knows that Bloom's account, like Heidegger's, is at best a reductionistic caricature of American souls today. I would even say that he needs less to defend Strauss, Tocqueville, and the *Federalist* than to defend the human liberty of most contemporary Americans, beings whose lives are remarkably apolitical. Ceaser is right to be indignant about what theorists have said to belittle and endanger America, but perhaps he should be more so about how they have misunderstood Americans. He needs to say more about the human greatness and misery of the guy in the jogging suit.

Bloom says the music of young Americans is nothing but the beat of mechanical rutting. But it is also full of anger and unfocused longing. It is lame, but only because the young lack words for their longings, not because their souls lack such longings. Bloom himself admits that the chaotic souls of the children of the divorced are not really calmed by the therapeutic platitudes of their psychologists, and that such children are becoming the norm in America. Americans still love and hate, and hate those who threaten what they love. They still experience the hard responsibilities connected with birth and death, and even ordinary lives cannot be lived well without considerable courage. And they also still have the responsibilities connected with being the beings with language or speech, which enables them to speak words that correspond, even if imperfectly, to what they really know about themselves and the world.

The souls of Americans today are less flat than disordered or deranged. As Walker Percy says, we're fairly loony.[31] Following Tocqueville's lead, we could say that madness is more common in America than ever before. We are restless in the midst of prosperity, unhappy in the best of environments.[32] We should be angry at the experts, the pragmatists, who aim to deprive us of the words that allow us to understand, and so live well with, our experiences. It is not true, as they say, that as words disappear the experiences do too. So a defense of America and Americans today is inseparable from a form of populism. And that populism is not merely Ceaser's excellent American chauvinism. Our own experts, our own intellectuals, are now much more our problem.

Until recently, the great threat to liberal democracy and human liberty was communism. Now it is therapeutic democracy, the tyranny of experts, and we can hardly blame the Europeans for our deconstruction. As Tocqueville predicted, the lie of socialism has been supplanted by the lullaby of pantheism, and the corresponding despotism is a disease of democracy, not mere anti-American snobbery.[33]

I wouldn't go so far as today's Heideggerian, who would, according to Ceaser, observe: "With the diversion of the Cold War behind us, it is possible to focus on the real threat to humanity. That threat is the barren and empty humanism found in America. The real war for the soul of humanity has just begun."[34] My view is that Americans still have souls, that what they say and do is not barren or empty. But the post–Cold War threat to the human soul is in some respects unprecedented, and it is very real.

Human nature continues to resist the pragmatists' best efforts at linguistic therapy. But emerging biotechnological breakthroughs promise to make the alteration of human nature routine; the goal will be, quite literally, the abolition of man—the being moved strongly by love and death. Even now it is not enough simply to *describe* the distinctive greatness and misery of human beings; human nature as a distinctive point of pride and as a good in itself must be defended as never before. We must show the goodness of Being and human beings in spite of human misery. It is not enough to defend the rare and questionable experience of the philosopher, as Bloom does. The experience of the goodness of human being is characteristically and best articulated by religion.

Religion can no longer be viewed as it was by the American founders, as primarily an instrument for the preservation of liberal democracy. Liberal democracy now has to be justified perhaps more than ever by the truth and goodness of religion. What used to be regarded as human nature may soon be only ambiguously natural. Because human nature might be eradicated or transformed by technology, we now have to show why what we have been given by nature and God is good for us. Unfortunately, the philosophers have not done well in defending the goodness of ordinary human lives. The Socratics, finally, only see the good in thought; the Lockeans see nothing good in nature at all; and the Rousseaueans only see good in what is less than human. Tocqueville, it is true, was devoted to human liberty in a way that to some extent defies reason, but he was not exactly a philosopher and was no lover of the ordinary, either.

Ceaser admits that his defense of the political life, the regime, is hardly a complete account of what shapes human lives or the human good. His next project may be to contribute to the conservative formulation of a public philosophy to defend liberal democracy. Such an effort, he says, involves rethinking "what will be our ground, our narrative, and our sentimental education." Conservatives must prepare to take on the pragmatists on all fronts; conservatives' "strategic" or rhetorical efforts must be more comprehensive than they have been so far. This project may even involve calling into question the liberalism of "our own founding." If Ceaser and others do move beyond the defense of our political life to a critical analysis of "the form and shape of our culture," they will discover that the shortcomings of the latter cannot really be blamed on our European critics or on recent currents in European thought.[35]

CHAPTER SIX

The New Liberalism

James Ceaser has given us the most brilliant and imaginative Strauss-inspired defense of America. But the most ambitious and able Strauss-inspired scholar to have actually attempted to influence American public policy is William Galston. Ceaser writes as a Republican moderate conservative, but Galston as a Democratic moderate liberal. Galston's efforts, in fact, have been to transform his party in a new or less ideological direction, both as a scholar and as an advisor to Democrats from Walter Mondale to Bill Clinton. And he had some success as a leading figure at the Progressive Policy Institute in forming "new" Democrats such as Clinton, Al Gore, and Joseph Lieberman. Galston's book *Liberal Purposes* (*LP*) is a wide-ranging attempt to understand America theoretically in the service of his moderate but liberal policy objectives.

Galston aims in *Liberal Purposes* to convince us that liberalism is a regime, a whole, a coherent understanding of the purposes of human life. "Liberalism contains within itself the resources it needs to declare and to

defend a conception of the good and virtuous life that is in no way trun-
cated or contemptible," he writes. He opposes the view of those "from
Irving Kristol to Jürgen Habermas," those on the critical but sympathetic
right and left, who say that liberalism depends on "the accumulated moral
capital of revealed religion and premodern moral philosophy," and that
the skepticism of liberalism more or less inevitably erodes those moral
resources over time (*LP,* 304).[1]

Galston correctly observes that both Marxists and conservatives argue that liberalism has within itself the seeds of its own destruction.
Galston disagrees, arguing that liberalism can free itself from illiberalism,
or what he loosely calls moral traditionalism. But Galston's argument is
unconvincing and rather obviously rhetorical. Galston wants contemporary liberals to accept him as one of their own and not to reject him as a
conservative critic. Like Tocqueville, who advised advertising oneself as
equality's friend in the services of moderating egalitarian extremism,
Galston proclaims that his friendly criticisms of contemporary liberals
are made within the perspective of liberalism. As a liberal partisan, he
corrects his fellow liberals only to secure better liberalism's perpetuation
and progress. But what he actually shows is that any stable society is not
wholly liberal, and that a regime devoted primarily to securing human
liberty does so by maintaining a host of tensions and contradictions.

Galston has written more candidly in other works about liberalism's
self-destructive character. Allan Bloom, his teacher, wrote a best-seller
that seemed to blame American relativism and apathetic "niceness" on
the alien infusion of Nietzscheanism into a healthy liberal context. Galston corrected that impression by pointing out that relativism is a late
moment in American liberalism's own development, the product of the
spreading of the Lockean spirit of individual choice or contract into
every area of human life.

Lockeanism is salutary only if properly limited, but it contains no
limits within itself. So, Galston argues, "Bloom's own account suggests

that modern liberal democracy is not stably well-ordered unless it is somehow mitigated by external forces (religion, traditional moral restraints,
aristocracy) with which it is at war and which it tends to corrode."[2]
Galston's own account of the excesses of contemporary liberal theorists
makes the same suggestion. But what most liberals call "illiberal" Galston
says we should now accept as "functional" from a liberal perspective.
According to Galston, we should incorporate religion, moral traditionalism, and aristocracy into liberalism because it cannot survive without
them. Galston humors liberal pretensions by declaring a compromise
victory.

My purpose in this chapter is to show some of the ways by which
Galston presents the forms of theoretical and practical incoherence that
sustain human liberty. I address a question that Galston acknowledges
remains unanswered: "whether the tensions I explore are wholly within
liberalism, or between liberalism and other sources of moral authority as
well" (LP, 16). That question is especially difficult because human liberty
itself is not one thing but many. Galston's liberalism at its best is actually
a moral pluralism that sees some intrinsic good in a variety of human
qualities, some of them illiberal.

Liberalism as a Regime

Galston argues that modern liberalism is a regime, which means that
liberal political decisions infuse every area of human endeavor. This view
of the "primacy of the political" means that the right of "conscientious
objection" does not exist, as many liberals believe. For one can only exempt oneself from the duties of a citizen by some claim of personal or
conscientious freedom, and though liberal regimes may allow more space
for personal freedom and diverse ways of life than others do, even they
must put the preservation of political order first. A certain kind of political order is required for the effective exercise of liberty. Thus, in Galston's

view, liberalism is far from morally neutral. Asserting definite claims about the human good, it favors some ways of life and tends to disrupt and even suppress others.

One liberal claim about the human good is that the deepest human longings and the highest human goals transcend the realm of politics. Religion, art, and philosophy are distorted by attempts at their political determination. And yet despite itself the liberal regime cannot help but shape them to a great extent. The amount of space allowed for such transcendent pursuits is a political or prudential decision, and that space can never be infinite. So liberalism's comprehensive political claim over citizens contradicts its claim about personal transcendence. The liberal citizen is free enough to know that he is not fundamentally a citizen, and the fact that he has that knowledge is in large part the result of a liberal political decision. Nonetheless, the liberal regime can, if it judges it necessary, treat citizens fundamentally as citizens or as instruments for securing its political perpetuation. Citizens, for instance, can be compelled to fight and die in battle. They also can, even must, be subjected to civic education, persuasion, and habituation with the purpose of attaching and devoting them rather uncritically to their political community.

Galston states the liberal dilemma with ironic simplicity: "To be a citizen of a liberal polity is to be required to surrender as much of our own private conscience as is necessary for the secure enjoyment of what remains" (*LP*, 250). Surrender, security, and enjoyment are not words usually associated with conscientious thought and action, let alone citizenship. Liberalism distorts both the conscience and the citizen. Galston concludes his book by acknowledging that liberalism is only very imperfectly a regime; he distinguishes it by its consciousness of its imperfection. Liberalism leaves the relationship between public citizen and private individual ill defined, giving itself "an endless task of imperfect adjustment" (*LP*, 304).

Ancient Liberalism

Galston regards Aristotle as a liberal. Aristotle held that human beings transcend political life through thought and that perhaps the only genuine human freedom is that of the philosopher. But Aristotle's philosophic way of life is possible, at best, for only a few; the many are chained to the way of life, laws, traditions, and mores of a particular political order. Political life cannot be transformed but only influenced indirectly by philosophers. Even philosophers depend on the existence of a stable political community, a stability that is endangered by the corrupting influence of the excessive politicization of philosophic skepticism. Aristotle viewed the primacy of the political as an ineradicable necessity rooted in human nature. Ancient liberalism did not intend to be the animating principle of any particular regime. For all political orders are fundamentally illiberal.

For an Aristotelian or ancient liberal, the claim of modern liberalism that all human beings transcend their regimes through their personal liberty is unsound. For one thing, the personal quality that enables this transcendence is usually left vague or undetermined. No one with any astuteness says that all human beings can become philosophers. Liberals who are also Christians can hold that transcendence occurs through God's grace and one's relationship with the personal God. But other liberals say, quite rightly, that Christian belief makes liberal consistency impossible. Galston himself calmly but persistently insists that Christianity and liberalism are in tension, if not necessarily at war. He also says that liberalism depends not at all on Christianity's own truth claim, agreeing with ancient and almost all modern and contemporary liberals.

It seems clear that ancient, Aristotelian liberalism, for Galston, is at its core Socratic. All liberalism depends finally on Socratic views of the truth and human liberation. Liberalism is really the protection of liberated reason, the way of life of the philosopher, from popular prejudice or traditionalism. Liberalism—properly understood—is good because it allows human beings to know the truth about their nature or condition, which is always being repressed by wisdom-hating fundamentalism. Liberalism is a good regime because, better than any other, it allows a few human beings to fulfill their natural potential to become rationally liberated. So for Socratic liberals, political and moral community and tradition are not good in and of themselves. These liberals' support for community and tradition is always functional or conditional. The unfortunate fact is that rational liberty cannot come into its own without their support.

Ancient liberalism affirms the contradictions of elitism, acknowledging that their abolition in the name of consistency would be at the expense of philosophy. Galston finds the elitism of ancient liberalism still present to some extent in the early modern liberalism of the American founders. He sometimes presents that elitism as a reflection of an ineradicable human problem, and he attempts to remind contemporary liberals of the consequences of the fact that liberalism always presupposes intellectual elitism. Galston contends that only a "few individuals will come to embrace the core commitments of liberal society through a process of rational inquiry," that is, "on the basis of purely philosophic considerations" (*LP*, 243–44, 265).

According to Galston, in practice American liberalism depends less on philosophical liberation than on a "civic pedagogy," primarily a rhetoric that attaches Americans to liberal principles and virtues as their own, not as true. It also depends on religiously based arguments and incentives that inquiring, rational liberals cannot accept as true. One indispensable liberal tenet, part of its self-conscious elitism, is that religion provides nothing "essential to the validity of liberal arguments." But religious belief supports liberal theory and practice in the minds and hearts of most citizens of a liberal regime. As George Washington said in his farewell address, the fundamental distinction is between the rational and the religious, and the former do not really regard the latter as liberals at all (*LP,* 265–66).

Liberalism is always, in practice, a liberal democracy, a mixed regime of the many democrats committed to equality and the few liberals committed to liberty. The liberals cannot free themselves from the necessity of acquiring the consent to rule from the democrats. So the liberals must deceive the democrats in order to rule. The many necessarily understand the foundation of liberal democracy differently from the few. Can Galston really persuade contemporary liberals to accept self-consciously the necessity of prudent deception, the contradiction or paradox that the pursuit of the truth depends on lies? As Tocqueville says, are not our times too dogmatically egalitarian, too opposed to privileging—as our intellectuals say—anyone or anything, for liberal intellectuals to acknowledge even to themselves that their partisanship is antiegalitarian?

Enlightenment Liberalism

The Enlightenment, for Galston, is the attempt to eradicate the contradictions present in ancient liberalism by transforming political order in accordance with reason. It represents the naïve educational theory that philosophic or critical education is *the* form of education for a liberal community. The aim is to make every human being a Socrates, *the* liberal hero or model.

But Galston recognizes that naïve liberals are not so naïve as to state their aim so directly. They define human excellence, and therefore education, as relentless self-examination, the radical questioning of all one has been given by society and even nature. That questioning is defended in terms of what is required for personal choice of one's own way of life, and so social diversity. But Socrates was no partisan of diversity. He thought one way of life was best for human beings, and otherwise naïve liberals really believe so too. So liberal education seeks to prevent us from choosing to act in accordance with tradition and authority because this would restrict true or rational choice. The only choice that finally passes the process of self-examination is a life devoted to critical self-examination, or the choice constantly to prepare for choice. Naïve liberals are so far opposed to favoring a genuine diversity of choices that they tend to view the closure that comes with moral choice as an arbitrary self-deprivation of liberty.

Contemporary liberals say they aim to expand the achievement of public religious neutrality to complete moral neutrality. They claim to relativize moral claims in the name of diversity. They oppose all hierarchy and repressive conformism. Everyone is free to do his or her own thing: Gays are free to be gay, women not to be wives and mothers, men to leave their wives and not support their children, citizens not to be patriotic, and conscientious objectors to follow their conscience without fear of the law. There are no public limits to choice.

But to his credit, Galston recognizes that modern Socratic liberals are not consistent in their promotion of public moral relativism. They do not question the goodness of freedom of thought, and they do not apply their relativistic method to Socrates' moralizing about the unexamined life. Their relativism seems mainly to be a strategy to liberate the mind and an intellectual elite from moral or popular control. Galston sees that the real offense of those who would closet gays or restrict divorce is that they would do so from a perspective that ranks moral order or duty above intellectual liberation. Modern Socratic liberals, in a way, are quite traditional in their view of the possibility of such liberation. They are partisans of the Socratic tradition.

Modern liberalism's model regime or utopia is, in the precise sense, an aristocracy of everyone. Its Enlightenment tendency is to correct ancient liberalism by universalizing or democratizing it. But this apparent correction of ancient elitism can also be viewed as its intensification. The aim is to impose intellectual liberation on everyone, even though all human experience suggests that most human beings do not want it and never really will. The error of modern liberalism is always, Galston says, that "the motives and satisfactions of a tiny elite somehow constitutes the (hidden) essence and desire of all human beings" (*LP*, 59). As Galston shows in his criticism of the libertarianism of Roberto Unger, the democratic aspiration of modern liberalism inevitably tends toward coercive utopianism. Galston believes, in fact, that the rise of the fundamentalist Right in America represents democratic opposition to the liberal propensity to tyrannize, and he even indicates his agreement with the view that the "secular humanism" of bureaucratic experts in American public education is a mild form of coercive utopianism (*LP*, 13–14).

Liberal Self-Destruction

Elite efforts to impose popular liberation inevitably inspire popular resistance. Galston disagrees with Bloom's thesis that the moral relativism of the intellectuals in contemporary America has emerged victorious. The fundamental political fact of America is the existence of a culture war, argues Galston, with the popular forces who support moral traditionalism offering strong and effective resistance to the liberal elitists. Liberals have to take the religious or moral criticism of liberalism seriously. If they simply show contempt for it, they are sure to be defeated politically.

Galston himself takes this traditionalist criticism seriously in a number of ways. And he instructs contemporary liberals by warning them that their liberated wisdom must be moderated by the requirements of consent if they are to be effective politically. One of Galston's main purposes, certainly, is to teach his fellow liberal Democrats what they must do to win democratic elections. By taking moral and cultural conservatives seriously as a force to be defeated, he appears less elitist and more pragmatic than other liberals.

If liberals cannot "recognize their partial dependence on" and forthrightly "accommodate" within their political theory "the moral restraints espoused by ordinary citizens," writes Galston, they "cannot regain in practice the general acceptance needed to guide public life in a constitutional democracy." Galston invites liberals to reflect on "the tenor and outcome of the 1988 U.S. presidential election," when Dukakis was demagogically and successfully branded as a liberal, a partisan of unbridled libertarian permissiveness. Liberals should rule, Galston says, on behalf of "the resumption of progressive politics," but they cannot present the abolition of moral restraints as their vision of progress and win elections. Unlike Dukakis, they must spiritedly defend themselves against those who claim they have no spirit (*LP,* 17–18).

Galston is in a sense more elitist than other liberals because he is less deluded about the possibility of popular liberation through persuasion. One reason Galston is not a conservative Republican is that he is more confident that popular, moralistic resistance will be an effective curb on liberal excesses than that liberals will succeed in curbing popular antiliberalism. The historical evidence, in his reading, mainly points to the fragility of liberty and the resilience of morality.

Galston's own liberal elitism is most extreme in the very unflattering view he sometimes gives of popular opposition to liberalism. It is, he claims, an "escape from freedom." Liberal openness is liberating and exhilarating for some, but others become confused and afraid. The latter "flee from the burdens of self-determination to the comforts of submission to authority." Liberals have to acknowledge that most human beings cannot live well with much freedom, and their psychological limitations are the cause of antiliberal politics (*LP,* 295).

But Galston sometimes complains that the modernist ideal of personal liberation is not Socratic at all. Modern liberals aim to liberate the self from all stable contexts, from all dogma and convention, but for nothing in particular. This radical, wholly negative form of liberation is,

as Socrates says, pure democracy or anarchy. Modern liberals have become too democratic to privilege even philosophy; they have forgotten
the purpose of human liberation.

Galston sees that the dominant tendency of modern liberalism has
been, over time, to free itself from the constraints of Socratic rationalism. The more liberalism frees itself from reason, the less conscious it
becomes of the true ground of its elitism. Hence liberals become more
able to flatter democratic audiences without the pain of deception. Universal liberation is more plausible on the vague premise "that everyone
could become creative, autonomous, a source of new values." Liberal
freedom becomes relativistic self-assertion. Once it does, liberals no longer
have, even among themselves, an argument for their elitism.[3]

The dominant form of contemporary liberalism, Galston reports, is
easygoing Kantianism. What makes Kant's thought attractive to intellectual elites today is its radical view of human freedom as freedom from
both "divine authority" and "any form of naturalism." That radically
negative freedom is what distinguishes human beings. Liberals radicalize
Kant by saying that freedom must not be bounded by morality or anything else, and so autonomy must be free from "rational constraint."
Kant's thought must be freed from what makes it most attractive to
Socratic liberals, "its broad agreement with Aristotle about what is highest in man." Libertarian or anarchist Kantianism is at the foundation of
today's "secular humanism," the identification of morality or autonomy
with unconstrained choice.[4]

Galston's criticism of easygoing Kantianism is of its libertarianism.
He knows, of course, that early modern liberalism was only inconsistently in agreement with Aristotle or Socrates about human purpose.
The American founders, whom Galston praises for their philosophic self-
awareness and their prudence, he views as Lockeans more than anything
else. Locke, to whom Galston often returns for his relative sobriety, based
his teaching about liberty on the state of nature. In that state, human

beings are both radically free from political and social ties and rational enough to invent solutions for their natural penury and fear. Locke, when he discusses human beings living in civil society, is perfectly aware that the functioning of human reason and the exercise of human liberty depend on proper socialization. But by nature human individuals remain unsocialized, and so they could not possibly be rational. Locke's teaching about nature, and so about the contractual basis of human political and social ties, is obviously inconsistent.

The American founders inconsistently accepted the state of nature teaching and also inconsistently tended to think of themselves as Socratic rationalists. The Lockean teaching is that the human desire to know has no support in nature. So the founders said both that the purpose of human reason is to free human beings from nature and that the rational life is man's natural perfection. Compared to thinkers and statesmen today, they may have been practically reasonable, but they were theoretically confused. This is why Galston criticizes Bloom for his suggestion that a return to the founders might be a cure for the intellectual malady of our time.[5]

The most consistent form of modern thinking, Galston says, is Rousseau's. If human beings are by nature free from all social ties, then they are by nature wholly irrational. They could not reason their way to property or government or even beyond the end of the day. What distinguishes human beings—their human liberty—emerges accidentally over time. What they had by nature—stupid contentment and an asocial self-sufficiency or inhuman liberty—was good. So human liberty is accidental or unchosen. It is not even choiceworthy because human beings become progressively more discontent or miserable as they become more self-conscious or aware of time. The most consistent version of modern liberalism denies the goodness of human liberty and human reason.

Kant attempted to restore the perception of the goodness of rational, human liberty on a Rousseauean foundation by allowing human beings to take proper pride in the dignity of their freedom from nature. For Kant, human beings have become unhappy, but their acquisition of reason has given them the dignity of moral choice. But Kant's separation of nature from morality produced a new inconsistency. We are divided, in effect, into animals and gods. We are both beings who seek happiness and beings who seek rational, moral consistency. For Kant, no animal can be moral or rational. But this means that man is not an animal. So Kant denies the obvious, the connection between what is highest in man and the rest of his being. He rationally but unrealistically denies natural evidence.

Easygoing Kantians free themselves from this impossible fanaticism. They return to the candor of Rousseau. They maintain that human existence, insofar as it is free from nature, is accidental and disordered. Human liberty is unlimited by nature. Dignity for the easygoing Kantian is not rooted in moral consistency but in the misery of our freedom, for which we deserve compassion. Our freedom divides our existence and makes us unhappy, but there is no reason not to use our freedom to pursue what happiness we can. We are mysteriously compelled to choose how best to live with our misery. The doctrine of autonomy or free choice means we cannot criticize those who choose narcotics or diversions over rational or moral consistency. They actually follow the philosopher Rousseau's choice of the negation of self-consciousness in a reverie, a perfectly anti-Socratic or antirational choice chosen in the name of reason.

To put it another way, if there is no natural support for reason, and if opposing reason to nature mainly makes us miserable, then how can an antirational choice in the name of happiness be criticized? Such a choice, in fact, might be called the most rational one, because it favors the rational, impersonal order of nature and opposes the disorder of human liberty. But the total negation of one's human liberty is impossible; no narcotic, diversion, or reverie works perfectly all the time. So easygoing Kantianism is based on the principle that human liberty is not good but inevitable. We are condemned to be deserving of compassion, but no one can blame us for whatever we might have to do to make it through our lives.

For Galston, liberalism seems eventually to want to destroy itself. Its foundation is Socratic, but its logic shows the examined life to be undeserving of privilege and finally impossible. Such a life is a particularly miserable, even irrational, choice as a human pursuit. But Galston sometimes turns our attention from the logic of this argument by suggesting that the fatal undermining of the Socratic view of liberty came not with Locke or some other modern thinker but with Christianity.[6]

Rousseaueanism, Galston suggests, is secularized Christianity. Both Christians and modern liberals say that man is mysteriously free from nature and the requirements of political life. Lockeans do not seem to reflect much on that freedom, but Christians attribute it to their creation in the image of a personal God. Rousseaueans, not believing in that God, say that freedom is purely accidental, bringing to light the foundation of Lockeanism. For Rousseaueans the accident of human liberty is an unfortunate evil from which human beings should be liberated, whereas Christians view their liberty as that of creatures who can know and rely upon their Creator. For Christians, human liberty is good.

Galston's own contempt for liberalism's self-destruction can be called partly Socratic and partly Aristotelian, and it is far from completely opposed to Christianity properly understood. He holds that liberation through the philosophic life may be the only genuine form of human liberty. But he also holds the Aristotelian view that an indispensable premise of moral virtue and political life—whether they are good for their own sake or are preconditions for philosophy—is personal responsibility for one's own conduct. That psychology of responsible liberty is opposed to the Rousseauean view that all human beings are essentially victims and so deserving of compassion. Both the non-secular Christians and the Aristotelians hold that human beings are free and responsible. They both have a moral, and so somewhat illiberal, view of liberty.

The Reasonableness of Traditionalism

From both an Aristotelian and a Christian perspective, contemporary secular humanism is not humanism at all. It rejects both Christian and Socratic views of the goodness of human liberty. American Christians today, Galston observes, perceive that "our system of public education . . . embodies a bias against authority and faith." They do not perceive that bias as Socratic, but is simply permissive and so opposed to the truth about human liberty. The Socratic Galston admits that, sociologically speaking, they are correct. The great threat to human liberty today is not that children "believe in something too deeply," but that they tend to have no deep beliefs at all (*LP*, 254–55).

Following Bloom, Galston makes the Socratic observation that one must begin with beliefs, opinions, and authorities in order to experience the exhilaration of rational liberation from them. Relativism acquired too easily and too early is a dogma that is especially closed to the truth. Bloom further argues that Americans, as a consequence, may have become incapable of rebelling against or otherwise responding to their mortality; they are no longer moved by it. Liberated from their awareness of death, they seem almost to have returned to their natural condition, as Rousseau describes it.

The dependence of philosophy on the cultivation of opinion by traditionalist parents and other authorities means that intellectual liberalism is endangered by excessive political liberalism. Philosophic liberation is from passionate, illiberal conviction, and political liberals, in their tendency to reduce all human relationships to calculation, contract, and consent, aim to undermine fatally such conviction. Philosophy or Socratic liberalism is parasitic. Its liberal political influence undermines the conditions of its existence.

From Galston's perspective, the relativistic, permissive liberalism of today's intellectual elite is too democratic. For him, popular, religiously based conservatism or traditionalism is permissive liberalism's benefi-cent—and in some sense truthful—corrective. The popular, salutary view is that elitist libertarianism is impractical; it ignores the requirements of everyday life. It is also willfully detached from the pleasurable, satisfying experiences that come with the performance of ordinary social duties. The forms of happiness associated with marriage, the family, friendship, love of God, and political life are distinctively human yet rooted in na-ture. Their enjoyment requires personal commitment and social stability and so moral resistance to change.

The popular view is that the libertarianism of easygoing Kantianism is ugly. It willfully ignores the fact that human liberty is necessarily lim-ited, and so cannot be detached from moral seriousness. Human beings cannot live or even think well without acknowledging some dependence on tradition and nature. Radical liberation, in truth, is dizzying and terri-fying, and nothing more. The insistent denial of intrinsic order and ne-cessity to human life is really a denial of death. That fantasy of total liberation is actually, in Galston's words, "more of a narcotic than the stable patterns of daily life could ever be."[7] According to Socrates, phi-losophy is first of all accepting one's mortality without flinching. So no conception of the self is less philosophical than the radically modern one.

The popular view that Galston affirms is that human beings have a finite existence in this world but infinite desires. So their deepest desires will forever elude satisfaction by any form of social transformation. Reli-giously grounded traditionalists place little faith in modern, Lockean-Rousseauean projects for such transformation. If the infinite desires of human beings are to be satisfied, it must be by an infinite Being. If such satisfaction is certainly impossible, then perhaps the relativists or anti-moralists are correct about life's futility and the need for narcotic fanta-sies. That is why the Christian traditionalist often believes that the funda-mental human choice is between Christianity and moral relativism. The

Socratic liberal would, of course, not agree. But he is put in a difficult situation. If the only genuine form of human liberation comes through philosophy, then the Rousseauean conclusion about human liberty leading to misery retains great force.

Contrary to contemporary liberals, traditionalists agree with Aristotle that no regime can "remain indifferent to the moral character of its citizenry."[8] The development of character usually depends on a stable family with two heterosexual parents, political stability, an educational system that does not oppose but reinforces parental concern with virtue and patriotism, and a vital religious life. Such socialization is indispensable for the exercise of liberty and personal responsibility. So Galston seems most in agreement with popular traditionalism when he says that his "guiding intuition is that the United States is in trouble because it has failed to attend to the dependence of sound politics on sound culture" (*LP*, 6). Culture, for Galston, means tradition, civic education, and religion. He is aware of Bloom's view that the heart of culture is religion. He is also aware of Bloom's Socratic distaste for the term. Galston's affirmation of culture makes him a very strange sort of liberal, but he remains a liberal because that affirmation is only partial.

Liberal Justice

One reason Galston remains a liberal is that he views the practical rationalism of Enlightenment liberalism as having produced undeniable moral progress. He sees as its goal the creation of a universal and homogeneous society, eradicating arbitrary and so unjust distinctions based on economic class, race, gender, and so forth. This society would minimize cruelty, the oppression of one group by another on behalf of some arbitrary or controversial view of the soul. Galston, for the most part, affirms in the name of justice the victories of universalistic liberal principles over moral traditionalism in America.

Liberal universalism is also a form of egalitarianism: "The full development of each individual is equal in moral weight to every other. . . . Thus a policy that neglects the educable retarded . . . is considered, in itself, as bad as one that reduces extraordinary gifts to mere normality."[9] Galston's interest in justice here is not really Socratic, and it produces inconsistencies in his liberal thought. What might be good for the retarded, the marginalized, and the unfortunate is not necessarily good for thought, unless the un-Socratic view that liberal political progress both reflects and is a cause of thought's progress is true. Is not the view that the retarded are equal in moral weight to the philosophers really a Christian one, even if it expresses itself in the form of the Rousseauean compassion of secularized Christianity? One indication that Galston inconsistently shies away from this conclusion is that he never seriously considers extending this concern to the unborn fetus; in fact, he regards those who do as illiberal. He shares the confusion of contemporary liberal Democrats, who want to embrace simultaneously libertarian permissiveness and compassionate duty.

Galston is aware that it is doubtful that liberal political thought has progressed in America since the time of the founders. The founders, as Lockean individualists, did not prefer one religion to another and were in principle antiracist and antisexist. So Galston presents the civil rights movement of the sixties as in one respect conservative, a call to eradicate the contradiction between the founding principles and the racism and sexism that had become part of our moral/religious tradition. Raising blacks and women to full citizenship was "long overdue," he writes. Galston even recalls Walter Mondale, a candidate he advised, as having said that "the changes that have swept through U.S. society are on balance not only consistent with but actually supportive of Americans' basic principles" (LP, 268, 272–73). He goes on to qualify Mondale's enthusiasm in light of evidence of social disintegration, but never does he reject it.

But Galston's analysis of culture or moral traditionalism in America actually seems to constitute a subtle criticism of the founders' liberalism as excessively abstract. They understood that liberalism needed moral and religious support, but they were vague about how that support would perpetuate itself. What Tocqueville called "distinctively American political culture" had to develop into a mixture of secular liberalism, Christian morality, and white Anglo-Saxon Protestant mores. This "moral traditionalism" was decidedly illiberal. It marginalized Catholics and Jews, subordinated blacks and women, and promoted "unquestioning patriotism" and respect for authority. It also included the more liberal virtues of self-reliance, self-restraint, and personal responsibility (*LP,* 267–68).

Galston is nearly silent on what allowed this vigorous moral particularism to develop. Tocqueville points to the limited authority of the national government and to "administrative decentralization" even within the states. The Constitution, against the intention of the leading founders, created a mixed regime, one including both the universal and homogeneous but limited national government and the relatively particularistic and illiberal states and localities. Because the Bill of Rights applied only to the national government, the states were relatively free from national supervision or correction.

Galston makes more than Tocqueville does of the white, male, and Protestant character of traditional American morality and mores. Tocqueville's description of American virtue is mostly that of the middle class, of beings who are free politically but compelled by their situation to work. Tocqueville's description of American Christianity includes not only Protestantism but Catholicism, however, and his emphasis is on the unprecedented freedom, equality, and responsibility women have in America.[10] Galston discredits the WASPishness of the past in the manner of a contemporary liberal. One reason he remains a liberal Democrat is that he believes that the nerve of the Republican Party remains traditionalist—that is, to Galston, racist and sexist. But there is no particular reason why Catholics, Jews, women, and blacks could not be incorporated (in fact they were) into traditional American culture. Personal responsibility, self-sufficiency, self-restraint, the family, religion, and patriotism are not sources of virtue that necessarily exclude particular American groups (except perhaps liberal intellectuals).

Galston's complex presentation of the civil rights movement of the sixties has it evolve from a conservative project aiming to purge the American tradition of racism and sexism to a more consistently liberal project viewing all moral traditionalism as repressive. The conservative antitraditionalism that liberated blacks and women became "an inspirational metaphor for other aggrieved groups," including the young, gays, atheists, and so on. It became an assault against all hierarchy on behalf of freedom and democracy. The radical democracy of liberal theory became the social or political movement of "expressive" individualism. Rather limply, Galston concludes that this movement came to embrace uncritically the "controversial premise that traditionalism *as a whole* was opposed to the actualization of liberal principles" (*LP,* 267–68).

The destruction of all hierarchy, all moral ranking, left only pure difference. So liberalism became the celebration of difference for its own sake. That celebration, Galston says, began with blacks, who came to demand not only equal citizenship but equal recognition of all features of their distinctive way of life. Celebration of the difference of groups is a marked departure from the founders' liberal individualism. What we now call multiculturalism is really a series of claims for exemptions from the requirements of common citizenship and personal responsibility.

The idea that blacks can be legitimately exempted from the American practice of moral virtue has not been good for blacks. Galston allows us to wonder whether that exemption was really a black demand or one largely made on their behalf by white liberals. The black precedent was the key for gay liberation. Yet there are differences. It is unclear, finally, what really separates white and black. Much of what we call black culture originated in the white South, and most middle-class blacks have contempt for public celebrations of, for instance, black English or underclass indolence. But if gays choose to define themselves primarily with reference to their sexual activity, then what separates them from heterosexual Americans is clear. Galston finally acknowledges, if only in a limited way, that defining gay and straight as just different choices or orientations undermines the family and so the proper inculcation of moral virtue.

Galston leaves us with the impression that the legacy of the sixties is ambiguous. The destruction of racism and sexism was progress; the assault on tradition and the celebration of pure difference were not. What broke down with amazing rapidity was the American mixture of liberalism and traditionalism. That breakdown is the cause of liberalism's immediate crisis and the repugnance that the relatively moral majority has toward it today. Galston cannot argue against the traditionalist critics who say liberalism is largely responsible for the "fearful toll" exacted by "epidemics of crime, drugs, and teenage pregnancy."

Was not that breakdown caused in part by excessive, imprudent zeal in the pursuit of liberalism's universal and homogeneous view of justice? But Galston affirms the liberal "tendency to employ constitutional law to extend the sway of liberal public values throughout the society" (*LP*, 273, 292). He agrees with the Supreme Court's meddlesome extremism in banning religious observances, creating new "rights" that leave the unborn without protection, and extending federal and judicial power to all aspects of our lives. But he remains aware that "pushed to their limit, the juridical principles and practices of a liberal society tend inevitably to corrode moralities that rest either on traditional forms of social organization or on the stern requirements of revealed religion" (*LP*, 279), and that liberalism's functioning depends on the vitality of such morality. Galston does, finally, try to establish limits to the consistent implementation of liberal constitutional principles in American lives, but they seem far too expansive.

Functional Traditionalism vs. Religious Belief

Galston usually holds that the traditional morality undermined by liberal principle and practice deserved to be undermined. But he also holds that liberalism cannot perpetuate itself if that morality is destroyed altogether. So he distinguishes between "intrinsic traditionalism," which understands traditional morality as good in itself (as part of divine law), and "functional traditionalism," which affirms certain parts of traditional morality not as good in themselves but as necessary supports for liberalism in practice. Intrinsic morality understands marriage as a sacred duty and divorce as intrinsically evil or sinful. Functional traditionalism opposes divorce in view of the "economic and psychological damage" it does to children, reducing "their capacity to become independent and contributing members of the community." A functional traditionalist approves of public policy that supports a particular tradition if a "plausible" connection can be made between that tradition and the exercise of personal freedom. But a functional traditionalism is also "wary" of the hierarchies of race, gender, and ethnicity inherent in intrinsic traditionalism. Galston's assumption is that traditions can be consciously liberalized to some extent while remaining effective (LP, 280–81).

For example, public policy can legitimately discourage divorce in view of its effects on children and can legitimately encourage heterosexual two-parent families over others in view of their better record in raising children. But that means that there is no rational basis for restricting divorce among those who are married without children. It may also mean there is no basis for not legalizing gay marriage, although public policy might discourage adoption by gay couples.

What Galston does not mention is that his alleged traditionalism here is Lockean. Locke transforms with impious humor the biblical teaching about marriage's indissolubility by saying that the stern divine injunction is that a couple must remain together until the children can fend for themselves. Marriage is for procreation, Locke says, and the marriage contract must include the acceptance of the responsibility that having children brings. But Locke cannot completely root the duty of parents to children in calculation and contract. The question Locke cannot answer about consent is the one Americans today apparently so often cannot answer: Why should one prefer the liberty of one's children to one's own liberty? Locke cannot explain why one would stay married just for the children's sake, and so our Lockean law does not compel that unreasonable choice. Locke's inconsistency, a time bomb at the core of his doctrine, is that liberalism in practice depends on the family, but family ties limit one's liberty in a way that cannot really be justified by liberal individualism.

Can "functional traditionalism," which is not at all an affirmation of sacred duty, really reverse or even retard the social disintegration caused by liberalism's nearly total victory over traditionalism? Galston says that "liberal notions of free choice and contractual relations . . . have permeated the previously sacramental understandings of marriage and the family. The notion of an irreversible, constitutive commitment has been undermined by the notions of liberalism and autonomy" (LP, 293). But Galston does not indicate how the sacramental understanding might be recovered from its capture by the individualistic spirit of contract. The reforms he recommends are sensible but far too minor to be of much consequence. He has not shown how religious duty, surely an indispensable foundation for "irreversible, constitutive commitment," can be incorporated into liberalism. Galston has not even explained how today's liberals might be induced to push for small pro-child restrictions in the divorce law. They may have some unease about the effects of easy divorce, but can they really be attracted to legislation that would actually restrict their choice? Galston, despite himself, shows us that liberalism depends on an "intrinsic traditionalism" that resists liberal assimilation or comprehension.

Galston's praise of functional traditionalism is in tension with his affirmation of the "informal gravitational influence liberalism has on individuals and institutions." He explains, for instance, how that influence has transformed American religion. American Catholic bishops have opposed Rome because their country's "liberal political culture encourages rational criticism of all forms of authority" (*LP*, 292). Because biblical religion depends on an authority beyond human reason, "political culture" opposes itself to religious culture, making the latter more liberal and less religious. So liberalism undermines the traditionalism that makes religion functional. As Tocqueville said, it was the Americans' decision to exempt religion from such rational criticism that allowed them to exercise their political liberty so well. Galston admits that the stability of Americans' political institutions still depends on the comparative strength of their religious commitments. So, in fact, American liberty is not well served by American bishops' applying their liberalism to ecclesiastical and theological questions, even though the gravitational pull of political liberty inclines them to do so.

Galston also describes liberalism's propensity to derange religion. As a result of liberalism's excesses, in his view, two extremist sects have developed: the secular humanists and the fundamentalists. Neither of them could be described as functional. The secular humanists are really easygoing Kantians or morally destructive relativists. The fundamentalists are spearheading a radical "traditionalist counteraction to liberalism," which now "threatens the centuries-old doctrine of religious toleration itself" (*LP*, 258). Another reason Galston is a liberal Democrat is that he genuinely fears that threat. He thinks that neoconservatives, such as Irving Kristol, who ally themselves with the Religious Right, are playing with fire.

Galston seeks to placate the fundamentalists by contending that political liberalism is compatible in principle with fundamentalism. A liberal view of political life can be combined with devotion to the discipline, traditionalism, and piety of a transpolitical religious community. But Galston admits that it is becoming increasingly difficult to do so because "any liberal commitment to key elements of both Socratic and Enlightenment rationalism has important corrosive effects on a wide range of psychological and social structures" (LP, 294). Genuine Christianity is becoming progressively more countercultural, and those who practice its way of life must have a "spirit of vigilant resistance" to maintain its integrity. As the need for resistance becomes more extreme, their opposition to liberalism should become stronger. Does vigilance inevitably approach fanaticism? The question is not as new as Galston believes. Tocqueville, writing in an allegedly more stable time, found religious enthusiasm, a reaction against liberal secularism, quite common in America.[11]

In fact, Galston usually writes as if his liberal doctrine of functional traditionalism is Tocquevillian. But in an article on Tocqueville's view of religion he admits that Tocqueville actually regarded Christianity as true in several senses. Tocqueville thought it might be possible to harmonize the spirit of liberty with that of religion because human beings have religious longings that liberalism cannot eradicate. Galston elsewhere acknowledges that human beings do have an "infinite longing" that can be satisfied only by an infinite object that also is a subject—a personal God. He agrees with Sartre that "in the absence of such an object, man truly is a useless passion."[12] The human need to pursue that infinite longing, which transcends political satisfaction, is one justification for the limitation on government that is part of liberalism. And if that longing is useless, then so are the human being's liberty and very self. Liberalism would seem to depend on the truth of both Christianity's psychological account of the transcendence of human individuality and the possibility, at least, that the God of revelation truly exists.

But Galston does not (at least usually) reach this conclusion about the truth of Christianity or biblical belief. He says that the main change since Tocqueville's time is that America is now too diverse to be called a Christian nation. Americans still need the moral guidance that religion provides, but gone is the Christian consensus Tocqueville described. So Galston's view is that we must return to the founders' view that liberalism does not or cannot depend on Christian morality in particular, but only on religion in general.[13] Is this need for post-Christian morality sociological, or is it connected with Galston's un-Tocquevillian silence about religious longing as an intrinsic part of the human condition? Surely Galston exaggerates the degree to which America actually has become post-Christian, and that exaggeration is a characteristic feature of contemporary liberal partisanship.

The Divided Self and Moral Pluralism

Galston sometimes admits that the human self properly understood is "the *divided* self." That self lies somewhere between "hyperindividualism," which abstracts from "social bonds or natural duties," and "hyperorganicism," which abstracts from the fact that to be human is to be "a demarcated being" with "an independent consciousness." Galston agrees that the "unencumbered self" criticized by fellow liberal communitarian Michael Sandel is neither realistic nor desirable. All human beings are shaped to some extent by their social attachments and commitments to family, friends, community, and so forth. But to be human is also to have the capacity to reflect on and even rebel against those commitments. The doctrine of rights, which all liberals, Galston says, affirm, depends on the possibility of many or most human beings using their "critical faculties" to obtain "critical distance" from authority and tradition. Galston adds that rights doctrine is not and cannot become a complete account of human morality or motivation. We need rights because the divided self makes love or affectionate attachment unreliable.[14]

Galston's most complete presentation of the liberal self rightly understood is at variance with ancient liberalism, as well as the liberalism of the founders. It is not based on the distinction between the very few who are deracinated philosophers and the many who are citizens. No human being achieves complete liberation from "social bonds," but many or most human beings achieve some liberation or rational distance from their society. "The liberal conception of the self," Galston observes, "requires the kind of reflective distance demonstrated by the ability to become aware of the contingency of one's own social position and the latent contradictions of one's society."[15] The liberal self may not become a philosopher, but it has many Socratic qualities, including the experience of social or political deracination and a sort of relativism. The liberal self is relatively open to the truth that it is not simply a social or political being.

At this point, it seems that the liberal must say more than that the divided self is a human possibility. He must defend the goodness of that self. Whereas the Socratic philosopher or radical individualist would say he must strive to overcome his dependence through more rigorous and critical reasoning, and the communitarian would say that the cure for his alienation or division is greater social or political devotion, Galston seems to say that the divided self is the true self. Human existence really *is* mixed or contradictory. We are partly social-political beings and partly individuals. Liberal societies, Galston says, reflect the truth both of human diversity and of "the inherent incapacity of the public sphere to encompass more than a portion of human activity, or to fulfill more than a part of human aspiration." Can we say that the disorder of liberal society mirrors the disorder of the human soul or self? As Tocqueville says, man is the beast with the angel in him, and that mixture is the source of both his misery and his greatness.[16] But is it really accurate to call a society that mirrors the soul liberal? The society he calls liberal, Galston admits, is really characterized by a "hard-to-describe 'inbetweenness'" (*LP*, 296, 301).

The self's division or alienation makes our existence miserably incoherent. We are inclined by nature to try to overcome it, to move toward communitarian (including socialist, republican, and traditional-ist) or libertarian consistency. It seems that, once again, liberalism de-pends to some extent on biblical religion. Our alienation must point to a greatness beyond, or imperfectly reflected in, human experience. Other-wise, we return to the misanthropic conclusion that to be human is to have our natural unity or coherence ruined by useless passion that truly points in no direction.

Galston elsewhere achieves greater precision by saying that the di-vided self is actually only partly liberal, and so the universal and homoge-neous society aimed at by liberalism is simply not good for human be-ings. Modern movement toward that society cannot simply be called human or moral progress. It brings moral gains, but also losses, and so liberalism can be called both better and worse than the more traditional regimes that preceded it. No regime, society, or self embodies perfectly the whole human good, and even the best imaginable human self or soul would be a mixture of human qualities in tension or contradiction.

Galston criticizes Richard Rorty's narrative of human progress to-ward the moral universality of "cosmopolitan altruism." That progress he describes as "the widening of moral sympathy to encompass endan-gered strangers." Galston does not deny that moral action based on such sensitivity is admirable. But the cultivation of such sympathy "entails significant moral costs," and preferences for one's family, friends, and community are no less morally worthy. Aristotle's account of friendship is "rooted in the finitude of our consciousness." The truth is that the human powers of knowing and loving are limited, and so a human being can have only a very few genuine friends. The fact that I have some as friends rather than others includes an element of irreducible arbitrari-ness: "That we effectively identify with one virtuous individual rather than another may be an accident of personal history, but once the sphere of available psychological space has been filled, it is impossible to broaden the sphere of deep connection." The liberal, universal, homogeneous, and abstract view of justice opposes itself to the conditions that make virtuous friendship possible.[17]

Rorty describes liberal development as a road that leads to "a world in which our capacity for solidarity overrides boundaries of family, class, ethnicity, politics, and religion." It "seems to require the negation of particularistic obligations and the attenuation of special emotional ties." But that negation could hardly be called progress, says Galston, because "those forms of human connection can hardly be set aside without moral loss."[18] Even today, despite liberalism's progress, Americans still say that friendship and the family, or love of a few particular human beings, are what makes life most worth living. Is that belief the deepest explanation of the popular rebellion against liberal theory? If so, then contrary to Galston's explanation, it is not mainly a negative escape from freedom that makes people traditionalists but a positive affirmation of human love.

We cannot help but recall here Bloom's Socratic objection to liberalism's excesses on behalf of love. Galston corrects Bloom on American relativism by noticing that most Americans are still capable of love and hate, and so they are capable of hating unfettered liberalism for threatening what they love most. He also opposes Bloom's inclination to accept too much of what Rousseau says about nature. Galston finds natural support for familial love even in men, and so he is more hopeful than Bloom concerning the family's future in the wake of women's liberation. A political activist and devoted father, Galston cannot help but have diverse experiences of the human good. To the extent that Galston really disagrees with Marxists and traditionalists on the inevitability of liberalism's self-destruction, it is because he has greater confidence that human nature, the nature of social beings who love and hate, can resist liberalism's historical progress.

Galston's criticism of Rorty is really a criticism of Christianity. The

Christian God loves all human beings in their particularity equally and intensely, and He calls on us to imitate Him in that love. But the powers of human knowing and loving are finite, and so any attempt to widen their scope dilutes them. One aspect of the project of liberal universalism is to weaken what it considers the unjust particularism and cruelty of human love by agreeing with God that justice requires that each individual extend his concern equally to every other. The combination of Christianity and liberal justice erodes friendship, family, political community, and virtue.

But Galston's criticism of Christianity is partial. He does not deny that its moral universalism is partly true. He agrees with Tocqueville that the coming of Christianity made manifest a truth that the pagan thinkers obscured: All human beings have souls and so are in some ways morally equal. But the danger of that view is that it denies the need for human beings to perceive and affirm human differences and to love particular human beings to the exclusion of others. Tocqueville might add that Galston's criticism of Christian universalism is actually Christian. The Christian God does not love human beings as abstractions or in general; He also favors the perpetuation of the conditions that secure human particularity or liberty. Only human beings capable of loving one another are capable of needing and so loving a personal God.

Galston, most deeply, is a moral pluralist. Moral pluralism is the recognition that liberal partisanship, like all human partisanship, is in pursuit of only part of the human good. To the extent that such partisanship has the character of secularized Christianity, it pursues the impossible goal of having all human beings love each other equally and intensely. That pursuit in some respects is good for the intellectual liberation associated with philosophy and for justice, but it is bad for human love, including even love of God and love of wisdom. The most radical practical aim of liberal theory is the replacement of love in all human relationships with the libertarian spirit of calculation and consent. But a life full of calculation and without the orientation or direction of love would be full of misery, and it would, as Rousseau said, quickly self-destruct. For liberty to be lovable, it must be constrained by love.

Liberalism is only partially good, and it is only good when mixed with illiberal elements. Liberalism is only good as part of a mixed regime, one with elements that elude its comprehension and control. Thus, it is genuinely perplexing that Galston does not conclude that the genuine partisans of moral pluralism today are conservatives. For conservatives, not liberals, are the ones aiming to protect local community, religion, and the family from liberal theory's corrosive effects, even while supporting the pluralism Galston rightly favors.

CHAPTER SEVEN

Natural Law
and the American Proposition

*J*ohn Courtney Murray is often regarded as the leading Catholic American "public philosopher" of the twentieth century. Yet his most ambitious effort to understand his nation in light of the Catholic tradition, *We Hold These Truths* (*WHTT*), seems, at first, not to be a book in the proper sense at all but merely a collection of essays written for various occasions over a decade. But in terms of purpose the book is a whole. It is also a whole in terms of argument. The book's thread of unity is its repeated exploration of what Murray calls "the American proposition," or what he also calls "the public consensus or public philosophy of America" (*WHTT*, viii).[1] Murray constantly defends his own "proposition . . . that only the theory of natural law can give an account of the public moral experience that is the public consensus" (*WHTT*, 109).

Citizen and Catholic

Murray means to show what is required to make the American moral experience intelligible, what makes America a whole composed of free and rational beings, creatures made in the image of God. *We Hold These Truths* is a work of political philosophy, although it is not only that. It shows how one of those "whom St. Thomas calls 'the wise'" can provide illumination and direction to moral and political life (*WHTT,* 111).

Through this demonstration, Murray says he fulfills his "duty" as a citizen to know and show the worthiness of what holds citizens together *as* citizens (*WHTT,* ix). But Murray writes not primarily as a citizen or even as a lover of philosophic reason but as a Catholic. He writes not only to show the compatibility between citizenship and the rational life but also the compatibility between reason and revelation, as well as between the political community (especially his political community) and revelation. He attempts to show how each of these human goods contributes to the development of the whole human person.

Although he was an American citizen, Murray noted that he viewed the American proposition primarily from the outside. The book's subtitle is *Catholic Reflections on the American Proposition,* not *A Catholic American's Reflections.* His existence and duty as a citizen were subordinate to his "Catholic faith and morality." The question for him was the compatibility of American democracy with this faith and morality, in contrast to the average American citizen, who would reverse the order of the question (*WHTT,* ix). For a Catholic, he asserted, *the* political question is "the right attitude to adopt toward the established polity" (*WHTT,* 43). Indeed, all Christians are called to judge their particular polity by a transpolitical, universal standard.

Murray criticized Catholic theorists whose acceptance of America is rooted only in expediency, that is, in their acceptance of what they do not have the power to change. According to their view, it is permissible for a

Catholic to be an American citizen not because America is good in itself but because the peace and security of any established polity is useful for the practice of one's faith. Catholic American citizens should do their civic duty, say these theorists, but they should do so without any principled devotion. From the perspective of a devoted citizen, the Catholic's relationship to his polity so understood seems parasitical and hence suspect.

Murray rejected the extreme Augustinianism or Platonism of this view even in theory as contrary to the harmonious or "integral" spirit of the doctrine of natural law (*WHTT,* 63, 182–85). The truth is that Catholics as Catholics can affirm the goodness of the American proposition or public philosophy with "conscience and conviction" (*WHTT,* 43). America is worthy of their devotion (although not, of course, of their highest devotion). Catholics as Catholics can be good American citizens. In one respect, as we shall see, they can even be the best.

Founding Principles

The reason for Murray's affirmation is "the evident coincidence of the principles which inspired the American Republic with the principles which are structural to the Western Christian political tradition" (*WHTT,* 43), those principles that in his mind received their fullest articulation in the Catholic tradition of natural law. This "coincidence," like all salutary coincidences, is fortuitous, even "providential" (*WHTT,* 30). Catholics did not, after all, found America, and the American founders undeniably exhibited hostility toward the Catholic Church. But Catholics, as Catholics, can still regard the principles of the American founding as good.

This coincidence is not some inexplicable accident. America, argues Murray, is a good polity because "the Fathers of the Republic" received as an inheritance and worked within the political tradition established by "the Fathers of the Church," their intellectual fathers (*WHTT,* 41–43). The

Republic's fathers viewed themselves as modern men rebelling against what their fathers had established. But the tradition was nonetheless vigorous, because their rebellion was not radical (not even as radical as they thought). "The Fathers [were] building better than they knew," says Murray (*WHTT,* 30, 66), because they remained, more than they knew, within the Catholic Church's "own tradition of thought, which is wider and deeper than any that America has elaborated" (*WHTT,* xi).

Catholic thought, more profound and more comprehensive than American thought, comprehends the Republic's fathers better than the authors of the American proposition did. Yet Catholic reflections on the American proposition cannot be sustained without some criticism and even some suspicion of the founding fathers (*WHTT,* 20). Murray explicitly follows Lincoln in affirming their proposition with a sort of filial piety while attempting to deepen and transform its meaning (*WHTT,* viii-ix). (Even the idea that America is devoted to a proposition was articulated not by the founders but by Lincoln.)[2] He writes of our "ancient heritage" as Lincoln spoke of our "ancient faith." The phrase "our fathers" comes from Lincoln, who blurs, for the sake of piety, and contrary to the Republic's fathers' rationalistic spirit of innovation, the distinction between our political and religious beginnings.

This indistinctness, for Murray, is more than merely rhetoric. The faith of the Republic and Catholic religion really do coincide in decisive respects—and without reducing American religion to "political religion," as Lincoln tends to do.[3] Lincoln's "abstract principle," for example, which Thomas Jefferson asserted in the midst of a revolution, finds its most profound articulation in the thought of Thomas Aquinas. Our "ancient faith" is also, in truth, a "rational faith" (*WHTT,* 10), as well as the Christian faith. Jefferson was more pious, more dependent on his Christian inheritance, than he knew.

Our Proposition and Our Crisis

Lincoln's tendency was to particularize the proposition, to make it seem less abstract or universal, to make it the American nation's own. The crisis the nation faced in his time, above all, was of *devotion* to the project the founders had given us. Murray's tendency, however, is to generalize the proposition, to make it less America's own by locating it in a larger, more rational, and more universal tradition of thought.

For Murray, the crisis faced by the nation—and by the West as a whole in his time—is the contemporary denial, from almost all quarters, that human beings really can hold moral truths in common. Murray makes clear what the crisis is before he makes clear what the proposition is. He does say that he does not agree with Lincoln that it is only that all men are created equal. He contends that Lincoln "asserted" the proposition's "imperiled part" in the midst of a "national crisis" (*WHTT*, vii-viii). Lincoln, it seems, self-consciously reduced the whole to a part because the crisis the proposition faced was only partial. The idea that moral truth can be held in common, which for Murray is the most crucial part of the American proposition, was not questioned by Lincoln's contemporaries.

Today, Murray says, "civil war" is "the basic fact of world society" (*WHTT*, viii). This conflict is essentially a series of "religious wars" over the "spiritual substance" of human existence and institutions—wars that lurk not far beneath the surface of "civic amity" of American religious pluralism (*WHTT*, 19, 24, 128). Murray asserts that "there is no element of the [American] theorem that is not menaced by active negation, and no thrust of the project that does not meet powerful opposition" (*WHTT*, viii). The proposition, conceived as Murray conceives it—as both natural law theory and as a historical project carried out in that theory's light—is now threatened, in its entirety, throughout the world.

The crisis is primarily theoretical. Devotion to the project is imperiled by the fact that the very foundations of the theory are no longer considered credible. There has been "a loss of confidence in the power of reason to fix the purposes of political life" (*WHTT,* 130). The defense of the American proposition today must be persuasive not only to Murray's fellow citizens, as their project, but to all human beings, as a truth that they can experience as true independently of their willing it. Murray, much more than Lincoln and the Republic's fathers, is compelled, for political reasons, to bring the transpolitical, "metaphysical" foundation of the proposition to light. He cannot begin with a defense of this or that part of the proposition. He must begin with a defense of the idea that there can be such a proposition. Therefore, he must argue for the existence of "a certain body of objective truth accessible to the reason of man" (*WHTT,* ix).

That such truths exist is the "traditional conviction" or "assertion" that has sustained the American proposition. If this faith in a "realist epistemology" is denied, Murray asserts, then "the American proposition is eviscerated . . . in one stroke" (*WHTT,* viii-ix). This denial is found almost everywhere today, perhaps especially in American universities, while the "traditional conviction" is defended in the American intellectual world only in the Catholic community (*WHTT,* 40–41).

Murray does not deny that the contemporary repudiation of the Republic's founders' way of defending their proposition is reasonable. Their propensity was to accept without much thought "the serene, and often naïve, certainties of the eighteenth century" (*WHTT,* viii). These certainties "have crumbled" in the face of what is "genuine and true" in the thought of "Darwin, Freud, and Marx" (*WHTT,* viii, 310). The founders' superficial version of natural law and natural rights thinking depended to a great extent on the Lockean abstraction of the prepolitical and presocial state of nature—an unempirical, even misanthropic beginning that, by itself, generates "individualistic, rationalistic nonsense." The idea of a Lockean state of nature is no longer credible anywhere. And so the fathers' certainties are our nonsense (*WHTT,* 310–16).

Insofar as the American proposition is understood to have originated in the thought of the Republic's fathers, we can legitimately question its axiomatic character (*WHTT,* viii). The founders focused on reason, not piety or uncritical traditionalism, as the proper moral and political standard. They were convinced that their proposition must pass the test of reason to constitute the public philosophy.[4] They themselves would recommend that the proposition now be abandoned unless a better argument than the one they gave for it could be found. Murray's contention is that there is indeed such an argument, and that only the Catholic tradition or community of thought, or the wise within it, can give American citizens what they most urgently need to perpetuate their proposition legitimately. It is in this sense that Murray asserts that Catholics are the best American citizens (*WHTT,* 43).

Today's defense of the American proposition cannot be as serene or superficial, nor as unconsciously traditional, as that of the founders. Murray explains that our reflection must be more profound, because the depths of the problem of human freedom "stand revealed to us" as they were not to the founders (*WHTT,* 321). They neither perceived nor affirmed the "naked essence" of the modern experiment, whereas we have no choice but to confront it (*WHTT,* 308).

According to Murray, the modern experiment is disintegrating even as it succeeds. It is constituted by the attempt to realize "the Cartesian dream." The "dream today is largely reality; man is the master and possessor of nature." But the owner of nature has achieved his conquest at the cost of "his own identity" (*WHTT,* 200). The conquest has been driven by an increasingly radical dissatisfaction with all traditional or "given" answers to the question, "What is man?" as dogmatic limitations to human freedom (*WHTT,* 126–28). We no longer understand ourselves to be limited or defined by our nature or God. Freedom, we believe, is primarily freedom from nature and God for self-creation. The modern faith centers on the belief that self-creation is possible, that the conquest of nature will somehow solve the problem of human freedom.

But the modern view of freedom is, at its core, only destructive or negative. It has been undeniably successful in its efforts to "destroy an order of political privilege and inaugurate an era of political equality." It has not been able, however, "to erect an order of social justice or inaugurate an order of freedom" (*WHTT,* 319). The modern view still consists of freedom from this or that limitation for nothing in particular. Its tendency, contrary to its intention, has been to obliterate everything that is distinctively human. Its effect has not been to raise man up to divinity but, as Eric Voegelin explained, to reduce him in theory to an indistinguishable part of some "monistic" social whole (*WHTT,* 130–31).

"Communism," Murray concludes, "is . . . political modernity carried to its logical conclusion," by which he means that "all that is implicit or unintentional in modernity . . . has become explicit or deliberate in the Communist system" (*WHTT,* 211). The modern experiment ends up revealing to itself that it cannot solve the problem of human liberty except by denying, quite unreasonably, and hence violently, that such liberty exists at all.[5] Murray asserts that communism marks the end of modern history and thought, though not the end of history itself. Its solution to the problem of human liberty is not empirical, only logical. The problem, in truth, remains unsolved. The end of history to which the communist system points is a "mirage" (*WHTT,* 215). The real human experience at the end of the destructiveness of the modern era is "a spiritual vacuum . . . at the heart of human existence" (*WHTT,* 216).

Postmodern Reflection

The filling of this vacuum is a task that "postmodern" man must perform in one way or another. Our "anxious reflection," writes Murray, concerns "how . . . these hollow emptinesses [should] be filled."[6] Our search is no longer primarily for a way of achieving liberation from this or that constraint but for a "definition of freedom," for the "positive content" of liberty, for "ordered liberty" (*WHTT,* 319). For us, then, there is of necessity "a new openness to the world of metaphysical and religious values" (*WHTT,* 320). The modern experiment has demonstrated that there is no purely secular or superficial solution to the problem of human liberty. (A reference to Nietzsche shows that Murray means, especially, to avoid the superficiality of Hegel and Marx [*WHTT,* 216].) Therefore, it is Murray's postmodern conviction that "the Basic Issues today can only be conceived in metaphysical and religious terms." Times are so untraditional that one must confront "the nature and structure of reality itself" (*WHTT,* 199). As a result of this confrontation, we postmoderns must make "a metaphysical decision in regard of the nature of man" (*WHTT,* 321).

Murray's description of the postmodern task as a "decision" in response to "anxious reflection" is meant to be more unsettling than it has been. It means that it is no longer possible to be a conservative, that one must think and act radically. It also means that decisions other than the one for natural law are possible.

Murray's postmodern metaphysical decision is a radically untraditional affirmation of the truth embodied in the Western tradition. Another possibility, the one Murray associates with Nietzsche, is the radically untraditional rejection of the metaphysical decision, which would also be, in its way, a metaphysical decision.[7] Murray understands that the result of the radically antimetaphysical decision, which modern thinkers prior to Nietzsche always fell short of making, would be the destruction of the West in theory and practice, the descent of the world into chaos and violence as a necessary precondition for the rebirth of human or spiritual life (*WHTT,* 216–17). The Nietzschean thesis is that the only way the "spiritual vacuum" can be filled is through this destruction, because the West now lacks the resources to fill it itself (*WHTT,* 290).

Murray agrees with Nietzsche, Heidegger, and existentialists of various varieties that a decision must be made in the face of the "impotent nihilism" (impotent because wholly secular) present at the end of modernity (*WHTT*, 12). The existentialist understands that such a decision is a resolution to define the future through one's own self-assertion. And for the existentialist, this resolution comes in response to the revelation of the falsity of the West's defining assertion that "values" or morality have some metaphysical foundation. Values must be asserted against the true emptiness of reality. A decision must be made because from a human or spiritual perspective there is nothing—but nothing—to be discovered.[8]

Murray's use of "decision" calls to mind existentialism's "decisionism," which, he recognizes, stands at the foundation of the relativism and tyrannical aspirations of contemporary social science (*WHTT*, 84, 322–24). He denies that mere assertiveness or will can solve the problem of nihilism, which arises when the problem of human freedom seems insoluble (*WHTT*, 12). He asks "whether the problem of freedom in the post-modern era can be satisfactorily dealt with in terms of philosophies (and theologies) which bear too heavily the stamp of modernity" (*WHTT*, 198). Murray argues that existentialism's postmodern solution does not constitute, at bottom, a rejection of modernity but rather an attempt to overcome modernity through the radicalization of its antimetaphysical bias. For the existentialist, the problem of freedom is still approached through self-creativity. All postmodern projects, except for the recovery of natural law, are, in Murray's view, nihilistic attempts to cover up the allegedly nihilistic truth about reality (*WHTT*, 217).

The emergence of the problem of nihilism signals the exhaustion of modernity. A decision must be made. To decide for natural law is, according to Murray, to "opt . . . for a metaphysics of right," for a standard that is not "subjective," a standard that exists independently of human decision. With this option, "objective law [or right] has the primacy over subjective rights" (*WHTT*, 327). It is the decision, finally, that human beings are not free to decide, that the moral order is not a product of their wills.

The Decision for Natural Law

But the metaphysical decision is not merely a decision. We cannot simply assert that "a metaphysics of right" exists. It depends on the discovery of the existence of "a metaphysic of nature, especially the idea that nature is a teleological concept" (*WHTT*, 327)—a concept, in other words, that orders and directs human freedom. Murray asserts that natural law doctrine is without "presuppositions," without elements that cannot be verified. In his view, the modern rejection of natural law is a radical error (*WHTT*, 109).

To say that we can discover a natural teleology and even a "natural theology" is extremely controversial, especially in our time. It is an assertion that seems to oppose the foundation of modern natural science. Whatever its shortcomings in coming to terms with the problem of human freedom, this science seems to have authoritatively discredited the idea that human beings can find a grounding for their freedom, their spiritual existence, in nature. Few postmodern thinkers are attracted to the metaphysical foundation of natural law doctrine because few believe that the postmodern era can root itself in discredited premodern presuppositions. Even some contemporary Thomists, including such very orthodox Catholics as Germain Grisez and John Finnis, accept the modern disjunction between nature and human freedom, and they transform Thomas's teaching accordingly. Others interested in recovering traditional morality, such as Alasdair MacIntyre, do not view the "speculative" or metaphysical component of the natural law tradition as recoverable.[9]

But the most telling example of this perceived tension between nature or metaphysical theory and morality is provided by Ernest Fortin. He calls for the full revitalization of the natural law tradition's theory against "the bland and emasculated versions that are now being offered of it."[10] Natural law theory, says Fortin, has "kept alive an ideal human wholeness . . . because its understanding of the moral life is not guided by the abstractions of modern science."[11] In Fortin's view, natural law does fuller justice to the concrete reality of the human person than does modern theory, which, in its various forms, always abstracts from phenomena that are distinctively human.

Fortin adds that there are problems with natural law theory, "particularly as regards its natural knowability." But he recommends that we ignore such "shortcomings," given the paucity of alternative theories and natural law's "particular suitability to a religious and cultural tradition such as ours."[12] But we cannot ignore his agreement with the modern critics of natural law theory that the perception of moral order often doesn't seem to be very natural. "The matter finally comes down to a choice between a truth that is good for the intellect alone and a salutary and beautifying truth that represents the good of the whole person."[13] He maintains that philosophers as philosophers do not believe that human beings can know the latter truth by nature.[14]

Fortin also holds that there is no "synthesis" that unites these two perceptions of truth. The "Great Tradition" is rooted not in a unity but in a fundamental tension.[15] The self-aware and candid partisan of revelation must concede that he cannot know "the good of the whole person" by nature alone. Unlike Murray, Fortin says that in the end the decision for revelation is contrary to the philosophers' rational account of nature. The decision for natural law is in the end a decision for revelation.

Even some thoughtful contemporary partisans of natural law question Murray's view that natural law doctrine concerning the natural or metaphysical foundation of moral order depends not at all on prerational and pre-empirical presuppositions. Murray does not, I think, adhere to that position consistently, much less demonstrate its truth.[16] As a whole, however, his book offers a more nuanced and more convincing defense of natural law.

For Murray, the "metaphysical decision" is really a decision in the sense that it is a choice from among plausible alternatives, none of which is wholly satisfactory to human reason. The choice for natural law—which according to Murray originates in part in human anger (*WHTT,* 316–18) or in the consciousness of a man protesting against injustice—may offend the intellect's desire for consistency or uniformity, which includes its desire to deny significance to human particularity or individuality. But it is still not a decision in the existentialist's sense, a willful imposition of human freedom. He also argues that it is the only theory that makes sense out of the American proposition. Natural law thus deserves to prevail over rival doctrines on empirical grounds alone.

Murray's affirmation of this conclusion is at the foundation of his critical defense of the American founding. He maintains that whatever theoretical pretensions the Republic's fathers might have had, the American Revolution "was less a revolution than a conservation" (*WHTT,* 31). He "radically distinguishes the conservative Christian tradition of America from the Jacobin laicist tradition of Continental Europe." American liberalism defines liberty in terms of nature and God, whereas Continental liberalism knows of no standard but "autonomous reason" (*WHTT,* 28).

Murray seems to say that natural law is part of a distinctively Christian tradition that the founding fathers perpetuated more than rejected. The evidence Murray presents for this interpretation is the Declaration of Independence, as interpreted by Lincoln. That "landmark of Western political theory" placed, in Lincoln's words, "this nation under God" (*WHTT,* 28–30). This acknowledgment of "the sovereignty of God over nations as well as individual[s]" is what "imparts to politics a fundamental human meaning." Politics, in America, is constituted and delimited by a "truth beyond politics," whereas for nations constituted by the Jacobin or secular liberal tradition, "religion is at best a purely private concern" (*WHTT,* 28). The foundation of the natural law tradition is the apprehension that human freedom is limited by God's sovereignty. Hence political freedom "knows itself to be bound by the imperatives of the moral law" (*WHTT,* 164).

Constitutionalizing the Declaration

The obvious objection to this interpretation of the American proposition is that the Constitution itself does not acknowledge the sovereignty of God but only the sovereignty of the people. Yet it is the document, as Murray himself says, that is the "object of reverence even to the point of worship among the American people."[17] Murray follows Lincoln in "constitutionalizing" the Declaration in order to save the Constitution from the moral superficiality of secularism. He says that "the Constitution of the United States has to be read in light of the Declaration of Independence," but the necessity here is less historical or empirical than moral. Only with such a reading can Murray say that "the famous American phrase 'We the people' . . . is the very negation of Jacobinism."[18] Other readings of the Constitution would reveal less continuity with the tradition.

Murray again follows Lincoln in neglecting interpretations of the Declaration that could point to the fathers' pretentious rationalism, to their at least partial kinship with the Jacobins.[19] The Declaration refers to "Nature's God" and the Creator, but nowhere distinguishes between the two. The only appropriate or consistent conclusion, Murray suggests, is that Thomas Jefferson was a Thomist. But "Nature's God," interpreted in light of Jefferson's thought as a whole, is actually the God of the secular philosophers. The phrase has an antirevelationist and even anticreationist connotation.[20]

In truth, the references to the biblical God in the Declaration were meant to humor those of the revolutionary generation less "enlightened" than the leading founders. The terms "Nature's God" and "the Creator" reflect very different theologies. For the political purpose of promoting revolutionary unity, the Declaration is, quite deliberately, theologically incoherent.[21] The synthesis Murray effects through his Thomistic natural law interpretation is imposed from without, even if it is the only possible synthesis.

For Murray, the incoherence of the Declaration, which he de-emphasizes but does not deny, reflects the incoherence of the modern political experiment as a whole. Even the Republic's fathers were modern enough to have rejected to some extent "the Christian revelation that man is a sacredness, and that his primatial *res sacra*, his freedom, is sought and found ultimately within the freedom of the Church" (*WHTT*, 215). They rejected the credibility of divine revelation, and they tried to free natural law from its influence. Madison and Jefferson, the most "enlightened" of the founders, also opposed, in their "anti-ecclesiasticism" (*WHTT*, 65), the church as an institution. But even they did not reject "the whole system of moral values, both individual and social, which had been elaborated under the influence of the Christian revelation" (*WHTT*, 214). Their values were, more than they knew, a Christian inheritance. "Men of the eighteenth century," Murray observes, had "intelligences [that] were very superficially Christian" (*WHTT*, 317), but they were Christian nonetheless.

The attempt of Jefferson and of the other leading fathers to dissociate the moral order of natural law from "Nature's God," that is, from illumination by revelation, was a pretentious impossibility. For, as Murray finally says, the whole American consensus, its proposition or public philosophy, "has its ultimate root" (*WHTT*, 81) in the Christian idea of personal sacredness. Murray insists that the proposition is eviscerated if this idea is denied. It turns out that "the spiritual substance of a free society" is always rooted in this "central Christian concept" (*WHTT*, 198), whether or not the proponents of freedom realize it.

It was a Christian discovery that "the whole of human life is not absorbed in the polis" (*WHTT*, 333) and that human dignity is not primarily "civil dignity" (*WHTT*, 52). The Christian knows, as the founders asserted, that the state "has only a relative value" in service to the person's transpolitical dignity (*WHTT,* 326). The Bill of Rights, in this light, was "a tributary to the tradition of natural law" (*WHTT,* 37), "a product of Christian 'history' and, hence, Christian presuppositions" (*WHTT,* 39). Its idea is that "man has certain original responsibilities primarily as man, antecedent to his status as citizen" (*WHTT,* 37). These responsibilities, as Madison said in his *Memorial and Remonstrance,* are the creature's duty, which he knows by his nature, to his Creator.

The First Amendment and Human Dignity

Murray claims to find in the religion clauses of the First Amendment the understanding of "the dignity of the person" he believes he ought to have found in Vatican II's "Declaration on Religious Freedom."[22] This dignity comes from the fact that the person is a "moral subject," capable of free and responsible choice. His freedom and responsibility, in turn, "are rooted in the given reality of man as man." By nature, he is aware that he should act freely "in accordance with his nature." He knows that he is or ought to be free from political coercion to obey "imperatives" given to him by "the transcendent order of truth." He is required, by his nature, to establish his proper, dutiful relationship with his Creator.[23]

The religion clauses of the First Amendment, Murray suggests, actually correct the impression given by the unamended Constitution's apparent indifference to the existence of God.[24] They establish the fact that American freedom is primarily freedom for religion (*WHTT,* 151). They link the Constitution less ambiguously with the Declaration. Perhaps they even make the Constitution's theological interpretation of the Declaration less ambiguous. Madison's theology in the *Memorial and Remonstrance,* even if presented only for political or rhetorical purposes, is more clearly or coherently part of the natural law tradition than is the theology of the Declaration.

Murray contends that the "dominant image of democratic society as ultimately monist in structure . . . and as ultimately secular in substance . . . represents the refined essence of political modernity. Its significance lies in the fact that it confronts us with an experiment in human freedom which has been based on a denial or disregard of the essential Christian contribution to human freedom, which is the theorem of the freedom of the church" (*WHTT,* 211). That image is surely dominant today, but Murray wants us to wonder to what extent it was dominant at the time of the American founding. In some large measure the leading founders did understand themselves as denying or disregarding the Christian contribution to human freedom, but Madison's *Memorial* and his defense of the sacredness of conscience cannot be understood coherently without that contribution in mind. Ultimately, freedom of conscience, democratically understood as freedom for every human being to do his duty to the Creator, can only be defended on Christian grounds.

Murray rightly writes that "among the rights of conscience is certainly not the right to debase the dignity of conscience by denying its dependence on God, ignoring the ultimate Lawgiver, and demanding respect for every private fancy."[25] That criticism is devastating for contemporary liberal moralists such as John Rawls and Richard Rorty, but Madison himself, in his public writings, never denied that dependence. That the effective exercise of freedom of conscience depends on freedom of the church Madison did not recognize clearly enough, but the First Amendment properly understood does defend that freedom.[26] Fortunately, Madison's apparent private atheism did not infuse every aspect of his public writing about the relationship between church and state.

Murray does say that the First Amendment implies no theology, that its substance is "simply political" (*WHTT,* 69), but that disarming assertion is negated by his argument taken as a whole. He also says that politics, for Americans, points beyond itself, that it gets "its human meaning" from the truth about human sacredness or dignity that lies beyond it.

Americans can agree about religious freedom "in the absence of a consensus with regard to the theological concepts that govern the total life and destiny of man" (*WHTT*, 72), but if their proposition or political consensus is to be intelligible, they must agree that for some reason or other human life and dignity transcend political life. In other words, they must affirm a metaphysical assertion that is distinctively Christian. It would appear that, in order to defend their proposition, Americans must acknowledge a limit to their theological pluralism. Religious pluralism, Murray says, "is inherently disintegrative of *all* consensus and community" (*WHTT*, 73; italics mine). Any community, if it is to be a community, must acknowledge its limitations. The First Amendment, as well as the Declaration, is part of the "conservative Christian tradition" because it is not merely political but implies a metaphysical decision about the nature of man. That the authors were not fully aware of that fact simply means that they built better than they knew.

Consider more precisely why Murray holds that our founding fathers built better than they knew: "The providential aspect of the matter, and the reason for the better building, can be found in the fact that the American political community was organized in an era when the tradition of natural law and natural rights was still vigorous" (*WHTT*, 30). Murray here repeats the view of the greatest nineteenth-century American Catholic political thinker, Orestes Brownson, that our fathers, as statesmen, were guided by Providence.[27] What they built was shaped by what they were given by tradition or God, and they built well because they let themselves, to some extent unconsciously, be guided by the invincible facts about human nature and American tradition. As good statesmen and political realists, they did not try to build the world anew on the basis of the Lockean abstract individual that Jefferson and Madison embraced in theory. Because of the providential aspect of our founding and the excellence of our statesmen, the American revolutionaries were far more conservative than the French. Their practice was better than their theory, and so Murray attempts to provide the theory that can justify and so perpetuate their project—the constitutional order they created under God—in our time.

How Natural Is Natural Law?

All that has been said about the Republic's fathers' accomplishment can be granted without addressing the problem that Fortin (but not Murray) says we should overlook: Is the understanding of natural law in the Catholic or Christian tradition theoretically correct or even plausible? The modern thinkers attempted to free natural law from revelation based on the premise that the human being does not, in fact, know himself to be a creature by nature. To experience the world as created and oneself as a creature requires knowledge that reason itself does not provide. For the originators of the modern project, the "creationist" metaphysics of Thomistic natural law is actually a combination of elements from reason and revelation. What is called natural law does not depend solely upon what we know by nature, and hence must be rejected in the name of nature.[28]

On some occasions, Murray seems to acknowledge the validity of this criticism. He says that all non-Christian thought tends to be "monistic." For Aristotle, "man in the end was only citizen, whose final destiny was to be achieved within the City" (*WHTT,* 15). He did not know of man's transpolitical dignity or sacredness. For the decisively post-Christian philosophers, Rousseau and his essentially secular successors, human distinctiveness or dignity is equated with citizenship. Their concern, according to Murray, was the recovery, against the influence of Christianity, of "the integrity of the political order." For them, the unifying consensus is essentially a "civic faith" that subordinates church to state (*WHTT,* 21). Murray even observes that "the chief phenomenon of modern times has been the development of secular civil religions."[29]

It appears at this point that Fortin is right: man does not know his genuine freedom or sacredness by the testimony of his nature alone, inasmuch as it was not discovered by those philosophers whose thought was unilluminated by revelation. Murray goes so far as to say that "Christianity freed man from nature by teaching him that he has an immortal soul," which he would have not known by his nature. By so doing, "it taught him his own uniqueness, his own individual worth, the dignity of his own person, the equality of all men, the unity of the human race" (*WHTT,* 192). Christianity freed human beings from what appears to unassisted reason to be the limits of their natures. Christianity, not nature, gave them their genuine worth or dignity.

Because of the influence of Christianity, Murray says, human beings no longer experience themselves primarily as citizens. In our Christian consciousness, "every fatherland" is, to some extent, "a foreign land" (*WHTT,* 15). We know we are not fully at home in or constrained definitively by our polity. Human beings know that, ultimately, they transcend their political communities.

The integrity of the political order cannot be restored in post-Christian times except by "totalitarian" means, because it requires the forceful suppression of this consciousness of personal freedom. The truth of St. Augustine's criticism of civil theology and even pagan natural theology cannot easily be eradicated from the world, precisely because the criticism is true. Post-Christian restoration, to the extent that it occurs, is never really a political restoration. Murray observes that the modern secularist must make "denials" that the pagan secularist did not. Hence, post-Christian "unification of social life" is not only more "forcible" but takes place on "a lower level than . . . Aristotle's" (*WHTT,* 133).

Totalitarian projects are revolts against the truth, especially the metaphysical truth about human existence. Perhaps Murray means to say that Christian revelation illuminated for human beings what they cannot know to be true independently of revelation about their sacredness or dignity. Genuinely self-conscious individuals cannot help but define themselves as more than parts of a political community, as beings that cannot simply be "absorbed" in some "monistic" whole. They know that a merely "civil theology" or even an impersonal "natural theology" does not address the most profound longings implanted in them by nature. In a discussion of the "imperatives" of his own nature, Murray says that "my situation is that of a creature before God" (*WHTT,* 329). He calls the modern denial of this situation "a basic betrayal of the existential structure of reality itself" (*WHTT,* 215). He also contends that "instinctively and by natural inclination the common man knows that he cannot be free if his basic human things are not sacredly immune from profanation by the power of the state and by other secular powers" (*WHTT,* 204).

Human beings know that they transcend the city as well as impersonal natural necessity. They know they are not God. They know they are not self-created. But do they know, by their natures as free and rational mortals, that they are free, as persons, under God? Is any other conclusion by a self-conscious mortal a rebellion against the truth, an antimetaphysical assertion? It is certainly true that post-Christian monism, culminating in communism, was at war with human self-consciousness. Murray understands this monism as being grounded in various scientific attempts to deny, in the name of reason's autonomy, the reality and sacredness of human transcendence or freedom (*WHTT,* 322–26). And the anticommunist dissidents Aleksandr Solzhenitsyn and Václav Havel understand the defeat of communism as a victory for human self-consciousness against efforts to subject Being and human beings completely to manipulation.

For Murray, unlike Fortin, the fundamental human decision is not between reason and revelation, but for natural law. It is for the proposition that human reason, as it attempts to come to terms with the apparently rationally unsatisfactory problem of human freedom, can be illuminated by revelation. Only in the light of its influence does reason remain genuinely empirical, does it avoid the intellect's characteristic propensity toward reductionism or "monism."

Citizens and Christians

The fundamentally Christian insight of natural law is that although the human being is a citizen or political animal, he is most fundamentally much more. This dualistic doctrine appears deficient to those committed to socialist idealism and to those who would revive the perspective of classical political philosophy, the "integral" perspective of the polis. From the perspective of the political community, the question remains whether natural law gives sufficient dignity to political life. To say, as Murray does, that the end of the political order is different from and subordinate to the total end of the human person—to say that citizenship is a means to a higher, more comprehensive end—undermines the devotion that the political community requires of its members in order to perpetuate itself. A large part—perhaps too large a part—of Murray's defense of America is that it is good for the church, and not simply good in itself. His key criticism of America is its failure to recognize sufficiently that the freedom it promotes and protects is ultimately the freedom of the church (*WHTT,* 69–72). Whether American political freedom is good in itself, Murray, the Christian, actually seems to leave an open question (*WHTT,* 195).

Rousseau's assertion that one "cannot be a citizen and a Christian at the same time" seems to retain some force against natural law theory. No dualistic account of human nature will be without tensions. Murray admits that any attempt at integration or "synthesis" will remain "ever precarious" (*WHTT,* 196). That is one reason why the American proposition requires constant "development on penalty of decadence" (*WHTT,* vii). The distinctiveness of natural law lies in its inclination toward integration or synthesis rather than reduction. It keeps alive, as Fortin says, "the ideal of human wholeness" without forgetting that it is to be actualized most fully in a personal and transpolitical sense.

Perhaps the most radical socialist and classical criticism of Christianity's denigration of politics is that it tends to make true communal devotion impossible and thus produce the loneliness of the isolated individual. This deracination, as Heidegger says, produces an anxious "homesickness" in modern human beings that cries out for some sort of radical cure.[30] This line of thinking suggests that Christianity produces the negative freedom that leads to totalitarianism. Hence postmodern thought must, in part, entail overcoming the effects of Christianity.

Murray's response here is to agree that if human freedom is freedom from political community or citizenship but for nothing in particular, or if it amounts to nothing more than the lonely freedom of the isolated conscience (*WHTT,* 206), then it is simply a source of misery and not worthy of human beings. Human self-consciousness or individuality might, as it grows, readily reach the nihilistic conclusion that it is itself no good. The "extreme individualism" of Lockean or "classical" liberalism (*WHTT,* 129), which is reflected to some extent in Madison's antiecclesiastical interpretation of the creature's freedom of conscience, generates the extreme collectivism of totalitarianism (*WHTT,* 213–14, 322).

This is why the understanding of freedom that Christianity brought into the world can be defended only as "freedom of the Church," freedom for membership in a "genuine intellectual community" (*WHTT,* 21), "an order of culture" (*WHTT,* 35) that transcends politics and resists politicization. Murray contends that the modern view of freedom has consisted in an attempt to find a "secular substitute" for freedom of the church (*WHTT,* 201). But experience has shown that there is no such replacement. The very idea of natural law, as opposed to the idea of the state of nature, suggests that the human person cannot sustain his liberty outside a community of thought and belief (*WHTT,* 331). Limited government or constitutionalism as a human good depends upon the possibility of such a community.

The truth of the matter is that people naturally long for liberation, and they know that true liberation cannot be simply political or historical. The American proposition is good primarily because, under its largely natural law understanding of freedom, religion is guaranteed full freedom to achieve its proper task of the spiritual liberation of man. No account of the American proposition or "moral consensus" is adequate that does not acknowledge all that is implied by this truth.[31]

Murray's Irony?

Murray's awareness of the fundamental inadequacy of America's political self-understanding today and as expressed by our leading founders, and his emphasis on the freedom of the church as the core of human freedom, can lead even a very careful reader to conclude that Murray does not really regard the American political order as worth defending and improving. This view of Murray, developed after a version of this chapter was published and largely in response to it, is weighty enough to deserve a response. According to Kenneth R. Craycraft, Murray's writing about America is ironic.[32] The American Catholic tutored by Murray's irony will live in America in peace, but not take his country seriously, because liberal America is hostile to the church's freedom and the true goal of human life. And that irony will, in fact, be generalized to include all secular authority, which is almost always hostile to the church's mission of evangelization.

Craycraft's understanding of irony mirrors that of the liberal bourgeois ironist Richard Rorty. Rorty uses irony to trivialize metaphysical and theological opinions in the name of peace and political liberty. Craycraft trivializes political liberty to preserve theological integrity. As Marc Guerra wittily and perceptively observes, Craycraft's anti-American and anti-political theological extremism resembles the anti-moral extremism of the Epicurean philosopher: Political morality is all nonsense, and I wash my hands of it.[33] So it is not surprising that Craycraft joins Rorty and Stanley Fish in what amounts to a postmodern negation of differences thought by both St. Thomas and the American founders to have been discovered by reason. For Craycraft, there is no such thing as religious freedom because in truth there is no real harmony between reason and revelation, or between political freedom and freedom of the church. There is no rational foundation to and no basis of argument about our beliefs. All we can really see, Fish and Rorty claim, are the incompatible myths or "narratives" of secular liberalism and Christianity. Because the political order can never really recognize the truth for which religious liberty ought to exist, Christians, like Epicureans, have no stake in the reigning political order.

Craycraft at least approaches Rorty's view that Christianity must look like madness to American liberals, and vice versa. So from the nation's very beginning Christians have been treated as madmen by our political leaders. Like the philosophers of old, Christians in America today have no alternative but to lie low. But we notice, against Craycraft, that the big differences between Epicurean philosophy and Christianity is that Christianity is for everyone. Christians are called to evangelize—and demand the freedom to do so—while the ancient philosophers were inclined to rest content as a fairly closeted and only in principle subversive minority. If the given order denies the freedom of the Church, Christians are called to be active and meddlesome dissidents. Their task is to get the reigning political order to recognize the Christian view of human liberty as somehow true, and in the American case that is far from impossible.

Not only that, Christian belief, unlike philosophic speculation, was never intended by the leading church fathers to undermine the duties of citizenship. It may be difficult to be a good Catholic and a good American citizen at the same time, but it is not impossible, and to try is certainly our duty. Let us not fall victim to the doctrine of Heideggerian moral equivalence: America and the Soviet Union are/were both modern regimes, and so neither is worthy of our loyalty. Not everything modern, in reality, is divorced from everything Christian, and the church really is still free to do her work in America. There are troubling signs, of course, that that may not always be so, but it is not inevitable that the atheistic view of American liberty will prevail.

Craycraft understands the argument I have presented in this chapter as "an excellent interpretation of Murray's Catholic correction of the founding principles."[34] But he chides me with a lack of boldness or radicalism. My presentation only "flirts with the idea that Murray rejected the Founding root and branch." He claims to boldly present the truth, based on the evidence I present: "Murray is not accepting the essential philosophy of Jefferson and improving it with a little theology." Instead, Murray "rejects" our founding fathers' "meaning out of hand, and articulates a distinctly Christian understanding of how a Christian can live in America."[35] The Christian lives in America, as St. Augustine and Stanley Hauerwas say, as an alien, by accepting the given order for the sake of peace but seeing nothing good or true about it.

Postmodernism Rightly Understood

But we have seen that Murray's postmodernism is quite different from Craycraft's. It is, if I may say so, postmodernism rightly understood.[36] Murray's view is that the culmination of modern nonfoundationalism in nihilism signals a return to Thomistic realism. The truth about moral and political reality is available to human beings as human beings, and so it is possible to assess the truth of human opinions about that reality. The reduction of human opinions about morality to incompatible values is more a modern than postmodern premise. Murray treats the founders' opinions concerning political and religious liberty as partly true, and so not wholly adequate justifications of the goodness of American practice. But part of the truth is better than no truth at all, and the main reason for this partial truth is our fathers' very incomplete rejection of the basic premises of Christian and realist thought. Their view needs to be refined and enlarged through its integration in the Thomistic view of natural law, which gives a more credible view of the liberty Americans cherish.

Americans' devotion to liberty, including intellectual liberty, has to be understood, as Brownson first explained, as devotion to *catholic* or universal truth, and the American premise that religious liberty is for the sake of that truth cannot be dismissed as Enlightenment propaganda without doing violence to most of our thinkers and our history. The Catholic task is to portray atheistic and purely subjectivistic views of liberty and truth as American heresy, and we can do so while acknowledging that some Americans from the founding generation until today have been seduced by such heresy. We can even acknowledge, from the perspective of the truth, that the theoretical views of our leading founders were distorted by the narrowness of antiecclesiastical prejudice, without denying the great good of their political accomplishments.

Murray writes not primarily as an ironist, but as both a loyal American and a loyal and believing Catholic. He writes as the best of Americans, providing, as a Catholic thinker, what his nation now needs most. And Catholics as Catholics have a genuine stake in how Americans view religious liberty. It may not make all the difference, but it makes a genuine difference, concerning the extent to which the Church can fulfill its universal mission in our particular country. What is good for Catholics, in this regard, is good for Americans: Our shared devotion must be to the truth about nature and God.

CHAPTER EIGHT

Religion, Philosophy,
and the American Founding

*J*ohn Courtney Murray presents America properly understood as based on a Thomistic foundation. But that interpretation might reasonably be viewed as too creative or partisan. In this chapter I want to consider the best version of the old view that America is basically a modern or Lockean project, the view recently articulated by Michael Zuckert in his book, *The Natural Rights Republic* (*NRR*). I will focus on the adequacy of Zuckert's interpretation of the American founding and religion. I do not mean to question this interpretation's historical accuracy, because Zuckert claims that what counts as historical evidence depends on one's perspective, and his perspective is that of philosophy, not history (*NRR*, 122). Zuckert maintains that Americans are free to judge the historical choices of their predecessors, and that they should take their bearings from the most rational or philosophic of the founders. From this perspective, the "founders" are simply those men who were most open to the philosophers' rationalism; therefore, the most philosophic of those men should be regarded as *the* founder. For Zuckert, then, Thomas Jefferson, author of the Declaration of Independence and *Notes on the State of Virginia*, is America's founder. This view of the founding did not, of course, originate with Zuckert. But I think he presents it in the most radical, penetrating, and honest way yet. His achievement is impressive.

Zuckert's rational or philosophic interpretation of America, in truth, is critical of the mainstream of American thought, both today and during the founding generation. It has been criticized most ably by Barry Shain, who has shown that most Americans of the founding generation were Calvinist Christians.[1] But I do not view Shain's criticism of Zuckert as decisive. My aim is to present a philosophical criticism of Zuckert's philosophical interpretation of America. I want to open the way for a defense of what Zuckert calls the continuity thesis. As John Courtney Murray claimed, the American founding, at its best, should be regarded as a modification, not a rejection, of the nation's Christian, natural law inheritance. While other writers emphasize the historical continuity between American and Christian and premodern forms of thought, I want to highlight the philosophic or rational necessity for taking that continuity seriously. After all, Zuckert may be right to suggest that if the choice is between historical traditionalism and philosophical rationalism, then it makes sense to celebrate American history as the progressive victory of reason over tradition. Following Zuckert's lead, I will focus my attention on Jefferson's thought, beginning with Zuckert's presentation of Jefferson. I should note that my presentation of the limitations of Jefferson's thought is not meant to detract from his greatness or from his deserved reputation as, in some ways, both the most admirable and the most philosophic of the founders.

America and Natural Rights

Zuckert defends "the centrality of the natural rights orientation" in understanding America (*NRR*, 6). This defense pits him against the understanding of America put forth by those who see America through the lenses of classical republicanism, contemporary communitarianism, and Protestant communalism. Beginning with Jefferson's Declaration, Zuckert argues, Americans have viewed government as concerned with "abstract individuals and their natural rights," with individuals freed from their political, social, and religious ties. This abstracted or not-fully-real "picture of the freely choosing individual" is opposed to the republican picture of political animals or engaged citizens and the communitarian and Christian picture of social or communally engaged beings (*NRR*, 21). The individual cannot act rationally if his view is distorted by the illusions of duty or love.

This perspective of radical liberation from communal and political life leads Zuckert readily to the conclusion that American political principles are not particularly American at all. They are "both accessible to and valid for all human beings"; they "are *simply* universal in character." A society formed by them is necessarily both "secular" and "open to the rational as such." That society is "cosmopolitan, not closed or sectarian." "To be an American" is not a matter of race, blood, culture, or faith, but "to accept those universal principles" (*NRR*, 126, emphasis added). That is, to be an American is to be open to philosophical truth by being uprooted from the social, political, and religious impediments to its acceptance. In Zuckert's view, to be an American is almost to be transpolitical, to be a member of the cosmopolis of philosophers, not the closed "cave" of citizens.

The Americans were the first to act on the modern philosopher John Locke's view that government comes from neither nature nor God, but is rather a human, rational construction to serve human purposes (*NRR*,

102). According to the Lockean Jefferson, author of the most philosophic book of the founding generation, *Notes on the State of Virginia*, human beings are different from the other animals because they "consciously understand their mortality and their vulnerability, and thus consciously shape the world so as to guarantee their survival" (*NRR*, 80). Other animals are merely concerned with immediate survival, but human beings pursue "security." Government is made by human beings to make themselves more secure as individuals, and it exists only to suit their convenience as individuals.

In Jefferson's mind, the American founders, freed from "monkish ignorance and superstition," came "to understand better than ever before how and why to make government." The result was "great improvements in their political life," and the rational expectation of more. The idea that government is a human construct is one source, Zuckert observes, "of the frequently noted progressive attitude to politics and society in America." And he seems to find that progressivism most reasonable (*NRR*, 103).

Zuckert explicitly contrasts the premodern with the modern or American view of political life. The former claims that "political life is understood as derived from God or nature," which "suggests a limit to what can be done with it." But the authentically American view is that government, as a human construct, is "open to indefinite improvement" (*NRR*, 103). So Zuckert affirms as America's and his own a philosophy of unlimited human freedom. Zuckert does acknowledge that the God of the Declaration is "Nature's God," but only to dismiss the idea that Jefferson relied at all on supernatural guidance. He adds that for Jefferson the only guidance nature provides human beings is negative: The drive for security points them away from nature. But there are no natural limits to the extent to which human beings might overcome nature through their own inventions, of which government is one. The movement away from nature is of indefinite duration.

Zuckert must go beyond the Declaration to explain that, for Jefferson, we really have no knowledge of even nature's God, for we do not really have any knowledge of nature at all. He attributes to the Jefferson of the *Notes* the view that "there is no 'nature-in-itself,' for the truth about nature varies with perspective." Human beings have no way of telling whether either some "natural theology" or some "atheistic or materialistic cosmology" is true. Because the available evidence is insufficient and our picture of nature necessarily varies with mood, "the thoughtful person stands undecided" concerning the truth about nature or the cosmos (*NRR*, 64–65). The drive for security shapes our moods which, in turn, shape the way we view nature as a whole. That drive away from insecurity, the only authentic natural standard, tells us not what nature is but only that we must escape from it. For political purposes especially, nature is not to be understood as some cosmos or rational design that exists independently of human making, but only as material to be exploited for human convenience. The human drive for security and so to eradicate human ignorance makes the "utilitarian" approach to science the only reasonable one. The American view of science is the same as the American view of government: both are useful constructs and nothing more.

The truth is, Zuckert argues, that "the security of these rights—the really valuable thing—is not supplied by God or nature but by human beings themselves when they institute government." What is really valuable human beings make for themselves. Christians say that human action was the cause of the Fall and that salvation comes from the supernatural grace of God. But for Jefferson, "Human action is more nearly the foundation for human salvation than the basis for a fall. The Declaration's history reverses the Bible's history" (*NRR*, 129). Zuckert contends that the Declaration's history is a tale of human self-liberation in the absence of a living, giving God. The Declaration's true significance has nothing to do with the rebellion against the British. It is the first political application of the Lockean theology of liberation, a theology, Zuckert believes, usually and wrongly thought to have Marxian roots.

So the natural rights orientation is really focused on human liberty, not nature or God. Zuckert rejects, for that reason, any version of the continuity thesis, the view that the Declaration or the founding is rooted in the nation's Christian, natural law inheritance. For him, the real alternative to the Declaration's politics is "the politics of the Puritans." Their Calvinist legislation, rooted in a distrust of "natural liberty," has, in Zuckert's view, "earned the censure of mankind as Puritanical" (*NRR*, 145). For the Calvinist-hating Jefferson and Zuckert, any moral legislation not rooted rather directly in the requirements of security is tyrannical. So Zuckert takes sides in the culture war, a war which between the liberals and the Puritans, he sees as characterizing American history. In his view, the liberals have won and have deserved to win most of the victories. For both philosophic and moral reasons Zuckert contests the view "that reform Christianity provides the key to the American political tradition" (*NRR*, 123–26).

Zuckert contends that the leading American founders adjusted themselves rhetorically to a citizenry that was largely Christian. But they aimed to transform the meaning of Christian language to make it compatible with "liberal rationalism." They did not aim somehow to do justice to both reason and revelation. The example of Jefferson shows they were not open at all to the possible truth of revelation. They used religion— and Jefferson, in particular, used it as little as possible—in the service of reason and liberty.

The Declaration's reference to the Creator and its appearance of an appeal to natural theology follow Locke's rhetorical example. Locke seems to ground his teaching on nature and rights in the human being's "relationship to the 'creator,' whose workmanship all human beings are." But his argument is more deeply grounded "in a *simply* nontheistic manner . . . in the self-grounding character of human selfhood." Rights originate in self-assertion, not in the authority of nature or God. So Locke's rhetorical theism "is an intermediate term between Christian theism and more strictly philosophic, but nontheistic reasoning" (*NRR*, 182, emphasis added). For Zuckert, authentic or strictly philosophic liberal rationalists know that all theistic reasoning is merely rhetorical. So Locke's theistic reasoning seduced Protestant American thinkers away from their distinctively Christian premises, while allowing them, if need be, to remain theists. America, Zuckert adds, has worked best when Christians have allowed themselves to be seduced, when religion and rights have seemed perfectly compatible (*NRR*, 200–01). Experience has shown that in a natural rights republic religion does not and should not completely wither away. But it has also shown that the "religious sensibilities" of Christianity could be employed to support the natural-rights republic. At its best, Zuckert holds, Christianity has been transformed into "the American civil religion" (*NRR*, 200). But the fact remains that Jefferson himself was a strictly philosophic thinker. He cannot be considered an atheist only to the extent that he held open the possibility that nature might have been ordered by some purposeful intelligence (*NRR*, 253n16).

Religion and Liberal Rationalism

The Lockean-Jeffersonian natural rights republic does allow a personal or private place for religion. The abstract individual consents to government for the limited purpose of enhanced security. Otherwise, he is free from government to pursue happiness. There is a right to pursue happiness, Zuckert explains, because human beings are unique in two ways: Unlike the other animals they pursue security *and* they pursue happiness. For Zuckert, the latter pursuit is actually a more genuine manifestation of human liberty.

The Lockean Zuckert says that "the idea of happiness, originating in the unique capacity of the human mind to form general ideas, supplies human beings with freedom, or *the nearest thing* to free will that is attainable" (*NRR*, 84, emphasis added). That is, the Christian teaching concerning free will is untrue. But the pursuit of happiness is less a product of natural determination than the pursuit of security. While pursuing security, human beings are free to choose the means, such as the construction of government, but not the end. But human beings desire to exist for more than mere survival, and so they imagine ideas or ends that transcend survival, and they believe that achieving them will make them happy. These various transcendent pursuits, or choices concerning purpose, are what form human lives into different shapes. And so human beings are free to pursue some spiritual or religious understanding of happiness according to how they imagine God.

But Locke and Jefferson hold that the pursuit of happiness, and not happiness itself, is distinctively human. Human happiness is, at best, unstable or transient. Every satisfaction is soon replaced by uneasiness, and the uneasiness renews the pursuit. In this view, restless discontent, not happiness, is the characteristic human condition. Human beings are "doomed to frustration in their pursuit of ever-elusive happiness," writes Zuckert, but they cannot help but pursue it (*NRR*, 84-85). Given the unalterable absence of solid evidence, what happiness is and how to pursue it properly remain a matter of free, personal choice. So nature directs human beings away "from a clear evil, death and suffering, to nothing in particular."[2] The positive dimension of distinctively human longing is pointless and in vain.

It might seem that Locke and Jefferson should praise the nobility of spiritual striving, the highest form of the futile human effort at transcendence (*NRR*, 85). But Zuckert explains that their tendency, instead, is to divert human attention away from religion, metaphysics, and philosophy. Their view is that the quest to know God and the good is more productive of misery than anything else, and it only gets in the way of what human beings can accomplish in the pursuit of security. The pursuit of happiness is subordinate to the pursuit of security, because al-though the latter may be more distinctively human, the former is more achievable.

So in Zuckert's view, Thomas Pangle is right to say that Jefferson's privatization of theological controversy is really an attempt to trivialize it. Jefferson thinks he knows that there is no metaphysical or theological truth accessible to human beings. True rational progress culminates in that skeptical conclusion. So the liberal, rational republic intentionally fosters religious indifference. Jefferson hoped that all Americans would soon comfortably and thoughtlessly accept the benignly vague theology of Unitarianism.[3] That uniformity would free rational discourse from the distortions of metaphysical and theological whimsy.

Richard Rorty, in this respect, justly claims to be Jefferson's heir. Both men have worked to make American thought superficial. Rorty, in fact, seems to go beyond Jefferson in more emphatically connecting the spiri-tual pursuit of happiness and the drive for security. The quest for God is really the quest for security, and so only with the personal access to eter-nity that comes at the culmination of that quest could a human being be happy. But all self-conscious mortals really know that that quest can never end. So Rorty's radical suggestion is that we aim to surrender self-consciousness in the name of happiness. He sees, perhaps quite rationally, that the doctrine that happiness is a futile target for self-conscious mor-tals is really anti-philosophic.[4]

The tendency of the leading founders was to turn human longing away from transcendent happiness and toward comfortable security. They tried, as much as possible, to identify the pursuit of happiness with the pursuit of security. And their intention in doing so was, as Zuckert con-tends, clearly anti-Christian. But we have to wonder to what extent their effort really depended upon, or at least is consonant with, Christian pre-mises. The liberal rationalist and the Christian Augustinian—or Calvin-ist—agree, against Aristotle and Socrates, that human beings cannot achieve happiness in this world through their own efforts. They also agree that human beings are unhappy, in large measure, because they experience themselves as insecure. Through their own efforts they really cannot acquire the security or freedom from contingency for which they long. The Christian shouts, while the liberal rationalist whispers, this truth about ineradicable insecurity.

But according to Zuckert, Jefferson's deepest experience of his "unique individuality" was occasioned by his sense of this ineradicable insecurity. As "most emphatically an individual," Jefferson was painfully dizzy in the face of the "abyss," of his "exposed situation" in nature. His personal experience was the same as that of the Christian Blaise Pascal, who is famous for expressing so eloquently how frightened he was by his unsupported existence nowhere in particular in the infinite universe. Jefferson's most personal experience, according to Zuckert, was of "the limits of human domination and use of nature." He was aware that the scientific and political attempts to dominate nature are futile diversions from the miserable experience of individuality, contingency, and vulnerability. Locke's abstract individual is not enough of a real individual to really encounter "the terrors of nature," but Jefferson himself was (NRR, 63–64).

So Zuckert shows us that Jefferson, the emphatic, unique individual, agrees with the Christian Pascal that the liberal rationalist pursuit of this-worldly security is not so rational after all, but a diversion from the truth about the limits of all human effort. The single-minded pursuit of security becomes a way of minimizing the unhappiness human beings feel when they encounter that truth. The main reason science and philosophy become active and utilitarian is to give human beings as little time as possible to reflect on the fact that the natural rights republic is rooted in the Lockean revelation of man's misery in God's absence. Philosophy and science, opposing leisure and idleness, become more an escape from, than the pursuit of, the truth. The Declaration's progressivism, its theology of liberation, is most unreasonable. It is manifestly less plausible than the Christian account of the Fall.

Tocqueville on American Unreasonableness

The best criticism of the American's unreasonable pursuit of diversion comes from Alexis de Tocqueville, who means in his *Democracy in America* to be a friendly critic of the leading founders. Tocqueville describes the Americans as pursuing happiness—skeptically defined as material enjoyment—but never taking time to enjoy life. They are, as Locke says, restless or uneasy in the midst of their abundance. But Tocqueville adds that they seem to be perversely proud of their misery. Their constant calculation on behalf of their pursuit is a sign of their human liberty. Actual happiness or enjoyment would be a sign of enslavement to nature or others. Americans' morality of self-interest in this respect is an assertion of individual human freedom against nature or instinct. They have quite consciously affirmed the Lockean-Jefferson doctrine that it is the mark of the free human being to spend his life pursuing what he cannot have.[5]

Preferring the pursuit of enjoyment to enjoyment or happiness itself may be free but it is surely not rational. Tocqueville takes this perversity as a convincing sign that Americans are beings with ineradicable spiritual needs. They feel the misery of God's absence intensely. They believe that reason leads to the conclusion that spiritual longings are insatiable, and so they must divert their efforts in a material direction. But that diversion of course, fails. Americans seem to know that material success cannot give them what they really need, and their attempts to divert themselves from what they really know becomes progressively less successful. For Tocqueville, the example of Americans—a whole people restless in the midst of abundance—contradicts the hope of liberal rationalism that spiritual needs can somehow be transformed or attenuated.[6]

Tocqueville accepts the French philosopher Jean-Jacques Rousseau's

criticism of Locke's individualistic extremism. Rousseau explains, in his
Discourse on Inequality, that Locke's psychology is flawed in its premise
that the human construction of good government will actually make
human beings feel more secure. They will be, objectively, more secure:
they will live longer, less risky lives. But they will tend to experience themselves as progressively less secure. The natural drive for personal security is
satisfied more with feeling than with fact. The fact is that the particular
human being will never really be secure. All human beings are dependent
on forces beyond their control; we all eventually die.

The establishment of peace and prosperity through good government gives human beings more to lose, and, despite their best efforts at
diversion, more time to reflect on the truth about their contingency and
mortality. And Cartesian or Lockean skeptical rationalism, the foundation of liberal democracy, deprives them of illusions about the providence of God and nature. Thus do human beings become more death-
haunted, more fearful and anxious, than ever before.[7] Especially penetrating contemporary observers, such as Aleksandr Solzhenitysn and
Walker Percy, echo Tocqueville when they report that what distinguishes
today's Americans, perhaps above all, is their inability to live well with
death. Beneath the thin veneer of American pragmatism, Solzhenitsyn
hears the howl of existentialism.[8]

If being human means acting to pursue happiness and security against
nature, and if that effort, contrary to human intention, makes human
beings progressively more anxious and restless, then human liberty ought
to be regarded as an unfortunate error. A truly human ethics would then
counsel that we ought not to strive to negate nature, but to negate human liberty and *return* to nature—that the futile pursuit of security and
happiness ought to be replaced by the security and contentment enjoyed
by every other animal. Human uniqueness would be regarded as an aber-
ration to be eradicated in accord with nature's general intention.[9] If Locke
and Jefferson are right about human freedom, then it is no good.

Locke and Jefferson might well say that to work for this eradication is unreasonable, that the human pursuits of security and happiness are natural or unalterable. But Rousseau responds that those pursuits are not natural, but historical. They are human creations or constructions that might well be deconstructed. Rousseau's correction of Locke, surely, is in accord with the basic Lockean premise that nature is inhuman and worthless, and so all human value is created in opposition to nature. According to Zuckert, the Declaration's theology is a tale of salvation through human ingenuity, but in fact Jefferson does not really believe that human beings can make themselves happy or secure. And according to Rousseau, the despair that comes with the absence of a living and giving God is really overcome through the hope that comes with the recognition that human misery is really a historical creation. By bringing history to an end, human beings can thus achieve for themselves what the Christian God promised.[10]

Tocqueville agrees with Zuckert's Jefferson that the human experience of unsupported individuality is of unlimited restlessness, painful disorientation, and practical paralysis; it is not rational at all.[11] So the abstract individual freed from the constraints of nature, family, community, and God does not experience himself as reasonable, happy, or secure. Tocqueville calls the Rousseauean judgment against this extreme experience of individuality "individualism."[12] Individualism is an apathetic, asocial, passionless existence, one without all distinctively human qualities. It is the judgment for the Rousseauean or wholly inhuman nature and against the abstract, deracinated or, in truth, unnatural individuality of the Lockean state of nature. That judgment is perfectly reasonable if human distinctiveness is defined in terms of futile, personal pursuits, and so it is the culmination of the liberal, democratic movement in thought. For Tocqueville, human liberty must be experienced as lovable if it is to sustain itself, and so it must be moderated or shaped by genuine experiences of familial, political, and religious love. In this sense, human beings really are communal and political beings by nature.

Tocqueville differs from Locke and Jefferson by recognizing and af-firming natural limits to human liberty. He does the same for the human longing for God, affirming the Socratic-Platonic-Christian view that human beings must believe that they are in some sense immortal if they are to act well.[13] For Tocqueville, the most reasonable understanding of freedom of religion must be as freedom for religious belief.

But Tocqueville goes further. He understands Americans as rightly believing that religious belief is indispensable for political liberty. Hu-man beings, even philosophers, cannot think or act freely without some salutary submission to intellectual and moral authority. The effort to achieve unlimited liberty, as we have seen, produces the conclusion that liberty is no good, and so it leads human beings to the willing acceptance of political bondage. The American choice, on the other hand, as pre-sented by Tocqueville, is for both political freedom and religious dogma, for a common moral and spiritual authority as a guide for personal and political choice.[14] So American religion, properly understood, cannot be trivialized or completely privatized. It is the basis of our political institu-tions and personal well-being.[15] Tocqueville's judgment concerning the Puritans is subtle and mixed, but he is clear that the American tradition of liberty cannot be understood without them.

Tocqueville shows us that the Lockean abstract individual of Jefferson's Declaration is no rationalist and, in the long run, no liberal. But having denied that Lockeanism is a reasonable account of human experience, I must add that I disagree with Zuckert's identification of Jefferson with Locke. That identification depends on making *Notes on Virginia* the authoritative text for understanding Jefferson, and slighting the self-understanding he presents in his letters.[16] Zuckert minimizes the letters' importance by saying that Jefferson was often concerned with being agreeable to his correspondents, not in saying what he really thought. But there is just too much evidence that the mature Jefferson thought of himself not as a Lockean but as an Epicurean. He claimed not to be in pursuit but in possession of happiness.[17]

Jefferson thought the Epicurean Jefferson was the most philosophical Jefferson. And if it is true that Jefferson expresses most completely the philosophic intention of the founding, we cannot avert our eyes from the adequacy of this form of ancient rationalism. It is also the case that Jefferson's affirmation of the philosophic doctrine of Epicurus is connected with his affirmation (ignored by Zuckert) of the moral teaching of Jesus—that is, Christianity.

Jefferson, Epicurus, and Jesus

Jefferson was indebted to modern writers such as Locke for his understanding of both political and natural science. But in his private and theoretical reflections, he says his ethical teachers were the ancient philosophers and Jesus. Some of these reflections are found in one of his letters to Doctor Benjamin Rush, his friend and partner in theoretical discussion. With Rush, Jefferson had no reason to fear speaking his mind. Gone, for the moment, were political and rhetorical considerations.

This letter fulfilled a promise Jefferson made to Rush in the midst of some "delightful conversations," which were a respite from the political crisis of 1798–99. Jefferson gives his views on "the Christian religion," which are "the result of a lifetime of reflections." These thoughts had occupied his mind whenever he could "justifiably abstract" it "from public affairs." Jefferson actually compares Christian with ancient philosophical ethics. He begins by denying that he accepts some "anti-Christian system." He asserts, in this private and theoretical moment, "I am a Christian," meaning that he accepts "the genuine principles of Jesus himself." Jefferson really holds that Jesus' "system of morals" is "the most perfect and sublime that has ever been taught by man" (to Benjamin Rush, 21 April 1803).[18]

But Jefferson did not regard Christian ethics as complete. He wrote in a later letter that "I . . . am an Epicurian [sic]." And he explained how he could be simultaneously a Christian and an Epicurean: "Epictetus and Epicurus give laws for governing ourselves, Jesus a supplement of the duties and charities we owe to others" (to William Short, 31 October 1819). The teaching of the ancient philosophers, Jefferson told Rush, "related chiefly to ourselves," to how we might achieve "tranquility of mind" through "government of passions." Because self-government is primary, Christianity is only a "supplement" (to Rush, 21 April 1803). Personal tranquility does not induce us to do our duties to others, and so Christianity is both secondary and morally superior to Epicureanism.

Jefferson's acceptance of the atheistic materialism of Epicureanism is actually, of course, strong evidence for Zuckert's dismissal of the authority of nature's or any other God. That atheism, Jefferson wrote, is the basis for "the consolation of a sound philosophy, equally indifferent to hope and fear" (to Short, 31 October 1819). To be beyond hope and fear, of course, is to be beyond being determined either by the drive for security or the pursuit of happiness. The tranquility of indifference *is* distinctively human happiness. For the Epicurean, happiness, understood as the pleasure associated with the overcoming of mental anxiety through truthful thought, is the achievable goal of life.[19] The Epicurean Jefferson employed reason to combat successfully the experience of "unique individuality" felt by the Pascalian Jefferson. He also used it to recognize the futility of the materialistic utilitarianism of the abstract individual inherent in the thought of the Lockean Jefferson.

Happiness, Jefferson emphasized, was achieved neither through hedonism or indolence, but through the practice of a certain kind of virtue (to Thomas Law, 13 June 1814). And the test of virtue is its utility in achieving mental tranquility.[20] For the Epicurean Jefferson, what is not useful in achieving that goal is not virtue. So the Epicurean will not be unjust, because injustice brings on mental anxiety. But neither will he exert himself on behalf of others in the name of justice or charity, because those exertions are not clearly useful.

The Epicurean Jefferson reconciled, in his own case, liberty with happiness. He was free from the chains of common opinion for his own self-government. And he knew that self-government in the precise sense is a way of life never lived by more than a very few (to Mrs. Cosway, 12 October 1786). Freedom from hope and fear is also freedom understood as self-sufficiency. The individual no longer desires what would make him dependent on others and others dependent on him. For this personal cultivation only, Jefferson recommended the study of the ancient philosophers. Jefferson's love of classical learning was not, as Eva Brann claims, a "noble and baseless preference."[21] The preference was personal, tranquil, and delightful. And it was a philosophically grounded one. But it was worse than useless in directing Jefferson toward his duties to others. It even revealed political leadership to be mere drudgery.[22]

The ancient philosophers recommended a way of life that points away from benevolence toward human beings in general. They taught, Jefferson reports, friendship toward their own kind, and the moral duties of patriotism and justice to those not of their kind. Epicurean philosophers know that patriotism and justice are qualities most human beings must have for their political community to sustain itself. And they also know that political order is useful for their tranquility. So the ancient philosophers "taught" or "inculcated" in nonphilosophers those political virtues, without really including them "within the circle of their benevolence" (to Rush, 21 April 1803).

The ancient philosophers' teaching concerning nonphilosophic virtue was part of their enlightened selfishness. And they did not even teach to be virtues—because they did not even regard as useful—"peace, charity, and love to our fellow men," the virtues that Jefferson regarded as particularly democratic. The ancient philosophers saw no reason at all to embrace "with benevolence the whole family of mankind" (to Rush, 21 April 1803).

Ancient philosophers spoke both candidly and truly when they opposed benevolence and moral duty. The philosophers' conceptions of moral duty are always tantamount to hypocritical moralism. And their moralism always distorts or mystifies the simple or subrational phenomenon of morality. So Jefferson ranked for Rush the ancient philosophers according to their candor. Plato is the least truthful, or the least openly selfish and elitist, of the philosophers. Cicero's Platonism was clear in his hypocritical attacks on Epicurus, whose views the Stoics in general shared. Jefferson praised Seneca for being less Stoic than most of the Stoics. Ranking still higher is Epictetus, the least Stoic of the Stoics. But it is in "the genuine . . . doctrine of Epicurus" that is found "everything rational in moral philosophy which Greece and Rome left us" (to Short, 31 October 1819). Epicurus is the most rational of the philosophers. Epicureanism, not Lockeanism, *is* rationalism for Jefferson.

There is no rational foundation for moral duty, and Epicureanism has the virtue of making clear this deficiency of rationalism for social animals. But perhaps that deficiency was not so clear to Epicurus himself. Jefferson seems to have absorbed some of the Christian criticism, expressed most eloquently by Augustine, of the selfish and self-deceptive pride of the philosophers. The Epicurean Jefferson fears, even more than Augustine, what reason and the reasonable can do to morality.

Jefferson knew that the Epicurean way of life is not for most people. His application of Epicurean precepts to his own life is a key point of distinction between his own and common opinion. His deepest rational opinions are selfishly undemocratic. And so to explain and justify the individual's, and especially the philosopher's, social and democratic responsibility to others, he turned from philosophy to Christianity. That turn is not merely rhetorical, because Jefferson held that the Epicurean account of human nature really is incomplete. Jefferson was actually more certain than most Christians that there is a natural foundation for the duties that social beings must have to each other. And so he does not agree with Augustine that there can be no justice without the loving subordination of the creature to the Creator. Jefferson's affirmation of Christian morality is wholly natural and has nothing to do with man's duties to God.

At first, it would seem that no Epicurean could approve of Christianity. In the Epicurean view, Christian hope and fear, rooted in doctrines concerning personal immortality, heaven, and hell, have no scientific or truthful foundation and produce anxiety. For the Epicurean, scientific recognition and acceptance of one's finitude are what secure freedom from death and what might come after death. The scientific liberation of the mind from the mystifications of metaphysics and theology through the discovery of the truth of atheistic materialism is the way to happiness.

But Jefferson actually believes that the atheistic materialist can be a true Christian. His acceptance of the moral system of Jesus has nothing to do with divine revelation, or especially Christ's divinity. Jefferson goes as far as to call "immaterialism" a Christian heresy that can be traced to those who wrote about Jesus, but not to Jesus himself (to Adams, 15 August 1820).[23] Jefferson merely affirms the "human excellence" of Jesus and his moral doctrine, which he claims is all that Jesus ever claimed for himself (to Rush, 21 April 1803). For Jefferson, Jesus gives a better account than the ancient philosophers of our duties to others, which Jefferson holds we are inclined to perform by our nature.

Jefferson held that "moral sense" (or "conscience" or "moral instinct") describes what nature gives beings "destined for society." This instinct, by directing human beings toward others and giving them pleasure when they perform their duties toward them, is the source of moral action.[24] We have a natural sensitivity to others' suffering that "prompts us irresistibly to feel and succor their distresses." The feeling of this pleasure, a source of happiness, is less distinctively human than the more free, futile, and selfish pursuit of happiness (to Carr, 10 August 1787; to Law, 13 June 1814). The moral instinct is given to social, not necessarily rational, beings. The Jefferson who describes the moral sense has a more positive view of human nature than does Zuckert's Lockean Jefferson. Nature does, after all, provide us with what we need to live well or happily as social beings. For Jefferson, there are two forms of distinctively human happiness, one rational and selfish and the other more subrational, instinctual, and social.

Action in response to moral sense or instinct is not clearly a manifestation of human liberty. Nonetheless, Jefferson does tend to use it to defend his view that all human beings equally possess natural rights. He argues that blacks may be intellectually inferior to whites, and implicitly that it is almost impossible to conceive of a black Epicurean. But blacks and whites are morally equal in their capacity to do their duties to others.[25] The possession of the moral sense, and so the capacity to distinguish between right and wrong, more clearly than reason makes the animal human.[26]

Jefferson contends that the moral instinct has nothing to do with "science" or the rational perception of truth. It also has nothing to do, contrary to Plato, with the perception of the beautiful. Because this natural goodness is so easily distorted by the "artificial rules" imposed by reason, "the ploughman" is more likely to act morally than "the professor" (to Carr, 10 August 1787). So it would seem that the rational conquest of nature actually produces moral decline. And it is far from clear how this subrational naturalization or allegedly complete demystification of Christianity can really be the foundation of natural rights, of equality in freedom. Perhaps the appropriate conclusion is that the Jeffersonian and American acceptance of the equal freedom and dignity of all human beings must be understood as an unreasonable Christian inheritance.

Jefferson's radical separation of the foundations of self-government (in reason) and moral duty (in instinct) actually makes Epicureanism morally salutary. The philosopher should leave morality alone because it is unreasonable. The "learned," such as the Platonists, act unphilosophically when they serve their "own interests" by "perverting" morality's true or Christian or "simple" doctrine (to Rush, 21 April 1803). The learned cleverly turn "primitive" into "Platonizing" Christianity, a perverse mixture which can distort beyond recognition each of its parts (to Adams, 13 October 1813).

Christian or true morality, Jefferson held, is most powerfully threatened by the Socratic dictum that knowledge is virtue. He wrote that the study of "moral philosophy" is "lost time," worse than useless (to Carr, 10 August 1787). There is, strictly speaking, no such thing. Morality must be democratic or common, because all human beings, both the "professor" and the "ploughman," must live in society. Because most human beings are not philosophers or scientists—that is, they are not primarily rational beings—moral sense must be rooted not in the "head" but the "heart," in sense or instinct. Jefferson, anticipating Rorty, says that this distinction is one between "science" and "sentiment" (to Cosway, 12 October 1786). Nature intends people who are not particularly reasonable to act socially or morally. It seems, in fact, that it is easier for such people to do so.

This understanding of moral sense or instinct seems to have been Jefferson's main debt to the Scottish Enlightenment, and it is a significant one. The term "moral sense" was first used in the way Jefferson used it by Francis Hutcheson, a professor of moral philosophy at the University of Glasgow. Hutcheson radically separated self-love from morality or benevolence. Because moral sense is an instinct, it owes nothing to reason. So it cannot be reduced by Lockean skepticism to mere self-interest.[27]

Hutcheson radically separated morality from reason to save morality from being merely a rationalization on behalf of passion. Reason, the Lockeans seemed to show, turns out to be incapable of directing human beings to some distinctive moral end. Human beings are not rational, moral animals by nature. If the rational animal is most fundamentally selfish, then the moral animal cannot be rational. Nature directs human beings to morality with instinct, and away from it with reason.

The selfish materialism Hutcheson finds at the root of modern rationalism Jefferson finds in ancient philosophy, in fact, in philosophy understood candidly at all times. Morality has to be separated from reason and become simply a feeling because the life of reason is always a life of personal selfishness. There is no rational foundation for charity, benevolence, and so forth, but Jefferson agreed with the Christians that such qualities are virtues nonetheless. The rational, abstract individual Zuckert finds described by the Declaration would not be fit for social life. What the Declaration abstracts from, in this view, is the goodness of nature. The Declaration has made both the rational life and the moral life more conducive to happiness than Locke seems to think. It remains unclear whether those two ways of life are merely in tension or fundamentally in conflict. Jefferson certainly held that the Christian Epicurean could reconcile tranquil self-government with doing his duties to others. But whether he actually did so in the case of the black slaves remains controversial.

The Unreasonableness of Christian Epicureanism

Jefferson had good reason to separate philosophy from morality, in opposition to the Declaration's Lockeanism. That does not mean that Christian Epicureanism is more reasonable than Lockeanism, much less the older natural law doctrine of Thomas Aquinas. The Thomistic account of natural law is an attempt to integrate reason and revelation by informing one by the other. Its premises are that revelation completes, not contradicts, reason, and that human beings are fitted to apprehend rationally moral ends given by nature. Jefferson does agree with Thomas—and calls himself a Christian because he does—by holding that human beings have a natural inclination to do their moral duties toward others. The ancient philosophers, he recognized, knew of no such inclination.

In Thomas's Christian correction of Aristotle, natural inclination and conscience replace, to some extent, moral and political education. Confidence in nature has a universalizing tendency on ethics. But for Thomas Aquinas, unlike Jefferson, nature intends these inclinations to be ordered and informed by reason. True human morality depends on the integration, not separation, of these natural goods.

Thomas Aquinas and Jefferson also agree that charity is not clearly a dictate of reason. Thomas Aquinas holds that the distinctively Christian virtues, the theological virtues, are "infused." They depend upon God's grace, upon the human being's friendship with a God who cares about his or her well-being and promises satisfaction of his or her deepest longings.[28] Charity cannot be a virtue for someone who accepts the Epicurean account of the human condition. Thomas Aquinas reasonably denies what Jefferson seems to believe, that there is a purely natural foundation for charity. In this respect, Aquinas is closer to the ancient philosophers than is Jefferson. Both Epicurus and Aquinas agree that Jefferson's secularized or naturalized Christian faith in the goodness of human nature is really ungrounded.

We know that Hutcheson's view of the moral sense was rejected by most of his contemporaries as incredible. They especially objected to the radical separation of morality and self-interest or self-consciousness.[29] The grounding of moral action in some instinctive moral sense, somehow shared by all human beings but having nothing to do with reason, now seems implausible to almost all of us. If morality is reduced simply to feeling, and can only be corrupted by reason, then it might be grounded in any feeling or experience. This doctrine, finally, is a short distance from the easygoing moral relativism Allan Bloom describes.

Jefferson, especially the Epicurean Jefferson, was not a moral relativist or nihilist. But the incredibility of his account of moral duty inevita-

bly leads to Rorty's view that morality has no foundation. Rorty's pragmatic corrections of Jefferson really do attempt to make Jefferson's
thought more reasonable or coherent. Rorty's pragmatism aims to universalize the Epicurean's experience of tranquil indifference to death.
And Rorty's description of contemporary sophisticated Americans as
politely apathetic suggests that universal indifference has been the true
or effectual goal of the modern philosophers' rhetoric. Rorty aims to
complete the project to which Jefferson contributed by purging the Bible
of its unreasonableness, reducing it to thoughtlessly conformist Unitarianism.[30]

Jefferson's partly Christian and partly Epicurean ethics seems, at first,
to reflect the tension between reason and revelation that, according to
Leo Strauss, is the secret to the West's vitality. But that appearance is
deceiving. Jefferson really dissolves that tension by not taking the moral
claims of either reason or revelation seriously enough. He says that neither, really, is the source of our duties to others.

Jefferson's limited revulsion against the philosophers' personal selfishness was not simply the result of his feelings. It owes a good deal to the
moral universalism of reason, as he must have learned from the Stoics, as
well as to the Christian criticism of the pagan philosophers' hypocritical
elitism. But Jefferson, in principle, reduced his moral revulsion to feelings because he accepted nothing from reason or revelation that would
lead him to practice the democratic or Christian virtues. That conclusion
is one of the deepest reasons why "neither God nor the good . . . were . . .
intended to be preoccupations" in the "republican university" designed
by Mr. Jefferson.[31] Jefferson's devotion to democracy, in the end, is based
on nothing more than his feelings, as well as his perception of the equality of all human beings.

Epicurean Christianity, Liberal Democracy, and Natural Rights
Zuckert's natural rights republic is also called a liberal democracy. The majority rules, but everyone's rights are protected. The premise of the doctrine of consent is that democracy and liberty are not fundamentally at odds. But for the Epicurean Jefferson, liberal democracy is a mixed regime, a combination of diverse and perhaps incompatible elements. Epicurus was a liberal, and Jesus a democrat, and their views concerning human happiness and duty do not really fit together. Jefferson's noble and partly successful project was to moderate the extremism of each one with the other. But they do not form a whole. And this incoherence is not just Jefferson's personal idiosyncracy: American intellectuals have often understood their country's principles as some combination of philosophical elitism and secularized Christianity or generalized benevolence. Consider today's (or maybe yesterday's) Democrat: both a card-carrying member of the ACLU and devoted to the welfare state's compassionate alleviation of human misery, both pro-choice and convinced the American nation should be viewed as a caring family.

Charles Griswold contends that Jefferson did not really do justice to both Epicurean personal selfishness and Christian moral duty. He reaches that stern conclusion by a careful examination of the crucial case of racially based slavery, where Jefferson's pursuit of Epicurean tranquility usually prevailed over his moral sense. Jefferson wrote eloquently against the injustice of enslaving black human beings. But after 1777 he never spoke out in public against the institution of slavery, took no risks to free his own slaves, and did not even act, when as president he could have, to improve the miserable situation of freed blacks. Jefferson's inaction and prevarications were, Griswold explains, "directly traceable to the underlying incoherence of his philosophical position." And, as Griswold adds, that inaction and incoherence are especially troubling because of his undeniable devotion to moral integrity and the pursuit of justice.

Jefferson was a great and admirable thinker and political actor, but, as he himself admitted, he was less than perfect on both counts.[32]

Jefferson finally had to choose between doing his duty to others—protecting blacks' rights, as his moral sense inclined—and maintaining his tranquil freedom from anxiety by convincing himself that he was already doing all that he could for unfortunate blacks, which was not much. The Epicurean could even calm himself with the thought that at least he was not contributing to the worsening of the injustice of slavery. But the truth is that Jefferson's deeds did not correspond to the eloquent and extreme condemnation of racially based slavery found in his words.

Completely demystified Christianity, in Jefferson's own case, was not a strong impetus to moral action. His inaction concerning slavery calls into question the natural strength of the moral sense, perhaps especially in the case of philosophers. The Abolitionists, more genuinely Christian, opposed slavery more resolutely because they believed that owning slaves was sinful. The enlightened Jefferson, finding Christian doctrines such as revelation, sin, guilt, judgment, and salvation not only incredible but repulsive, tended not to take bold risks on behalf of racial justice. Jefferson hated Calvinism perhaps more than any other leading founder.[33] But perhaps that anti-theological passion made him too "reasonable," too cautious. Could original sin better account for man's nature than some combination of reason and generalized benevolence?

According to Zuckert, the protection of rights and especially the white denial of black rights caused Jefferson to find a very limited place for public belief and even God. The Declaration's "We hold these truths to be self-evident," properly understood, means that most Americans must accept the self-evidence of natural rights by conviction. Only a few scientists or philosophers will really see the true foundation of natural rights in the self's drive for security. The few know, and the many must believe in what the few know (*NRR*, 46–49).

Zuckert quotes—indeed, surely over-quotes—Jefferson's most uncharacteristic assertion about God. Found in Query XVIII in *Notes on the State of Virginia*, it is part of an attack on the injustice and antidemocratic moral corruption caused by the presence of slavery in Virginia: "And can the liberties of a nation be thought secure when we have removed their only firm basis, a conviction in the minds of the people that these liberties are the gift of God. That they are not to be violated but with his wrath."[34] Zuckert contends that Jefferson's point is that the effective security of rights depends on the belief of most Americans that rights are God-given and that their violation will be punished by God. This untrue belief is the core of the American civil religion, which, as Lincoln emphasized far more insistently later, is an unphilosophical but indispensable support for the natural rights republic. (There is actually little other significant evidence of Jefferson's support for civic or public religion. He usually differed from his fellow enlightened American educational theorists Noah Webster, Benjamin Franklin, and Dr. Rush in his extreme opposition to it.)[35]

But Zuckert's interpretation apparently does not apply to the philosophical Jefferson. For Jefferson, disbelief in the God-givenness of rights and the wrathful God caused him to do less than he might have to secure the rights of others. And this moral deficiency was shared with many or most of the other leading founders. According to Harry Jaffa, "the widespread lack of concern over the moral challenge of Negro slavery to the doctrine of universal rights in the revolutionary generation can be traced to the egoistic quality of those rights in their Lockean foundation."[36] And, of course, Lockean and Epicurean selfishness are not really that far apart; virtue in both cases consists in what is useful in securing one's own happiness.

It also seems to me that Lockean-Epicurean calculation even dominates Jefferson's assertion about the violation of rights and God's wrath. Here is Jefferson's next sentence: "Indeed I tremble for my country when I reflect that God is just; that his justice cannot sleep forever; that consid-

ering numbers, nature, *and natural means only*, a revolution in the wheel of
fortune, an exchange in situations is among possible events; that it may
become probable through supernatural interference" (emphasis added).
Human fortunes change; those on top eventually lose power. God's justice would be found in the violation of the rights of the oppressors by the
formerly oppressed.

For Jefferson, acting in the fear of God means acting in the fear of
what will happen when blacks—increasing in numbers—eventually take
power. Whites should respect their rights now in expectation that blacks
will respect theirs later. It is unclear what Jefferson means by "supernatural interference," but the calculation that leads to rights-protection works
perfectly well without it. So here again we have "Nature's God," or no
supernatural divine judgment at all. The problem remains that such calculation did not prove persuasive for slaveholders, a category that included Jefferson himself. Still, Jefferson opposes using the biblical God
as the foundation of ethics for either the many or the few. Jefferson's
philosophical reflections are not only far from passing the test of reason;
his liberal rationalism is deficient from the perspective of the effectual
protection of rights.

Rational Continuity?

If liberal rationalism, uprooted from nature and God, and grounded
wholly in either the activity of the self-constituting self or the serenity of
the Epicurean atheist, is not simply rational, then the continuity thesis—
the view that the American founding, at its best, is indebted to classical
and Christian thought—merits some reexamination. Zuckert's assertion,
which follows that of Harry Jaffa, that the American founders used "created" and "by nature" interchangeably is suspect, especially if "by nature"
means the Lockean view of nature (*NRR*, 25). Whatever Jefferson and the
other leading founders thought personally and privately, the public pre-

sentation of the Creator was characteristically made with the intention of making clear that human beings are creatures, that is, beings not only with rights but with duties to God. The best example here, of course, is Madison's *Memorial and Remonstrance,* where he says, "Before any man can be considered as a member of Civil Society, he must be considered as a subject of the Governor of the Universe."[37] The God who governs subjects is a personal God.

For Madison, the duty of the creature is part of the "property" that government protects, not controls. He even claimed that "conscience is the most sacred of all property; other property depending in part on positive law, the exercise of that being a natural and inalienable right."[38] Acting according to conscience is the most perfect manifestation of one's freedom, of one's real ownership of one's self, of self-determination. The performance of this duty is evidence that one is not simply determined by one's political order, by the drive for security, or by the futile pursuit of happiness. Both Jefferson and Madison agree that that freedom is the one which is most natural, because it is the least dependent on political support. But Jefferson, in Madison's view, is wrong to reduce conscience to some subrational instinct or moral sense.

This idea of inner moral freedom, not clearly present in Jefferson, perhaps is not wholly defensible without some biblical-Christian support. The founding idea of "created nature" can be the basis for affirming the truth of the ancient or classical or even Epicurean assertion that reason points the way to an understanding of moral virtue and happiness that exists independently of human making. But it is also the basis for seeing all human beings as equally persons created in the image of a personal, free, and rational God. To experience oneself as created is to view democratically the accessibility of the true understanding of human duty through conscience. That experience is available not only to the gifted and fortunate few, the followers of Socrates or Epicurus, but to all human beings. The democratization of the transpolitical search for truth and the conviction that this search can be the foundation of human duty and human society may well be decisively biblical and Christian.

Madison and Jefferson's rather extreme opposition to the public promulgation of civil theology and political religion can be understood in terms of this understanding of the limits of politics for free and social beings. Political life perhaps really does largely consist of cooperative and coercive efforts to provide for bodily needs. But it does not extend to the formation of conscience, and it does not provide fully for human fulfillment. On that point, the Epicurean Jefferson and the Christian agree. So the creature and the Epicurean would agree with George Anastaplo's criticism of even Lincoln's very moderate political religion. It is, in part, "yearning for a comprehensive vision which can be reflected in practical affairs," and so less reasonable than authentic Christianity's acknowledgment of intractable limits to political reform and human ingenuity in general.[39] Perhaps Lincoln's identification of American religious passion with a merely political enterprise contributed decisively to the nearly fatal weakening of American religious thought and sentiment we see now. The same identification is found in the atheistic pragmatist Richard Rorty's *Achieving Our Country,* and Rorty is honest enough to admit that he is using what remains of the American religious impulse to create a world where religion, philosophy, and self-conscious mortality will all wither away.[40]

Pierre Manent explains that the Lockean-Jeffersonian American solution presented by Zuckert is a characteristically modern rebellion against the confusion characteristic of medieval Europe in practice and Thomism in theory. The human being, for most medieval thinkers, had two ends, one natural, the other supernatural. The human or political world—constituted by the empire and the emperor—aimed to understand itself as naturally self-sufficient. But the spiritual or supernatural world—represented by the Church—claimed to be superior to the natural or political world, and so free from temporal power and control. And the perfection of the supernatural world made the natural one seem unjust and unfulfilling by comparison. As a result, people were burdened by two seemingly incompatible forms of domination. Both the government and the Church were oppressive and ineffective.[41]

The modern solution was to free the human being from both natural and supernatural domination. So the human being had to be freed from all dependence connected with his sociability, from being a political animal or a social being under God. In the name of both human freedom and good government, the modern philosophers invented the abstract individual, who consents to government he in turn invents to satisfy his fundamentally asocial needs. But this allegedly self-constituting individual, in truth, lacks the resources to constitute himself. His liberated will is insufficiently directed and too limited to really be effective, and that is because modern liberation is achieved, in large measure, through the abstraction from, or denial of, the social, political, and spiritual longings characteristic of real human beings. And so, as Tocqueville predicts and the history of our century—even in America—confirms, human self-assertion culminates in self-surrender and even the view that the self was never really there at all.

The audacious—in important ways noble or liberating, but fundamentally unreasonable—attempt to free human beings from nature and God has clearly been unsuccessful. Liberal rationalism, understood as individualistic self-assertion, can no longer be defended as an adequate account of human liberty. But, as Walker Percy says, the anthropology of the founding was, in truth, a "mishmash" of incompatible elements.[42] The Declaration, for example, presents the human being as free, rational, and dignified, but it is also unclear or incoherent on the foundation of those distinctively human qualities. The various assertions concerning inalienable rights, Nature's God, and the Creator (who is both Supreme Judge and the source of Divine Providence) cannot really be harmonized. So we do well, in our time, to highlight those aspects of the founding that can contribute to a dissent from the more extreme and, in truth, discredited claims of liberalism, and to attempt to reconstitute liberalism on a less secular and less individualistic foundation. On the most fundamental questions, Jefferson ought not to be our only guide.

CHAPTER NINE

Religion and the
American Idea of Liberty

I have presented two versions of the traditional view that America begins with the Declaration of Independence. But let me now balance that view with a bit of pious impiety: The place of religion, of God, in the Declaration is ambiguous, incoherent, and so open to a number of interpretations. The result is that Americans characteristically argue about the relationship between religious truth and political order on an unstable foundation.

One reason for the Declaration's incoherence in this matter, although not the only one, is that its four references to God have two different sources. Two come from Jefferson, two were added by Congress. Jefferson's are not meant to be specifically biblical. They are, in fact, rather antibiblical. Congress's two additions mean to invoke the biblical or personal God.

Jefferson referred to "Nature's God" and the "Creator" who "endowed" men with "inalienable rights." Nature's God, as we have seen, is the philosophical alternative to the biblical God, and the endowing is clearly something that happened in the indefinite past. God then left human beings alone, in freedom, to fend for themselves as needy and insecure beings. They have rights, not duties, because God asks nothing of them and they have no reason to be grateful. They have to invent government, because it was not God-given, to make themselves secure. Rights might have been God-given, but they are evidence of natural human insecurity and misery, and not something for which to be grateful. God has no right to tell us what to do, and nature guides us only negatively. We are to use our freedom, or rational creativity, to move as far away from our natural condition, the misery and penury of the Lockean state of nature, as we can.[1]

Calling the Declaration wholly Lockean may be a faithful reflection of the Jefferson of 1776. But that interpretation does some violence to the text of the Declaration itself and is unabashedly elitist. The premise, as we saw in the last chapter, is that the document should be interpreted philosophically, according to the most philosophic or rational of the founders. But even Jefferson, following the rhetorical example of Locke, implies that God is more than an impersonal and indifferent Being when he calls Him the Creator of all men and of each man. If Nature's God is a Creator God, would He not also be the personal God of the Bible? But on the basis of the Lockean doctrine of right, that could not be. So the term Creator would seem to be an imprecise and misleading piece of rhetoric, and we suspect that the Declaration was written to be misunderstood. Yet the Declaration also calls God "the Supreme Judge of the World" and claims to rely on "the Protection of Divine Providence." And these two attributes are clearly those of the Creator God.

The Declaration might be interpreted as Lockean or virtually atheistic only by focusing solely on the doctrine of rights and the mind of Jefferson, as Michael Zuckert does. Alternatively it might be interpreted as relying on a biblical understanding because of the textual implications that there is a Creator God to whom we are responsible. For those aiming at consistency, or reconciling the God of Nature with the providential, judgmental Creator, there is even room for a Thomistic, natural law interpretation of the Declaration. That interpretation was not, of course, intended by the document's authors. But as John Courtney Murray thought, they might have built better than they knew.[2]

On religion, it is roughly true to say that at the time of the founding Americans were divided into the pious many and the "free-thinking" few. But there were some, such as the famous preachers who reconciled in their sermons the revolutionary doctrine of rights with the biblical God, who straddled the fence between the two factions.[3] One aim of the Declaration, as realistically revised by Congress, was to unite the two factions on the level of preaching. The result is that the Declaration is less Christian than the many and more Christian than the few would hope. For both free thinkers and believing Christians the Declaration is, in truth, a corrupt document. One thing a man ought not to compromise on is God. But the founding compromise also calls to mind, if only accidentally, the old doctrine of natural law: What human beings can know about God through their natural powers does not contradict what they can know through revelation. Revelation completes, not opposes, nature.

Any compromise between the claims of secular liberalism and those of revelation points to a truth rejected by both Thomas Jefferson and many Christians, especially Calvinists.[4] What we know by nature may well point to the possibility that the world and man were created. In defense of this view, we could observe that St. Thomas Aquinas himself was not only a harmonizer but a compromiser. His commentary on Aristotle's *Ethics* lessened the difference between pagan magnanimity and Christian humility, but it did not eradicate it. His account of Aristotelian virtue seen through Christian eyes is best termed a compromise. But it also suggests that the natural law position lying between Augustinianism and Aristotelianism might be discovered through reflection on a humble

critique of magnanimity and a proud critique of humility. We know by
nature of both our aspiration for virtuous independence and our fundamental dependence; we know of our individuality and its limitations. We
also experience the irreducible and inextinguishable tension between pride
and love. Magnanimity and humility correspond to real human longings,
to experiences which can be distorted but not eradicated by rights, which
represent an abstract understanding of human longings suitable to invented, abstract, individuals.[5] So an Aristotelian or Thomistic interpretation of the Declaration would have to begin with its insufficiency, its
silence on virtue. For the doctrine of rights propels an abstract being—
the individual—toward an unreal and unvirtuous independence from
nature and God.

The doctrine of natural law understands the human being not as
liberated or isolated, but as a social being. That being also longs by nature
to know and love God. The latter longing must be expressed socially, for
instance, in a church or synagogue. But that is a controversial statement.
Government is limited, even Madison agreed, by the human being's natural knowledge of his duties to his Creator. But Madison presented the
performance of that duty as a matter of individual conscience, not as a
matter of membership in an organized religious body.[6]

Madison and Jefferson, in fact, thought that perhaps the greatest
threat to human liberty was the tyrannical impulse of organized religion,
the church. They despised "religious slavery" even more than racially based
chattel slavery.[7] The doctrine of rights, they seemed to hope, would above
all free human beings forever from the thrall of monkish ignorance and
superstition, which they pretty much identified with belief in the truth
of revelation (see Jefferson's letter to Roger C. Weightman, 24 June 1826).
Jefferson, especially, hoped and expected that the churches of Christianity, with the benign or virtually empty exception of Unitarianism, would
simply wither away in America. In 1822 he wrote during the midst of a
Great Awakening that "I trust that there is not a *young man* now living in

the United States that will not die a Unitarian" (letter to Dr. Benjamin Waterhouse, 26 June 1822; emphasis in original).

The century just ended has been full of evidence that Jefferson and Madison's Machiavellian view about the Christian threat to human liberty is profoundly wrong. The three most antiliberal and murderous regimes of all time were atheistic. And the most philosophic of the anticommunist dissidents, Aleksandr Solzhenitsyn and Václav Havel, both connected the ideological war against truth and liberty to the atheism and materialism first relatively latent but eventually dominant in Enlightenment or modern thought. Anthropocentric humanism, the humanism of Locke and Jefferson, turned out not to be a humanism at all. Human beings cannot live well or courageously unless they somehow experience themselves as responsible to what is above them, unless they can live well in truth about their purposes and limitations. They need a point of view that transcends time in order to resist the lies of their time and place, to resist evil. And that point of view cannot be merely conscientious or private. It points, as Havel said, to a dissident community or polis; and for the dissidents, at the heart of that community is the church.[8]

A characteristically American answer to that criticism is that communism was a deformation of modern principle, one that mixed Christian eschatology with modern science. Communism failed according to the standard of the effective protection of rights, and so now American liberal democracy is the only viable model for the world. Americans, as Francis Fukuyama has mused, may now live in freedom and dignity according to their human nature, but without God, at the end of history.[9] But the same Fukuyama just a decade later claims that human nature has no future. Biotechnology will soon be able to free us from our distinctively human qualities in the name of the modern goals of equality, happiness, and security, and we have become too libertarian or rights-obsessed to resist technological progress from a moral or religious point of view. What the possession of rights allows us to pursue with very incomplete success we will now be able to have easily through chemicals, gene therapy, and nanobots. And we already have the popular Ritalin and Prozac, nature-altering pills that allow us to be much less moved by fundamental human experiences. The abolition of man seems perhaps more likely than ever.[10] The challenges to human liberty in the century now beginning may even surpass those of the twentieth.

The case for the natural law (as opposed to natural rights) interpretation of the Declaration gains force from the challenges we now face. The Declaration might reasonably be viewed as presenting a mishmash anthropology, one that presents Americans as free and dignified but without explaining clearly the foundation of human freedom and dignity.[11] It stands between Thomistic realism and modern materialism and atheism. But its greatness, its inspiration, comes from its devotion to the thought that human beings can know the truth about their natures as different from those of the other animals and that of God. That is, because of their natures as the beings with language or speech, human beings can know the truth about other animals, and they are open to and long for the truth about God.[12]

The Declaration's—and so America's—dignity comes from its affirmation, however ambiguous and incomplete, of moral and metaphysical realism. An openness to the truth and the courageous and responsible resistance to theoretical or ideological lies are, Havel said, evidence that Being and man are not simply subject to manipulation. That most human beings can live well, even better, in light of the truth about themselves is the only thought that can shore up resistance to today's destructive mixture of libertarianism and technology, both of which are legacies of the Declaration wrongly understood.[13]

This interpretation of the Declaration is to some extent a criticism of the Declaration and America as they actually are. But obviously even the best interpretations of the Declaration have been selective in their use of evidence and criticism. The revival of the Lockean interpretation, best presented in the work of Michael Zuckert, is critical of the communitarian and Christian strands of American thought in the eighteenth century and today, as well as of understandings of rights that are not strictly Lockean. Lincoln's egalitarian interpretation is an implicit criticism of the selfishness of the founding Lockeanism, of men who knew that slavery was wrong but were not devoted enough to doing everything they could to eradicate it.[14] John Courtney Murray, the best proponent of the natural law interpretation of the Declaration, knew that he was following Lincoln's example of using American history and founding thought creatively in dealing with the crisis of his time.[15] At all times in our history, the Declaration has been the preeminent vehicle for hashing out the places of philosophy, religion, politics, and personal interests in America's self-understanding. That argument cannot come to an unambiguous end; it will remain far from self-evident what exactly Americans mean by equality, liberty, and happiness.

In this chapter I want to prepare the way for a natural law interpretation of the Declaration in three stages. First, I will show that using Jefferson's thought as the guide to the Declaration leads us too easily to the easygoing pragmatism of Richard Rorty, which is incapable of taking either truth or virtue seriously. Second, I will explain why even the more sober view of most of the leading founders that religion is an indispensable support for liberty and happiness is inadequate, for it too does not take seriously religious truth. Finally, I will begin to show the proper place of religion in the American view of liberty with the assistance of Christopher Lasch and Alexis de Tocqueville.

Jefferson and Rorty

Jefferson, in his later letters, saw the insufficiency of the doctrine of rights. He knew that it was based on the view that human beings are free by nature to pursue security and happiness, but never really to achieve it. So

Jefferson's most considered personal view was not Lockean, but Epicurean. Human beings, he believed, can achieve security and happiness by
employing reason to free themselves from hope and fear. The purpose of
reason, most fundamentally, is to reveal the ineradicable limits of being a
self-conscious mortal, and it is with the serene acceptance of that truth
that it is possible to live a life that is both rational and happy. This philosophic life, Jefferson thought, is for the rare few, and it is intrinsically
selfish.[16] But, Jefferson also believed that human beings are fitted by
nature, if not by reason, for society, and so they are given by nature a
moral sense or instinct that guides them to serve others. We are not naturally isolated individuals but social beings, and when doing our social
duties we not only pursue happiness but are happy.

The classical Epicureans thought that most human beings needed
the security that comes with belief in providential gods. But Jefferson
thought that the gods could be cast aside. He thought that most human
beings could be satisfied with the teaching of the secularized Jesus, while
not being particularly concerned one way or another with God or the
good. Jefferson also relied on utilitarian science or technology to occupy
Americans' thought and time and divert them from existential concerns.

Jefferson, the Epicurean, agrees with the Christian Pascal that the
Lockean pursuit of security is not rational, since it depends on being
diverted from the truth about the limitations of all human effort.[17] The
single-minded pursuit of security and comfort, as Tocqueville explains in
Democracy in America (*DA*), becomes a way of minimizing the unhappiness
human beings experience in light of that truth. Philosophy and science,
actively opposing idleness and leisure, become more an escape from, rather
than a way of pursuing, the truth. But American restlessness, the relentless pursuit and purchase of diversions, is itself uncomfortable and anxious (*DA*, vol. 2, pt. 2, ch. 13). So more radical efforts than Jefferson's or
Locke's are required to effectively subordinate truth to comfort.

Today's most influential professor of philosophy, Richard Rorty, is nothing but a pragmatist; he is in no way an Epicurean.[18] Human beings, according to Rorty, need not and cannot use reason to live beyond hope and fear. But they need not be concerned with death, for death can be talked in and out of existence like every other human experience. Not reason but imagination and sentiment can conquer the obsessions of existentialism. Hope need not disappear; it can be banalized or focused on modest goals human beings can really achieve. Perhaps the most substantial difference between Rorty and Jefferson is that Rorty does not exempt the few, the philosophers, from the pragmatic view of the truth. To do so would be, as Jefferson admits, selfish or parasitical, and Rorty views the Socratic view of truth as just another ungrounded fantasy.[19] The ironist, Rorty would say, must be ironic about his irony, given that he can show neither its utility nor its truth.

Jefferson and Rorty agree that theology and metaphysics can largely if not completely be purged from American experience. And both want to make the great majority of human beings more banal for their own and society's good. They aim to free human beings from the repressive cruelty of the spiritual imagination for whatever the individual deems happiness to be. Religious belief, in their view, must be no more than a harmless private fantasy and not a project to tyrannize over others. Rorty attempts to manipulate feelings or sentiments to universalize the Epicurean's tranquil indifference to the truth. His linguistic therapy attempts to improve upon the words of Jesus by bringing cruelty to an end. Truth must be subordinated to comfort, because most or all human beings cannot be expected to take comfort in the truth. The success of Lockean science or technology must be supplemented with Rorty's therapy for it to achieve its goal of bringing fear and anxiety to an end.

Even if we ignore Jefferson's Epicureanism, we can still say that a wholly Lockean understanding of the Declaration culminates in a denial of the real limits to human liberty and so undermines limited government. As Zuckert observes, Lockean politics is progressivist.[20] The abstract individual moves indefinitely away from nature by perfecting his various inventions. For Locke, the ability to invent or recreate oneself through abstraction is the point of human freedom and distinctiveness. So Zuckert follows Locke by writing about the self-constituting self and by dismissing any idea of natural limits to human liberty as "biologism."[21] A genuinely Lockean history of America as described by Zuckert would be similar to the Hegelian history of America described by Rorty.[22]

Jefferson himself at times embraced limits to political reform based on the Declaration by adopting a spirited localism and by speaking (but never acting) against racially based slavery. But the Lockean-Jeffersonian Zuckert understands the Fourteenth Amendment as completing the Constitution by directing the national government to compel the states to abide by the principles of the Declaration.[23] And on that foundation the reconstruction of American life has become progressively more complete. Americans, over time, have accepted more fully the self-understanding of the abstract individual. The government has implemented more fully the Constitution's radical individualism—its antiracism, antisexism, anticlassism, and its silence on, or hostility toward, religion. American lives have become more free and uprooted, more democratic and atomistic. Americans have come closer to understanding all human endeavors through the language of rights. But in becoming more consistently pro-choice, they have actually found it progressively more difficult to choose against the reigning institutions and ideas. The spheres in which we can choose against rights on behalf of love and pride, not to mention truth, have shrunk. Carey McWilliams observes that the dominant American ideology—the lie that we are merely abstract or self-created individuals— "pursues Americans into the most private places and to the very foundation of the self."[24]

Extending the domain of choice to unprecedented places has made Americans more anxious and self-obsessed, and so they also are more in need of Rorty's death- or self-denying therapy. As they have become more individualistic, they have become more open to the thought that the individual, the "I," is an illusion.[25] Rorty may have hit on what a self-constituting self most wants to do: deconstruct itself as a cruel illusion. The completion of individualism or free self-invention is the imaginative creation of the capacity to believe anything about oneself that leads to comfort. The self does not want to be afraid or to be cruel or to die, and those things are all consequences of taking the truth seriously. The language of rights culminates in the right to therapy, to self-esteem through self-denial. If chemicals and computers are added to Rorty's politically correct words, as now seems likely, this peculiar form of self-denial may actually become self-destruction.

Functional Traditionalism

Most leading American thinkers, even Rorty, have seen the need to use religious devotion to limit the drift of individualism toward self-obsession. Rorty promotes devotion to a progressivist civil theology, and in doing so he thinks, with good reason, that he continues an American tradition that began with Whitman and Lincoln.[26] But the leading founders were minimalists when it came to politicizing religious devotion, because they saw the resulting enthusiasm as threatening the limits of constitutional government. Jefferson almost managed to avoid enthusiasm for civil religion altogether.

From a Christian or natural law perspective, the leading founders were right not to reduce religion to a means of ideological indoctrination. They all recognized to some extent or another that the responsible exercise of rights depends on the perpetuation of some illiberal or non–rights-based institutions and practices. As Thomas West shows, they did not regard their support for the traditional, "patriarchal" family, including severe laws restricting divorce and extramarital sex, as incompatible with their devotion to the protection of individual rights. Children had to be raised well to use their freedom well, and women and children are more secure and men are more responsible when constrained by a settled family structure. The leading founders would have regarded our libertarian views concerning women's liberation and divorce as most unrealistic and so as destructive of liberty. They knew the difference between the abstract individual of Lockean theory and real human persons. But their judgment concerning illiberal means was made on liberal grounds. Traditional practices and beliefs are not to be valued for their own sake, and unnecessary rights-denying repression is also to be eliminated. American law was liberalized considerably, West also shows, as a result of the American revolution. As far as is possible, the liberated individual is to become reality.[27]

The founding view that "traditionalism," a term that incorporates and degrades religion, can be justified as "functional" for liberalism remains alive today. Now it seems to have become a conservative or neoconservative view, or at least a "new" and unexpected form of liberalism. Nobody defends functional traditionalism with more comprehensiveness or candor today than the liberal William Galston. He is candid enough, in fact, both to make clear his liberal partisanship and to show its human limits.[28]

Galston distinguishes functional traditionalism from "intrinsic traditionalism," which affirms certain beliefs and practices because they are intrinsically good as part of divine law. The great merit of Galston's portrayal of the functional traditionalist is that he gives the benefit of the doubt to tradition-based public policy. All that he requires, as a liberal, is a plausible connection between the policy and the responsible exercise of personal liberty. But he remains particularly wary of policies permeating all traditional institutions that perpetuate the hierarchies of racism, sexism, classism, or even heterosexism. He, in fact, has a hard time restraining his doubt, his democratic skepticism.[29]

Divorce among married couples with children, Galston concludes, can be discouraged, while heterosexual two-parent families should be encouraged in view of their record in raising children. But there is no rational basis for keeping childless couples from getting divorced, and none for keeping gay couples from getting married, although they can be discouraged or perhaps prohibited from adopting children. Galston does not emphasize that these distinctions are less traditionalist than Lockean. God and nature intend, Locke says, for marriages to last until children reach maturity. Then the contract can be terminated pretty much at will.

God, of course, is not recorded as having said any such thing. And Locke's functionalist impiety did not hold up over time. Galston admits that the main cause of the growth of divorce and parental irresponsibility in general is that choice and contract have largely replaced the "sacramental" understanding of marriage. The sacramental view, of course, is intrinsic, not functional, and Galston shows us no way of restoring it given the dysfunctionality of its disappearance. The "irreversible, constitutive commitment" required for most good marriages cannot be incorporated into the liberal or rights-oriented view of the world. In the latter, marriage must be understood to exist, like government, for the security and happiness of the individual.[30]

Galston agrees with his teacher, Allan Bloom, that both easy divorce and women's liberation impede the ability of children to love, trust, and learn. But neither would be in favor of restoring the bygone world of religious authority that constrained individuality by subordinating women and by chaining them, and men, to children in the name of love for one another and God. We can admire Tocqueville's description of the superiority of American women, whom he portrays as wisely sacrificing their claims for justice to perpetuate familial love in a democratic time. But Tocqueville knew that women could justly assert their rights at any time, and that eventually they would (DA, vol. 2, pt. 3, chs. 8–12). The thinking associated with functional traditionalism culminates in a whiny,

ambivalent, and ironic nostalgia for what has been lost. It lacks the commitment or somewhat illiberal understanding of the human good required to formulate a plausible program for recovery. Functional traditionalists cannot even formulate a rhetoric for the restoration of what
they really regard as a necessary illusion.

Galston's ambivalence is clear in his praise for both functional traditionalism and the "informal gravitational influence liberalism has on
both individuals and institutions." His example of that influence is the
American Catholic bishops' resistance to Rome. Their "liberal political
culture" leads them to challenge all forms of authority.[31] But the application of liberal skepticism to theological and ecclesiastical questions leads
the church to be less of a bastion against divorce and for the family. What
would be most functional, in Galston's eyes, is a church that is anti-
divorce but fairly permissive on abortion and homosexuality and has an
egalitarian view of the sexes. But if the church were to cave in selectively to
liberalism on such fundamental questions, then surely it would lose its
teaching authority. And the church presents its teaching on abortion,
homosexuality, and so forth, as rooted not just in the Bible and revelation but in reason as well. Its rational understanding of what human
beings are is as antiliberal as its interpretation of divine law.

Galston clearly sees that the definition of man as the being with
rights is both empirically incorrect and socially destructive. He acknowledges that "cultural change" is the most important factor in "civic decline," the decline of responsible liberalism in America. He praises Alan
Ehrenhalt's documentation of that decline in Chicago.[32] But he does not
take seriously enough Ehrenhalt's case for communal authority.[33] The
"social capital" required to produce responsible individuals depends upon
a stable community or neighborhood. And a community is held together
by respect, obedience, fidelity, sacrifice, and restraint, virtues that flow
from persons and institutions with genuine authority. Responsible liberalism depends on the cultivation of illiberal virtues, and central to that

cultivation is the church. The church, to perform its function, has to command an uncompromising belief in its own moral authority. In Ehrenhalt's account, people in the Chicago communities he surveys used to believe that the centers of life were the family, the neighborhood, and the church, and that political freedom is good because it allows them to submit to transpolitical communal authority.

Because ours is a free country, it was always possible for individuals too stifled by such authority to escape, and the countervailing forces of liberal principles and the free market stood in tension with the authority of the church and parents. Ehrenhalt's story is about the gradual victory of those individualizing or atomizing forces, and an important step in the decline of authority is the churches' surrender of their vigilant spirit of moral resistance. He criticizes today's communitarians for believing that the love or warmth of community can be recaptured without the common authority and discipline that liberals view as repressive. Unlike most functionalist traditionalists, Ehrenhalt wonders whether the deficiency of liberalism is its elitism. The story of liberal progress is typically told by the malcontent who can remember nothing good about, say, nun-run parochial schools. But everyone knows that those schools prepared most children for life as parents, citizens, and parishioners (and the liberal critics for their lives as writers) far better than most schools do now.

There is always something unrealistic about the liberal memory; the being with rights characteristically does not acknowledge his debts to others and to communities. And so his understanding of what a human being is is also bound to be unrealistic. Galston contends that if the sociologist Alan Wolfe is right and libertarian moral permissiveness has now become the doctrine of the middle class, then America is in the midst of an unprecedented social experiment that is bound to fail as soon as peace and prosperity do. But, responsible liberal that he is, Galston finds that virtually none of his fellow liberals are "prepared to accept restraints on choice and entitlement to create a stronger society that can endure."[34] The liberal individual has so abstracted himself from his social context that he really believes he can do without it.

Finding today's liberals short on love and gratitude, Galston appeals to their pride, their elitism. For the leading founders, he writes, a fundamental purpose of liberalism was that it protects the free-thinking few, the followers of Socrates (or Epicurus), from the moralistic or religious many. Most people will always be too afraid or too dumb to be free, and the naïve mistake of contemporary liberal theory is to treat all Americans as if they could live like Socrates. Galston asks liberals to remember they are and will always be more free than most people, the democrats. But they, the few, must humor the morality of the many, or else they will suffer the fate of Socrates. Following the example of the leading founders, particularly George Washington, they should use religious or traditional language in a deceptive way, while always remembering that it contributes nothing to the truth of liberal arguments. The few can rule the many in a democracy only by being clever and making concessions to popular sensibilities.[35]

For your own good, Galston in essence says to the liberal elite, watch what you say. But this good advice concedes too much to liberal pretensions to be effective. It allows liberals to believe they are more or less completely right on the big questions, and it does not give them enough reason to be afraid. Even if they lose some elections, liberals still dominate the media and the universities, and the American Constitution is much better than the Athenian Assembly when it comes to protecting rights. But most importantly, the elitism of functionalist traditionalism misconceives the religious objection to American liberalism by trivializing it.

Secular Humanism vs. Orthodoxy

Galston acknowledges that liberalism does not so much weaken as derange American religion. The churches are no longer regarded as a normal and constitutive part of the American moral community, as they were in Tocqueville's day or even in the Chicago of Mayor Daley. So they feel out of place and under assault. Galston is especially concerned with the growth of the fundamentalist Religious Right, whose angry reaction to the imperial excesses of liberalism he believes now threatens the very idea of religious toleration. In fact, he claims that one reason he remains a liberal Democrat is that he fears the Religious Right more than the permissive Left. But the truth is that the Religious Right, with every passing day, is becoming a more oppressed minority. As I write these words, it is impossible honestly to maintain that the main danger to liberty in America comes from too much religiously inspired political activism. What might have been true in seventeenth-century Europe, or even at the time of the founding, is clearly not true now. Tocqueville guides us better than the *Federalist*; the main malady of liberalism's individualistic progress is its culmination in apathy and the atrophy of the social passions of love and pride.

The political theorist Jeremy Rabkin denies that American political life in recent years should be described as a culture war in which the moral conservatives have largely lost to the moral libertarians. That pessimistic view, he argues, blinds conservatives to the limited but real victories they won in the 1990s, with the Supreme Court in *Planned Parenthood v. Casey* allowing limited room for anti-abortion legislation and Clinton co-opting some of the conservative agenda concerning families and faith. Besides, withdrawal from political life, as some conservatives have advocated, is just plain un-American. Our history is full of political movements animated by religious fervor, and those movements have often succeeded. Rabkin argues that no good can come from the opinion that our nation has become so morally and politically rotten that nothing can be done in public life to improve it. But Rabkin's chastisement of religious believers seems motivated more by political than by religious reasons. He knows that American conservatism is done for if the Religious Right is not an active part of the conservative coalition.[36]

Two conservative Catholics, Gary D. Glenn and John Stack, respond that there has always been some tension between the requirements of America's modern or liberal political life and Catholic belief. But that tension was livable for Catholics as long as the claims of government over American lives were modest and political life itself was really not wholly liberal. According to Glenn and Stack, however, the Supreme Court has since 1940 imposed a more comprehensive "civil liberties" regime on America, and both the Court and liberal theorists now hold that Catholics are expected to abandon in public life their religious beliefs when they conflict with the established principles of this new, more comprehensively liberal, regime. If it is true that Catholics must deny what they really believe to be true about religion and morality, about the family, sexual morality, and abortion, in order to participate in public life (as Mario Cuomo famously said), then they should withdraw from it to save their souls. Catholics today, say Glenn and Stack, must think of themselves as political and cultural outsiders in America, and they must regard themselves as living in a moral and political order increasingly hostile to what their Church teaches to be true.[37]

America's leading sociologist of religion, James Davison Hunter, is famous for both coining the term "culture war" and for not taking a stand in that war. But in his most recent work, *The Death of Character: Moral Education in an Age Without Good or Evil*, Hunter sides with cultural conservatives against the mainstream of contemporary American education, even religious education. He notes that there has been a conservative political backlash against the therapeutic orientation of moral education in the schools. Conservatives typically criticize this approach, which emphasizes self-expression and values clarification over self-restraint and moral truth. But, says Hunter, the problem is that the "neoclassical" (think William Bennett) and communitarian programs tend to be little more than the abstract affirmation of traditional moral values intertwined with the same old therapeutic techniques. The process of implementation dilutes the moral intention almost beyond recognition.

Hunter shows that the easygoing, antiauthoritarian premises of secular psychology are omnipresent in our educational institutions, and even the wills of conservative political leaders are too weak—they do not want to be accused of not being inclusive—to take the extreme measures required to dislodge the experts. The experts' prattling about democratizing all of society—making even children full participants in communal decision-making—triumphs over efforts to arouse the majority on behalf of character formation. And the most important part of the story is the diffusion of academic psychology into popular culture. Calculation about one's own emotional well-being has, to an amazing and unprecedented extent, become the language of moral discourse among otherwise ordinary Americans.[38]

The same problem exists even in the Sunday School educational efforts of evangelical Protestant churches. These Protestants often claim that therapeutic secular psychology is value-neutral, and that therefore its insights and language can be employed in the service of biblical morality. But Hunter's reading of leading Evangelical authors like James Dobson shows that the therapeutic language has, in fact, compromised biblical morality. The language of "self-esteem" and personal "acceptance," more than virtuous obedience to God's law, frames the presentation of biblical moral standards, and it is often hard to distinguish between the advice of Evangelical ministers and that of secular family therapists.[39]

Traditional or orthodox Catholics and Jews know, of course, that Protestants characteristically lack an intellectual tradition of moral realism to defend revealed morality against moral individualism. Certainly the best Catholic and Jewish culturally conservative thought is better rooted in theological and philosophical tradition and less cloying than their Protestant equivalents. Yet Hunter does overstate some of the differences between today's relatively orthodox Catholics and Protestants. C. S. Lewis, among the most anti-therapeutic of writers, is loved by them

both, and Catholic and Jewish moral teaching at the level of the particular parish or synagogue is itself also often diluted and distorted by the
language of therapeutic expertise. Most importantly, the time and attention lavished by Evangelical parents on their children cannot really be
accounted for in therapeutic terms. Hunter is surely right to conclude
that the churches, in their moral teaching, provide surprisingly little support for a character-based cultural conservatism, but he finally confesses
that perhaps what matters most is their practice.

Virtue cannot be detached from the practices—forms of habituation—and beliefs of a particular, religiously based way of life, the way of
life Ehrenhalt found among working-class ethnic Catholics in the 1950s.
That way of life, Hunter explains, integrates the efforts of parents, teachers, ministers of religion, and other communal institutions. All adults are
concerned in more or less the same way with the rearing of children, and
"intellectual and moral virtues are not only naturally interwoven in a
distinctive moral ethos but embedded within" the community's structure.[40] The crisis of character is most of all rooted in the scarcity of that
sort of community in America today. It is difficult, writes Hunter, and
maybe impossible, to think of another time or place "where the individual has been so disconnected, both socially and metaphysically, from
stable communities—spectacularly free to determine one's fate, to be sure,
yet at the same time, restless and with few if any bearings for the journey."[41]

The shallowness and self-indulgence of our moral education mirrors
the absence of genuine moral culture in America. Our talk about inclu-
siveness and diversity barely masks our pathetic inability to think and
argue about the content of character. Genuine diversity, the result of a
variety of religiously based moral communities, actually scares us, and
our experts are devoted to its eradication. But some such communities
do still exist, and Hunter slights the extent to which they are still being
formed by serious believers. Many Evangelical communities, for example,
now aim quite consciously to shape the lives of their members in a coun-

tercultural way, and the explosive growth of the homeschooling movement is also directed by a truthful concern with the character of children.

Today's liberals are usually not willing to learn the requirements for the formation of character and the effective cultivation of virtue from these seriously religious Americans. Today, membership in a disciplined, pious, transpolitical religious community is nothing if not a countercultural act. The vigilance of these communities must be thorough, and they cannot help but seem somewhat fanatical. The dominant liberal theorists, Rorty and John Rawls, feel confident that liberal society can now dismiss them as nuts. But antiliberal animus is not found only among fundamentalists or other unsophisticated believers in biblical inerrancy. It must be felt by anyone who believes in the biblical God and who believes that people cannot live well outside the authority of religious community. Anger is directed not only against the elite but perhaps more ominously against the elite-compromised majority, against a people deformed by the language of therapeutic liberalism.

Most Americans, if Wolfe and Hunter are right, have reduced religion to a morally undemanding source of comfort.[42] They want to be called virtuous children of God in order to enhance their self-esteem, but they don't want their lives limited or directed in any harsh or demanding way. They want to feel at home without feeling bound by the responsibilities of creature, father, or citizen.[43] Most Americans agree with the liberals that religion exists to be of service to, or to provide therapy for, the being with rights. Most "mainstream" Protestants and a large number of Catholics and Jews view themselves as religious progressives. That is, they are Kantians, believing that the God of the Bible must be judged according to our free and rational understanding of rights. In this view, theology and religious community are primarily vehicles for the pursuit of the latest social justice project, and so the recently fashionable theology of liberation has been displaced by the more libertarian or individualistic feminist and gay theologies.

Progressive or liberal theology seems functional only to those who believe that Americans are not yet liberated enough, that the problems of democracy can be solved with more democracy. But it is not functional for those who attend church because they want to know and love God and are anxious and lonely in the face of death. The general rule, we now know, is that the more liberal or progressive a church becomes, the more members it loses. It is quite understandable that if their church implies that the Bible consists of nothing but symbols to be appropriated by the spirit of liberalism, then most believers will say the hell with it. Therefore, most Americans who define themselves as members of religious communities do not define themselves as progressives.

Progressive theology is opposed not so much by fundamentalism as by orthodoxy, by those who believe that there is a God to be known, loved, and obeyed, and that this truth is to be shared by human beings in common.[44] Orthodoxy takes on a variety of forms among Protestants, Catholics, Mormons, and Jews, all of which have tended to divide into progressive and orthodox factions. Some orthodox thought (such as that found in the journal *First Things*) is as erudite as any form of secular liberalism today, and studies show that the average orthodox American is better educated than the average secularist.[45] The orthodox believer has a point of view with which to oppose the culture's dominant materialism and relativism, and he often believes that the development of liberalism has shown that the two human alternatives are orthodox belief and moral nihilism.

Orthodox belief in America today is not primarily a remnant of decaying traditionalism. Most such believers have chosen or converted to a way of life usually not shared with equivalent intensity by their fathers. They may turn to tradition because they find life without it dysfunctional, but they also connect their tradition with what they view as true regarding doctrine, human beings, and their relationship with God. Some have said that we are probably nearing the end of what we have largely failed to perceive as another Great Awakening, a powerful spiritual reaction against the soul-deadening excesses of liberalism.[46] Such periodic revivals, rooted in part in the Christian disdain for routine on behalf of the spirit, have made the process of secularization unpredictable in America. According to Tocqueville, they are evidence that human beings, by nature, have religious longings that can only be distorted, not destroyed (*DA*, vol. 2, pt. 2, ch. 12).[47] The current Great Awakening is more orthodox and more opposed to spiritual subjectivism than its predecessors; it is a reaction against the "mainstream" theological tendency to replace dogma and what the Bible actually says with subjective emotionality. Even the Southern Baptists are moving toward doctrinal conformity and away from their own tradition of individualism. Led by a great Pope, the Catholic establishment is joining the Baptists in becoming less democratic, and young Catholics, especially younger Catholic priests, certainly seem to have become more orthodox.

Orthodox believers are not reliable political conservatives. They have little use for either country-club Republicans or therapeutic Democrats, and especially today they often tend to put little hope in political reform. They sometimes ally with libertarians against big government, since their experience has typically been that wherever government goes, God and moral responsibility disappear. And they see, with Hunter, no way to reform our public institutions, particularly our schools.[48] Their political aim is to protect the freedom of churches and parents to educate children and exercise authority. But they are further than anyone from the nerve of libertarian morality. Politically and intellectually, they face the dominant culture as dissidents, seeing in the nation's pro-choice agenda a brutality toward women and children, toward the weak and vulnerable, to which most Americans are blind. They regard the progressive view that life gets more moral and easier as it gets more rights-oriented and individualistic as a lie. In the South, I have discovered, their heroes are often Patrick Henry, Stonewall Jackson, and Aleksandr Solzhenitsyn. They sometimes ask whether the American regime—increasingly shaped by pro-choice judicial imperialism—is legitimate, whether it any longer deserves their loyalty.

The intrinsic morality of the orthodox is also functional. They lead disciplined, meaningful, family-oriented lives, and studies show that, as a result, their lives are healthier and happier than those of most Americans.[49] My experience with the home-schooled is that they are especially well prepared in every way for higher education. And the best orthodox colleges, such as Thomas Aquinas College in California, are among the firmest supporters of liberal education against political correctness and the imperatives of technical specialization. But liberalism is only ambiguously functional for the orthodox. It is not functional because the America Tocqueville describes is not theirs: There is no longer a commonly accepted religious morality from which even the free thinkers dare not dissent in public. President Clinton, to be sure, still had to mouth Christian words, but he supported precious little of orthodox Christian morality. The contempt the orthodox have for Clinton they also tend to have for the America that tolerated him. Most dysfunctional is the open contempt serious believers and liberals now have for each other. Not only do they think each other immoral, they think each other blind to the most basic facts of life.

Both the liberals and the orthodox believe that human beings can only live well in light of the truth, but today they deny they have much to learn from each other about what that truth is. Neither the orthodox nor the liberals regard policy concerning abortion, gay rights, or divorce as subject to determination by a national argument according to the principles of the Declaration rightly understood. Nor do they regard them as subject to prudential compromise because both sides of the argument contain some truth. They need, but are very far from, the common meeting ground of natural law. They need a realistic consideration of the nature of the whole human person.

Most Americans are confused and conflicted enough to stand somewhere between the orthodox and the liberals. They typically think of themselves as liberated individuals, but they also typically regard the family and church as intrinsically good, as what makes life most worth living. They complain about the absence of common decency and character, but they refuse to accept constraints on their personal freedom. They want to be both pro-life and pro-choice.[50] They tend to mouth liberal or therapeutic platitudes more than ever, but they do not really often experience them as true. As Allan Bloom notes, what the therapist tells the children of divorce does not really calm the chaotic anger in their souls.[51] The orthodox are right to say that liberals have worked, with some success, to deprive Americans of words that correspond to their real longings, but they are wrong to say (as some do) that the words they need can only be found in the Bible. Both the liberals and the orthodox underestimate how much human beings can really know about their condition by nature, but the liberals in particular underestimate how reasonable the psychological understanding of the religious really is. The liberals, in the name of reason, should think about what the orthodox know about the social and religious nature of man.

Religious Truth

A characteristic failing of liberal thinkers, from the leading founders until today, is their condescending approach to religion. They usually regard it as a sign of human weakness, something to be humored or, better, overcome. Perhaps the finest opponent of this sort of elitism in our time was Christopher Lasch, a critic of the abstract individual's capture by therapy, of the replacement of psychoanalysis—which was, in his mind, the last moment of the Socratic tradition—with psychotherapy. One reason I rely on Lasch here is that he did not think or write from a specifically religious perspective. He was neither an orthodox believer nor a functional traditionalist. He was only concerned with what he knew to be true about the way human beings should live.

Lasch sees today's liberal elite's preference for an abstract reality created by mental labor as itself rooted in weakness, a pitiful revolt against moral realism or the morally demanding life required of all conscious beings who know they are going to die. The members of that elite believe they have freed themselves through thought from the need for religion. But their effort to create an alternative reality is really a denial of the goodness of the experiences of real, particular men and women. Lasch's moral populism, his preference for those who primarily do manual over those who primarily do mental labor, reflects his choice for a real man living a real, moral life with the love and earned respect of others over the regressive self-denial of the man seceding from a common human reality to live immersed in a self- or class-created fantasy.[52]

Lasch complains that in modern liberal writing religion is "consistently treated as a source of intellectual and emotional security, and not as a challenge to complacency and pride."[53] And so we proudly believe that believers languish in the thrall of monkish ignorance and superstition. Religion, in fact, may allow human beings to speculate more clearly about human purpose and even experience more deeply the temptation of despair. Is faith really a more unreasonable response to existentialism than pragmatism? It has certainly been more friendly to contemplation and to liberal education, in America and elsewhere.

Lasch learned from William James that "the deepest variety of religious faith . . . always, in every age, arises out of a background of despair. Religious faith asserts the goodness of being in the face of suffering and evil."[54] Authentic religion, for Lasch, is not rooted in the effort to "clothe human purposes with a spurious air of sanctity," but in "a disinterested love of Being in general," which is why he prefers "an honest atheist . . . to a culture Christian."[55] Liberals tend to begin by denying the necessary existence of suffering for human beings or the reality of evil. Rebuffed by both, they end up denying that human life as we actually experience it, and so Being itself, is good. As a rebel against the hard responsibilities and suffering associated with birth and death, the liberal cannot help but end up being pro-choice on even birth and death, advocating both abortion and euthanasia. The assertion that we can choose against the goodness of human life as such barely masks despair over the character of Being, about what we are given and on what we must depend.

"Alienation," Lasch adds, "is the normal condition of human existence. Rebellion against God is the natural reaction to the discovery that the world was not made for our own personal convenience."[56] Liberals, succumbing to a natural human weakness, work to eradicate human alienation from the world. They forget that alienation is the price to be paid for being human, the precondition for the human goods we actually experience. The truth is that we should accept gratefully our partial alienation or separation from each other, the world, and God. We should be grateful for being compelled to live in a morally demanding and invigorating way, for not being fully at home in this world.

At the very heart of the modern doctrine of autonomy, the American Thomist Marion Montgomery notices, is the denial of our gifts, our givenness, of what is mysteriously beyond our control but nonetheless good for us. The truth is that "the very gifts which make us particular also define finitudes in us. Without the limit of gifts, we would not be at all."[57] The denial of God through human overcoming is finally the denial that anything at all need or should remain mysterious, the belief that neither thought nor action need depend on what is beyond our comprehension and control. It is a denial of the necessary conditions of our own being. It is misanthropic.

It is a mistake to view religion as a childish form of dependence, the conjuring up of an illusory father figure. The orthodox, in fact, oppose those who childishly deny our dependence, our ineradicable and beneficial limitations. The fundamental human experience, as Flannery O'Connor says, is of limitation. So Lasch concludes that our proud, elitist, individualistic dismissal of the authority of religion is a sign that "the normal rebellion *against* dependence," against the truth, "is more pervasive than it used to be."[58] That rebellion gains strength from our amazing technological mastery of nature, but we have not freed ourselves so far from love and death. If Solzhenitsyn is right, our rebellious self-centeredness has made us more lonely and death-haunted than ever before.[59] But our rebellion against God and religion has deprived us of the language to tell the truth to ourselves about, and to live well with, our fundamental experiences.

In the face of this misery, the Jeffersonian view that we are free to pursue happiness has perversely and irrationally evolved to the point that we now think we have the right to be happy. We are now allowed, even encouraged, to break all ties that bind us to each other and God if we are no longer happy with them. Of course, we cannot be happy with them for long if we view them in terms of rights, and so all human relationships are threatened as never before. Beings that calculate incessantly about how to be happy rarely are; even the Lockean-Jeffersonian view is that human beings were born to pursue happiness, not to achieve it.

Human beings have been given the responsibility to live morally in light of what they really know about human purpose and limitations. Human happiness, not as a right but rather as a somewhat inexplicable gift, comes from doing what we must do in the name of courage, love, and truth. We have been given the capability of affirming the goodness of our being in the face of suffering and evil, and happiness, contrary to both Jefferson's Epicurean and Jefferson's Jesus, is not incompatible with our duties to others and what we really know. In fact it most often comes from fulfilling them.

Pride

Revealed religion, especially, presents the evidence needed to puncture human pride. It is always aimed against the pretensions of a liberated elite. But Lasch also emphasizes that pride is to some extent justified. There is an inevitable disproportion between our aspirations and our accomplishments, but we can be proud of our accomplishments nonetheless. And real men know they are worthy to give and receive earned respect.[60] In the American case, religion, perhaps especially Christianity, actually supports both humility and magnanimity. The Lockean doctrine of rights is based on the premise that our rational freedom is enslaved to our bodily needs. Its most visible achievement, technology, promises and delivers bodily comfort and security. In principle, of course, it also delivers unprecedented leisure, but we too are busy, too much in pursuit of diversions, really to use that leisure well. The extreme or unrealistic pride of the abstract individual is enveloped by the unrealistic humility of the view that human beings are nothing but bodies in motion, or just an extremely clever species of animal. Democrats, Tocqueville observes, are characteristically too skeptical of spiritual pretensions really to have an appropriately elevated opinion of themselves and their possibilities. The effectual truth of the liberal effort to use that skepticism to free society from religion contributes, in the long term, to human brutalization (*DA*, vol. 2, pt. 2, ch. 15–17).

Tocqueville actually calls Christianity America's most precious inheritance from aristocratic times, when men had a greater pride and confidence in their capabilities as individuals. He agrees with Nietzsche that Christianity is Platonism for the people, but he gives that thought a very positive spin. The Platonists or Socratics have always opposed the materialists with their doctrine of the immortality of the soul. That belief can cause apolitical and apathetic otherworldliness, and the modern thinkers were right to oppose its excesses by emphasizing the appropriateness of material pursuits. But they went too far. Without the belief that they somehow transcend time, human beings will not produce enduring accomplishments. What aristocrats built and wrote was intended to persist, and so every detail was constructed with the greatest care. Today all human activity suffers from the thought that nothing human endures, and so nothing is worthy of our best efforts (*DA*, vol. 2, pt. 2, ch. 15). We tend to be present-minded pragmatists, immersed in working for immediate comfort, or anxious existentialists, too aware of our contingency and the futility of all we do. Without the help of religion, we think so little of ourselves that we say we neither long for nor have access to immortality. But what we say contradicts what we experience; our deeper thought is that the longing remains but its satisfaction is impossible (*DA*, vol. 2, pt. 2, chs. 12–13).

Tocqueville's deepest personal shortcoming is that he agreed with this democratic or modern philosophic perception that our fundamental experience of the truth is that it is terrible, that religion, even at its best, is a proud illusion. He longed to but could not affirm the goodness of being, and he knew that his devotion to political liberty was partly a diversion from what he really knew. And so his defense of pride was never wholly free from despair. But his candid analysis of his own troubled soul allowed him to see the depths of the divided soul in America.[61] Americans, in effect, live six days of the week as if nature and God were hostile to human existence, and they must work incessantly to fend them off. But on the seventh day, they rest, believing that God provides, the soul is immortal, and all is well with the world. Tocqueville affirms those contradictory impulses as a reflection of the mixed and elusive character of human liberty. And he believes that without that day of rest, the day of leisurely contemplation of the truth about God, Being, and the soul, Americans would find their human liberty unendurable. At least they had some awareness, one day a week, that being human is good and that moral virtue is not just useful but the source of human happiness. The churches should never have surrendered Sunday (*DA*, vol. 2, pt. 2, ch. 15)!

American clergy, Tocqueville observes, can only limit the excesses of materialism. They will lose their influence if they are too obviously unfriendly to democratic pretensions. He recommends that the orthodox not despair over democratic politics and culture, but he also praises the liberal Americans he knows for exempting common religious morality from democratic skepticism. He knows that orthodox extremism would be a likely human response to moral secularism. Americans bragged that religious dogma was useful for political liberty, but he notices that they also actually longed to love God and were anxious in the face of death. Tocqueville criticizes American clergy for unnecessarily connecting religion too closely to this world. What they say must come from a perspective outside democracy, and insofar as they can they must exercise undemocratic authority over their people (*DA*, vol. 1, pt. 2, ch. 9; vol. 2, pt. 1, chs. 2, 5–7; vol. 2, pt. 2, chs. 9 and 12).

Religion can serve human liberty in democratic times by challenging, most prudently, democracy's most cherished dogmas. The central democratic judgment is in favor of individualism: It is better to succumb to apathetic individualism or immersion in private fantasies than to be moved by the social passions, pride and love, because they make us miserable more than anything else (*DA*, vol. 2, pt. 2, ch. 3). Liberated thought culminates in Rorty's belief that we should be free from the misery of being human, while religion affirms the thought that it is better to live in truth and love despite the accompanying misery. The abstract, rights-obsessed individual is created by abstracting from love and pride, from the natural gifts that sustain individuality and more than compensate for human misery.

Tocqueville favored a greater separation of church and state than actually exists in America today. The fundamental reason for that separation is to protect religion from democracy, from skepticism about spiritual distinctions, personal authority, the goodness of the truth, and God.

Americans, he writes, went as far as imaginatively to separate the brain into two parts, one governed by the churches, the other by democracy. So the separation of church and state means, most of all, that democratic procedures and modes of thought do not apply to the church, to theological dogma, and to moral duty (*DA,* vol. 1, pt. 2, ch. 9). American society, as John Courtney Murray asserted more recently, ought to be divided into liberal and illiberal realms, and the primary danger to liberty in our time is the "monistic" or tyrannical tendency of liberalism, one based on the denial of the religious, transpolitical, and social dimensions of human freedom.[62]

The Divided Self

Tocqueville presents Americans as divided or alienated, and he is concerned about the unstable character of their rather self-conscious inconsistency. They are partly democratic and partly not, and the danger is that their love of equality will overwhelm human love as it actually exists in particular families, churches, and political life. Tocqueville, like Lasch, defends this division or alienation as reflecting the truth about human nature. The human being is the beast with the angel in him, and so unable to live with the consistency and contentment of either a beast or an angel (*DA,* vol. 2, pt. 2, ch. 16). Human greatness is inseparable from human misery, and human goods are not those of a pure spirit or mind or a simple body. Revealed religion, far more than liberalism, understands the person as qualitatively distinct from both mind and body.

How the divided self is best understood in terms of natural law is a complicated issue. But I will recall what I said near the beginning of this chapter. St. Thomas regarded magnanimity and humility, pride and love, as two interdependent human goods in conflict or tension, and each of those moods, based on virtue, reveals part of the truth about human nature. Similarly, Leo Strauss writes that the tension or conflict between reason and revelation is the source of the vitality of the West. And so the victory of one or the other would be fatal. In principle, Strauss says, we have to choose. But in fact we can live the tension, and reason may well be of service in making it livable. Reason cannot show that revelation is true, but perhaps it does point to its possible truth. And without some debt to revelation or some form of orthodoxy or moral community, the reasonable person may not properly or fully appreciate the goodness of human life. Every human life is more than the life of the mind, and every human life is more than a body in motion.

Chapter Ten

Percy and Tocqueville on
American Aristocracy and Democracy

Alexis de Tocqueville's *Democracy in America* (*DA*) is, with good reason, understood as the best critical analysis of the American way of life. The book is a measured account of the strengths and weaknesses, virtues and vices, of what Tocqueville presents as the two fundamental political or social alternatives: democracy and aristocracy. His standard of judgment of each way of life comes from a standpoint beyond both aristocratic and democratic partisanship.[1] His ability to see further than the partisans comes, in part, from his privileged position as a member of an aristocratic family near the beginning of his nation's democracy. Tocqueville admits that, personally, his judgments are more aristocratic than democratic, but the standpoint from which he attempts to judge democracy is not his own, but God's. He finally sides with democratic justice over aristocratic excellence. And despite his own lack of belief in a personal God, his analysis of the truth about human nature is a form of Christian or Pascalian psychology.[2]

The most Tocquevillian American writer of our own time is the phi-losopher-novelist Walker Percy. Like Tocqueville's *Democracy in America*, his books are also, in part, measured judgments concerning the strengths and weaknesses of American democracy. He too was born to an aristo-cratic family and raised by an authentic aristocrat in the midst of a de-mocracy. Percy, it seems, was even better situated than Tocqueville to view his nation through aristocratic eyes. The standpoint by which Percy at-tempts to judge aristocracy and democracy is also that of the Christian God, and his analysis of the truth about human nature is also largely a form of Christian or Pascalian psychology. Percy is also better able than Tocqueville to view his nation with Christian eyes, for he actually was a believing Christian.

In this final chapter I present a broad comparison of the thoughts of Tocqueville and Percy on the relationship between American democracy and American aristocracy. At first glance, this comparison seems strange. Percy's novels and prose do not seem at all like *Democracy in America*. And although Percy and Tocqueville both wrote to tell their contemporaries what to do, their advice seems quite different. Tocqueville's can be sum-marized as, "Exercise political responsibility in order to perpetuate hu-man liberty." But Percy's primary concern was not to defend political liberty or America. Because of his Christian faith and his understanding of what a human being is, he knew that the greatness and misery of human liberty would continue even if the bomb fell or if America, in its decadence, collapsed into ruins. Percy's advice, finally, was for us to "ac-cept the truth of the Thomistic or realistic view of human nature and acknowledge the possibility that the Good News of biblical revelation is true."[3] His work means to be a prelude to a return to faith; he traces a path that Tocqueville admits he could not find.[4]

Tocqueville and Percy understood modern intellectual politics to be animated by the goal of eradicating loneliness, that is, the creation of a wholly predictable world of human beings, a world in which we will be fully at home. The goal is less socialism than pantheism, a unity without the distinctiveness of human individuality. Tocqueville says that pantheism is the most seductive and consistent democratic intellectual doctrine, and that defenders of liberty must war against it (*DA*, vol. 2, pt. 1, ch. 7). Percy contends that modern science is perfectly compatible with the self-negation of New Age religion or Buddhism. But it is radically opposed to the predicament of the particular human person in search of the personal God described by Christianity. Percy sees that the complete success of modern science and modern democracy would produce subhuman beings unmoved by love or hate or death, no longer with spiritual needs nor tormented by a longing for immortality. They would be thoughtlessly immersed in the contentment of the present, and easily controlled by what Tocqueville calls schoolmaster-despots, or what Percy calls pop-Cartesian experts. As long as there are free human beings, Percy and Tocqueville add, they will be marked by an "incurable God-directedness."[5] The scientist seeking to explain, without God, all that exists aims to cure the human being of his liberty, his distinctiveness.

But both Tocqueville and Percy describe an America marked by the failure of this modern project. In a world designed to make them fully at home, Americans feel less at home and more like aliens than ever. Tocqueville describes Americans as restless in the midst of prosperity—anxious, confused, and death-haunted. Percy says that modern science, by providing a progressively more complete explanation of all that exists except the human self or soul, makes human beings feel more displaced than ever.[6] The Cartesian experts' material explanation of our troubles is finally incredible, but all other alternative scientific explanations seem also to have been discredited. So the success of popularized science is perfectly compatible with the grossest of superstitions, of unfettered romanticism: We might do or believe anything.[7]

For Tocqueville and Percy, the Cartesian destruction of aristocratic illusion reveals much that is true about human nature, and they aim to reduce our confusion or alienation by giving a distinctively human explanation of that truth. They aim, as Percy says, to make us more at home with our homelessness, by connecting our seemingly inexplicable experiences with our nature as social beings who search for the truth. They aim to make us "ambiguously at home."[8]

Wondering and Wandering

Percy's most memorable characters, Binx Bolling of *The Moviegoer* and Will Barrett of *The Last Gentleman,* are disoriented, detached inhabitants of democracies. They are wanderers, but they are also searchers or wonderers. They wander because they wonder. The being who wonders about the way things really are and finds joy in truthful discovery necessarily experiences himself as a wanderer or a leftover in the cosmos. Only when Binx and Will become able to wonder about themselves as wonderers and wanderers, when they are no longer diverted in one way or another, are they somewhat at home with their ineradicable homelessness.

Percy opens his most theoretical work, *Lost in the Cosmos,* with a quote from Nietzsche, which includes this observation: "We are unknown, we knowers, to ourselves . . . Of necessity, we remain strangers to ourselves... as far as ourselves are concerned we are not knowers." The being that knows the cosmos is a leftover from the cosmos he knows. As a knower, he finds himself elusive; he cannot know himself the way he knows a rock, a frog, or a galaxy. But this does not mean he does not know anything at all, as some Nietzscheans say. It does not even mean that his existence is merely accidental or without natural purpose. Nature is heterogeneous; our mode of being, what we have been given by nature, cannot be integrated into non-human being. We alone are knowers by nature, and that is why we find ourselves elusive.

This understanding of the human being as the wonderer and wanderer is not, in fact, wholly Pascalian or Nietzschean. Percy is no existentialist; he accepts the existentialist criticism of the impersonality of scientism, but he also writes that "the existentialists have their flaws," and "one of them is their contempt for science."[9] Percy views himself as a Thomist, doing justice to both Greek or philosophic wondering and Christian wandering. He claims that Binx Bolling "recreates within himself and within the confines of a single weekend of New Orleans a microcosm of the spiritual history of the West, from the Roman patrician reading his Greek philosophers to the 13th century pilgrim who leaves home and takes to the road."[10] Percy the Christian realist means to show the true relationship between knowing and wandering by nature. The knower is, necessarily, a wanderer, an alien, a pilgrim on the road to somewhere.

This understanding of what it means to be human is not, of course, a prominent theme in Tocqueville's writing. But it is there. "There is no need," he observes, "to traverse earth and sky to find a wondrous being full of contrasts. . . . I have only to contemplate myself, man comes from nothing, passes through time, and disappears forever in the bosom of God. He is seen but for a moment between two abysses, and then is lost." Man, Tocqueville goes on, is not "wholly ignorant of himself," but he cannot see himself "clearly." Much of "the nature of man" is "sufficiently veiled" to leave him in "impenetrable darkness, a darkness in which he ever gropes, forever in vain, trying to understand himself." Man, for Tocqueville, is by nature a wanderer (coming from and disappearing into nothing seemingly for no reason) and a wonderer (especially about himself), who is largely but not completely in the dark when it comes to self-understanding (*DA,* vol. 2, pt. 1, ch. 17).

This mixture of knowledge and ignorance, Percy and Tocqueville agree, is what makes the human being, among other things, a poetic animal. And the desires this mixture engenders are what make him trouble to himself and others. Percy turned to the writing of novels to illuminate the predicament of the being who wanders and wonders. Novel-writing is a way of overcoming the abstractness inherent in modern understandings of the human being as either angels (theorists) or pigs (consumers), or as beings with natural rights to pursue bodily enjoyment. *Democracy in America*, of course, is a quite singular form of literature that is in some ways closer to poetry than philosophy.

Tocqueville and Percy present the perspective of the wanderer and wonderer as, in one way, radically democratic. It is what emerges, Tocqueville says, when the idealism or illusions of aristocracy are purged from the imagination (*DA*, vol. 2, pt. 1, ch. 17). Percy's wandering characters are inhabitants of a democracy where the aristocratic code of honor of their ancestors has become discredited and largely irrelevant for understanding the world. But in another way this view of the human being is not democratic at all. It distinguishes radically between human experience and that of the other animals, who do not engage in self-contemplation or exist between two abysses. It emphasizes the predicament of the democratic individual, uprooted from tradition, time, and place, but not determined by impersonal forces and so not really comprehended by the expertise of materialistic science.[11]

Tocqueville's presentation of the predicament of the dizzying, paralyzing dislocation in a democracy is particularly striking. For him, that perception of unadorned truth is really something like radical contingency, or what Percy calls "pure possibility." He criticizes democracy for destroying the convictions that lead thought and action in the direction of liberty. He says that the active and effective exercise of political liberty depends on the acceptance of the truth of religious dogma and, even better, a proud, aristocratic confidence in ruling oneself and others. Human beings need the salutary bondage of tradition and religion—or trust in the opinions of others on all sorts of matters—in order to think and act freely (*DA*, vol. 2, pt. 1, ch. 2). Liberty to sustain itself must be lovable and so limited. The human experience of liberty as pure possibility or self-constitution out of nothing is, in fact, hateful. Uncertainty about the fundamental questions leads democrats to degrade themselves by taking refuge in the certainty of materialism and deference to public opinion. Public opinion, often expressed in the impersonal language of popularized science and seemingly determined by no one in particular, rules in a democracy because individuals have no standpoint by which to resist it (*DA*, vol. 2, pt. 1, chs. 2–5).

Pure Possibility vs. Human Reality

Percy's Will Barrett in *The Last Gentleman* (*LG*) is an isolated, highly self-conscious individual. He spends his time thinking by himself, mainly about himself. His recurring question is, "What to do?" He has been abandoned by his father, who committed suicide, and by his family's aristocratic way of life, and he lives in a free and prosperous environment. As the abandoned "last of the line," he is free "to see things afresh," but too free, as it turns out. His life appears to him as "pure possibility"; an indefinitely large number of choices or life-plans are open to him. But he lacks the resources from tradition or religion to think clearly about himself, connect with others, and really focus on his past and future. So he does not know what to think. Freed up from authority and personal dependence on others or God, he believes he must not only think but know before he can act. He is paralyzed by the fact that what he wants—perfect self-knowledge—is not available to a human being, the being who thinks (*LG*, 3–5).[12]

Will finds he cannot "engineer" his identity through the expert principles of popularized science and the self-knowledge they provide (*LG*, 41). He will, he thinks for a while, achieve self-knowledge through rational self-creation, but the self-conscious effort "to adapt myself to my environment and score on interpersonal relationships" proves futile and just too hard (*LG*, 284). The abstract or fuzzy principles of that science (such as "personal growth" and "creativity") never really account for or identify his distinctively human longings. He has enough irony, partly a residue of his father's aristocratic distance and partly by nature, to know enough never quite to fall for the idea that the pop Cartesian sciences of personal identity and human relationships can tell him what to do. Although "he made the highest possible scores on psychological aptitude tests, especially in the areas of problem-solving and goal-seeking," he still "could not think what to do between tests" (LG, 9). And he is constantly seeking out a new father figure, a personal authority. He becomes obsessed with the scientific genius, Sutter Vaught, who might really be the expert (father substitute) who can tell him what to do. Despite his reliance on reason, Will remains superstitiously open to signs of all kinds. But even if there really are signs in nature pointing to what human beings are for, he is too caught up in solitary thought to notice them. And like us pop Cartesians, he does not know what to look for: "Often nowadays people do not know what to do and so live out their lives as if they were waiting for some sign or another" (LG, 6).

Will does know that the democratic utopia of pure possibility, of life unconstrained by necessity, is hell. As the novel's narrator says, "Lucky is the man who does not secretly believe that every possibility is open to him" (LG, 4). He knows he is miserable in good environments, and he also knows he feels better when confronted unexpectedly by necessity, such as the natural necessity of a hurricane or the honorable challenge of fighting off redneck racists. Then he knows what to do. For a moment, "things became as clear as they used to be in the old honorable days" (LG, 325). But opportunities to deal with natural catastrophes or engage in honorable combat are rare in our democratic world. So his more pedestrian efforts to keep his anger "pure and honorable" are quickly overwhelmed by irony. And he notices that although people are often as angry as they ever were, they are now embarrassed by their "unspendable rage" (LG, 144, 148). He knows that "the American revolution had succeeded beyond the wildest dreams . . . so that practically everyone in the United States is free to sit around a cozy fire in ski pants" (*LG*, 22). But because he cannot be happy simply enjoying the leisure produced by prosperity, he does not know what to do. He knows enough to resist being diverted, but he has no idea from what he might be diverted (*LG*, 241). "An immense melancholy overtook him" (*LG*, 10) for no reason experts could readily explain, and he notices that his experience is, although not often acknowledged, not uncommon among free and prosperous Americans (*LG*, 46), when they are, for example, trying to be entertained or diverted by paintings in Manhattan's Metropolitan Museum of Art (*LG*, 26–28). The hateful experience of the pure possibility engendered by Socratic democracy is becoming common.

Will cannot help but long for a different result to the Civil War, a result that would have given him and his family political power and purpose. He also hopes for apocalyptic destruction, which would make action necessary and possible again. The novel's narrator explains that "if a young man lives in the sphere of the possible and waits for something to happen, what he is waiting for is war or the end of the world" (*LG*, 10). Partly because he is traumatized by his father's ready embrace of it, Will does not know how to think about the ineradicable necessity of death. He also does not know how to think about God or religion or love because he believes that all there is to think with are Cartesian principles. His view of love is nostalgically romanticized, and far too detached from physical love. He wants both disembodied purity, or angelic mother-love, and the rawest of physical sex. But he cannot connect the two in a single human person. The woman he thinks he loves he does not really know, and so he is often confused by what she says and does. He can see her only abstractly, as "a certain someone" (*LG*, 151), because he cannot think about women or nature as they really are.

Will has "the old itch for omniscience," longing one moment "for carnal knowledge, the next for perfect angelic knowledge." He is so detached from the world of human beings he cannot help but think of himself as a scientific spectator: "He had to know without being known" (*LG*, 170). The knowledge he thinks he longs for is actually quite incompatible with his more human longing for love. His engineer's effort at both detachment and control must turn into wonder about what is real—especially real, troubled human beings who are born and die—before he can know the first thing about love and friendship.

Will's detachment from the past, from others, and from reality itself serves as the cause of his psychological and physiological disorders. He suffers from intermittent amnesia and *déja vus*. He is often confused about time. As a being facing pure possibility, he cannot be sure he is anywhere in particular. Time and place are, in human experience, intertwined. To uproot human beings radically from their connections with the past, with particular persons and places, deprives them of the precondition of all human identity and genuine self-consciousness. Most human beings live in the past or in the future, and so rarely live well as human beings in the present. But being deprived of the past and the future does not really give us the present, as it does for Rousseau's natural man. The experience of pure possibility places us nowhere in particular, not even in the present. As Will puts it, pure possibility inheres when "what a man can be the next minute bears no relation to what he is or what he was the minute before" (*LG*, 356).

We all are saddled with some experience of homelessness and homesickness. But unmoderated or uncompensated, this experience makes thought and action in light of the truth about the human situation impossible. Pure possibility can never lead to actuality, which is why the radical democracy first described by Socrates is neither possible nor desirable. It is also why the relativism described by Allan Bloom sometimes leads not to mindless contentment but miserable disorientation and conscious or unconscious despair. For Tocqueville and Percy, Pascal far more than Rousseau better describes the condition of many Americans today.

Percy describes this condition as postmodern. The postmodern world, he argues, emerged when modern language was exposed as empty and exhausted.[13] The expert language repeated with little conviction by Will about having "much to learn about the psychological insights of the World's great religion" and "rewarding interpersonal relationships" between consenting adults seems to consist of no more than silly platitudes. For Percy, the nihilistic revelation of the emptiness of modern science or "humanism" when wholly detached from Christian and aristocratic premises is the main cause of the angry, ideological slaughter of our century, beginning with Verdun and continuing through our apparently compassionate affirmation of euthanasia, abortion, and other forms of killing. Death, the thinking goes, is better than the low quality of life we now live, despite our health, wealth, and freedom.[14] Actual death, apparently, is better than what Percy calls "death in life" (*Signposts in a Strange Land* [*SSL*], 162).

But Percy's own view of the future of human beings is far from despairing or even radically pessimistic. He opens *The Last Gentleman* with a quote from the German Catholic philosopher and theologian Romano Guardini: "We now know that the modern world is coming to an end . . . at the same time, the unbeliever will emerge from the fogs of secularism. He will cease to reap benefit from the values and forces developed by the very revelation he denies . . . Loneliness in faith will be terrible. Love will disappear from the public world, but the more precious will be the love which flows from one lonely person to another . . . the world will be filled with animosity and danger, but it will be a world open and clean." The modern world was a mixture of Christianity and modern science; it avoided nihilism only insofar as the values derived from revelation retained some credibility and force. In Percy's eyes, even our Declaration of Independence should be viewed as reflecting a "mishmash" anthropology that understands human beings partly as creatures given language by nature and partly as organisms well or badly adjusted to their environment (*SSL*, 228–29). The modern world ends when "the fogs of secular-ism," which obscured even the vision of Mr. Jefferson, are replaced by the clarity of the unbeliever.

Percy, like Guardini, does not share the apocalyptic view of many unbelievers who see clearly enough the modern world's end. The end of that world is not the end of what makes life worth living. Love, in fact, remains possible in the ruins of the modern world, whether those ruins are merely intellectual or the actual destruction of the great cities and suburbs we built in order to be at home. Percy writes often of the inevi-table return of social, political, and spiritual life in the ruins. And Will Barrett's experience of postmodern loneliness is the prelude to his own love, the love of one lonely disoriented self for another. That "after-mod-ern" love is more precious and true than the more socially supported love that preceded it.[15] Will ends up joyfully connected (*LG*, 409) with a soli-tary, despairing scientist who believes that suicide is the only reasonable response to postmodern emptiness, to being "doomed to the transcen-dence of abstraction" (*LG*, 354). We can expect that these two friends will find joy in pursuing the truth about the fundamental human questions. His new friendship with Sutter Vaught is the culmination of Will's jour-ney. The story of the novel is one in which he gradually comes to think less abstractly, sees the reality of nature and human nature more clearly, and finally locates himself to some extent in the world of his fellow human beings, especially those who know best that they are wanderers and wonderers by nature. Will needed a friend more than a father, which doesn't mean he still doesn't need a father.

The very possibility of really being conscious—or knowing with—another human being is a refutation of dogmatic disbelief and the no-tion of the primacy of solitude. Will Barrett and Sutter Vaught at the novel's end are finally ready to talk with each other about the true cause of human homelessness, and the real possibility of human and divine love. Freed from various diversions, they are now able to think about love and death—and therefore the responsibilities given to the being with language—as natural limitations to human possibility. Because they have found some definition to human liberty—and identity for their selves or souls—they are no longer in a position to rule out God.

Tocqueville does not share all of Percy's hopefulness about love in the ruins because he does not share either Percy's religious faith or his faith in the persistence of human nature, the resistance of Being and human being to human manipulation. Tocqueville recommends that political leaders and thinkers do whatever they can to perpetuate the heart-enlarging aristocratic inheritances—the family, religion, local government, and voluntary association—that the Americans fortunately but mistakenly view as democratic. Exercised in the limiting and directing context of these institutions, American liberty seems lovable, but the disappearance of these institutions would make the restless isolation of individuality too extreme to bear. The result would be extreme individualism and soft despotism.[16]

Tocqueville does not write of love as a compensation for loneliness in the ruins, but instead of the likely coming of an apathetic existence without love or hate. But he does find some hope in the deranged longings of Americans (*DA*, vol. 2, pt. 2, ch. 12). Percy also finds apathy or "death in life" in America, and he even thinks it has become common. But he also sees it as superficial, as masking anger and despair. Human longings—love, hate, and anger—remain barely submerged beneath therapeutic platitudes.

From one perspective, Tocqueville wants to use aristocratic illusions to protect Americans from too much unadorned, democratic truth. The experience of dizzying disorientation would also blind them to another part of the truth, to what is really good and genuinely excellent about distinctively human life. Too much truth of one kind negates the perception of another kind, the kind which includes and supports the being who can know the truth. Unlike Percy, Tocqueville cannot quite free himself from a certain aristocratic pessimism about the destructive consequences of democracy's progressively more complete victory. But he avoids fatalism by holding to the aristocratic view that nothing about the future is absolutely inevitable. Human beings are not simply playthings of forces beyond their control. We cannot be certain that the right kind of action by the few who are especially devoted to liberty will not have a lasting effect (*DA*, vol. 2, pt. 1, ch. 20).

Defending the possibility of political life is considerably more important for Tocqueville than for Percy. Tocqueville was fearful that political life would disappear entirely, and for him political life was what made life worth living. When the opportunity was available to him, Tocqueville was a political actor. He wrote only when denied a place on the political stage, and almost all of his writing was about politics. He did not write about metaphysical or theological questions. The impossibility of answering them made him miserable. He knew well enough that his political devotion was partly in the service of the truth and partly a diversion.[17] By contrast, Percy's writing was less political than theological and metaphysical, and his personal interest in political engagement was minimal. He minded doing nothing much less than Tocqueville, because his leisurely thoughts did not point in the direction of misery in the absence of God. Percy was a believer, and he held that discovering the truth, loving other human beings, and being transparent before a loving, personal God, was what makes life worth living. (A more complete list would include the other good things of the world, including bourbon [*SSL*, 102–7].) But he also knew Tocqueville's misery, the misery of doubtful intellectual solitude, and, like Tocqueville, he saw it all around him in America's democracy.

Aristocrats and Democrats

One temptation in calling attention to any difference between Percy and Tocqueville is making Tocqueville appear to be entirely aristocratic and

Percy entirely Christian. The truth is that both their analyses of American democracy owe something to aristocracy and something to Christianity. They both came from aristocratic backgrounds; their most immediate family members thought of themselves, in fact, as dispossessed aristocrats. From their privileged positions between democracy and aristocracy, they both accepted much of the aristocratic criticism of democracy and the democratic criticism of aristocracy. They both aimed to evaluate democratic and aristocratic partisanship from a more comprehensive perspective.

Tocqueville employs the divine perspective to criticize the democratic propensity to think with general ideas, ones which abstract from the true complexity of human nature. Such general thinking is, in one way, powerful. It is the foundation of modern science and modern government, the government grounded in the consent of the being with rights. No one can deny that modern science and modern government have provided human beings with unprecedented freedom, security, and comfort. But in terms of comprehending reality, general ideas are really a sign of human weakness. The omniscient God has "no need of general ideas," writes Tocqueville, and so he "does not view the human race collectively." He sees each of us as we are, as both similar to and different from the rest of nature and other human beings. His "gaze of necessity includes the whole of created things" and "distinctively and simultaneously all of mankind and each single man" (DA, vol. 2, pt. 1, ch. 3). God is critical of democratic thinking, but he is perhaps just as critical of aristocratic thinking. Aristocrats think too particularly. They attribute too much to the action of great individuals; they exaggerate the extent to which they, in their greatness, transcend the realm of material determination. They coldly and mistakenly tend to reduce human beings not of their class to subhumanity (DA, vol. 2, pt. 1, ch. 20; vol. 2, pt. 2, ch. 8; vol. 2, pt. 3, ch. 1).

Tocqueville's most general judgment is that aristocrats are better at producing, appreciating, and perpetuating human excellence, whereas democrats are better at providing for prosperity and justice. He admits that his personal judgment is for aristocracy, for liberty understood as excellence, but his judgment, he admits, is due to his human weakness. It is not the "divine view." What seems to Tocqueville to be decline is to God progress. God, he imagines, finally prefers democratic justice to aristocratic excellence, but He also prefers that the former be as compatible as possible with the latter. Human beings should be equally free, not equally degraded (*DA*, vol. 2, pt. 4, ch. 8).

"Jesus Christ had to come down to earth," Tocqueville contends, "to make human beings understand that they were naturally free and equal." Jesus Christ teaches that all human beings are qualitatively different from the other animals by nature. He overcame the aristocratic prejudice, shared by even the ancient philosophers, that understood most human beings as slaves to the given political order. There is, in truth, "an equal right of all at birth to liberty," and with that right—rooted more in the Christian understanding of the person than the Lockean doctrine of the abstract individual—in mind, aristocratic claims for excellence must be reformed or generalized (*DA*, vol. 2, pt. 1, ch. 3). For Tocqueville, the unprecedented sight in America of a whole people restless in the midst of prosperity showed the truth of Christian psychology, whether or not the Christian God actually exists. All human beings have ineradicable spiritual longings, and they all are capable of the miserable greatness of experiencing themselves as dislocated in the absence of God (*DA*, vol. 2, pt. 2, ch. 12-13; vol. 1, pt. 2, ch. 8).

Tocqueville's view of God is decisively Christian, and that God, in His way, leads Tocqueville to moderate his understandable but merely human contempt for democratic mediocrity. But he also views Christianity, in democratic times, as itself partly democratic and partly aristocratic. He calls it "the most precious inheritance from aristocratic times." Christianity was, in fact, the religion of European aristocracy. Its spiritual concerns, especially its belief about the immaterial nature of the human soul, are not democratic (*DA*, vol. 2, pt. 2, ch. 15). The viewpoint of the Christian God, which is that all human beings are more than matter and have restless longings that point beyond this world to Him, corrects both democrats and aristocrats in the name of the truth about human liberty. The distinctively Christian Pascal, in truth, was neither an aristocrat nor a democrat (*DA*, vol. 2, pt. 1, ch. 10).

Percy the Aristocrat

Tocqueville understood that the aristocratic criticism of America's democracy came not only from the hereditary aristocrats of Europe. He found two exceptions to the dominance of middle-class democracy in America: the Native Americans and the southern masters (*DA*, vol. 1, pt. 2, ch. 10). And he saw the South, formed by such leaders, as an aristocratic society. He would have seen the Civil War, more clearly than most of our (democratic) historians, as a conflict between the democratic and aristocratic ways of life. The southerner, he noticed, "has the taste, prejudices, weaknesses, and grandeur of every aristocracy" (*DA*, vol. 1, pt. 2, ch. 10). And the southern aristocrat, of course, is better situated than even the European to see the weaknesses of American democracy.

Tocqueville quite astutely predicted, decades before the war, that northern civilization would prevail and America would "become assimilated" (*DA*, vol. 1, pt. 2, ch. 10). He predicted, in effect, the New South, the Sunbelt of the suburbs—the golf courses, Chevy dealerships, vulgar fundamentalism, and nouveau bourgeois happiness mocked so effectively by Percy in his novels. The South to which Will returns in *The Last Gentleman* "was happy, victorious, Christian, rich, patriotic, and Republican" (*LG*, 185). From a middle-class perspective, the South is now more American than the rest of America. This, not residual racism, explains why the Republican Party has moved South. The Republicans, aristocratic southerners notice, seem always to side with the winners. But, Percy notes, for a Pascalian all that the victory means is that "in the Sunbelt the diversions of technology, restoration, climate, media, sports, and fun are more successful" (*SSL*, 158).

Even in the 1830s, Tocqueville observed the southern aristocrats turning "their melancholy gaze inward and back to the past," knowing that their way of life, their cause, was lost (*DA*, vol. 1, pt. 2, ch. 10). He also saw, of course, the South's aristocracy as flawed in a way its predecessors were not and so more deserving of destruction: It depended on racially based or modern slavery, which was much more brutalizing and soul-destroying than its ancient counterparts. The southerner, with a confused mixture of ancient pride and modern materialism, had come to believe that the black, because of the color of his skin, was somehow less than a human being by nature.

The southern aristocracy that existed when Walker Percy was born had affirmed the humanity of the black, but not his right to rule himself. He was viewed by that class as a laborer, by nature unable to plan for his own future. The aristocratic consciousness of southern leaders had become in that sense more purely paternalistic. Those aristocrats thought whites with property and power had a responsibility, a duty, to provide for those who could not provide for themselves. Percy agreed with Tocqueville that the virtues and vices of his immediate ancestors were pretty much those of any aristocracy. These virtues were purified not only by slavery's end, but by the memory of their noble defeat by the North in the war. They had proven themselves better, they thought, by their willingness to die for a cause that was lost, and by being unable to live well under the sway of the North's inhuman, technological, vulgarly democratic principles. Not only were they defeated by the North, Percy reports, they had lost political power to democratic forces in the South "around 1890" (*SSL*, 334). The aristocratic southerners stood nobly in ineffectual criticism of democrats North and South at the time of Walker Percy's birth.

The aristocratic southerners, Percy reports, were only Christian in a secondary sense. "The greatness of the South, like the greatness of the English squirearchy, had always a stronger Greek flavor than it ever had Christian." The southerners were primarily Stoics, followers of Epictetus and especially the philosopher-emperor Marcus Aurelius. They understood themselves as Roman patricians reading Greek philosophy. But their stoicism was less an ancient philosophy than a code of action. It was "the stern inner summons to man's full estate . . . , toward generosity toward his fellow men and above all to his inferiors—not because they were made in the image of God and lovable in themselves, but because to do them an injustice would be to defile the inner fortress which was oneself" (*SSL*, 84–85). Put more simply, "if you are a good man, then you will be magnanimous toward other men and therefore especially toward the Negro" (*SSL*, 98). Living according to this code, Percy acknowledges in Aristotelian fashion, is "the nobility of . . . natural perfection," "a flowering of human individuality" (*SSL*, 85). One form of human perfection is the performance of duty whatever its consequences, and that resolution is a fortress against the contingencies of fortune and death, of all things human.

Aristocratic Despair

But in almost all cases that fortress is far from purely personal. Knowledge of duty usually depends on the code of honor of an aristocratic class. It also depends on the opportunity to do one's duty on a stage of some significance. And so the nobility of natural perfection disappears as democracy progresses. As the social influence of the aristocratic class declines, the morality of magnanimous nobility provides less and less personal guidance, and the remaining aristocrats cannot avoid the loneliness of isolation and irrelevance. Honor recedes, Tocqueville explains, as the aristocratic preference, say, for violence over cunning makes less and less social sense (*DA*, vol. 2, pt. 3, ch. 18). And paternalistic nobility is overwhelmed by the insolent clamor for equal rights by those the aristocrats protected (*SSL*, 86). The aristocrat feels the sting of ingratitude for what were his genuinely noble deeds—his defending of his people, for example, from the lawless, murderous white trash who populated the Klan. Southern stoicism culminates in the angry impotence and despair of men who no longer know what to do.

Will Barrett is, in an obvious sense, "the last gentleman," the last of his lineage to be affected by his southern family's view about how to act nobly. Will was formed by his father, but his father committed suicide because there was nothing left for his kind to do. As the novel's narrator explains:

> Over the years his father's family had turned ironical and lost its gift for action. It was an honorable and violent family, but gradually the violence had been deflected and turned inward. The great-grandfather knew what was what and said so and did not care what anyone thought. He even wore a pistol in the holster like a Western hero and once met the Grand Wizard of the Ku Klux Klan in a barber shop and invited him then and there to shoot it out in the street. The next generation, the grandfather seemed to know what was what but he was not really so sure. He was brave but gave much thought to the business of being brave. He would have shot it out with the Grand Wizard if only he could have been made certain it was the thing to do. The father was a brave man too and he said he didn't care what others thought, but he did care. More than anything else, he wished to act with honor and be thought of well by other men. So living for him was a strain. He became ironical. For him it was not a small thing to walk down the street on an ordinary September morning. In the end he was killed by his own irony and sadness and by the strain of living out an ordinary day in a perfect dance of honor. (*LG*, 9–10)

Honorable action depends on self-certainty and opportunities for the noble risk of life. But self-certainty depends on being raised a certain way and on experiencing the pleasures and duties of that way of life. The enemy of honor is excessive self-consciousness or an ironic detachment from one's way of life. Honor, without renewal in war and the other dangers associated with political rule, becomes more questionable and empty over time. Honor has to be more than a "dance," or form without content. It has to be connected with the requirements of a certain way of life. If life depends on noble action, and there is nothing left to do, then ordinary life becomes unendurable misery. And noble action, of course, is not possible if there is no audience to see it for what it is. Those who say they do not care what others think are usually in a position to know they are admired. For the Christians, this problem of an audience might be solved by God Himself, but for the noble southern Stoics there is no solace in a providential, personal God. They refuse to succumb to such illusory hope. As Percy says, for the Stoic, strictly speaking, there is no hope; the Stoic claims to live beyond hope and fear (SSL, 86).

But later in the novel Will remembers that his father, Ed Barrett, did act nobly. He gave speeches "to the D.A.R. on the subject of *noblesse oblige* and our duty to the Negro," and he gave that "strange bunch of noble-women . . . proper hell" (LG, 208). Far more importantly, he ran out of town a lawless Klan mob that had sworn to kill him. The mob's claim was that Ed Barrett "loved niggers and helped the Jews and the Catholics and betrayed [his] own people." But the mob was too Christian to under-stand the aristocrat. He acted out of duty, and for himself, and not out of love. His son discovered soon enough that his father was governed not at all by love. The father told his son that his apparent victory was not real. The reason the mob left town, he said, was that "they found out that we are like them after all and so there was no reason for them to stay." There used to be a distinction between men of honor and "the fornicators and bribers and takers of bribes," but no longer (LG, 330). The mob, the democrats, had won. His father's only choice was his refusal to choose them, and the only way not to do so was suicide. So perhaps Ed Barrett was not so ironical at the end. He acted nobly but quite alone, despite the nearness of his loving son.

Ed Barrett (like Carl Sagan) in fact generalized about the cosmos from his own loneliness. He took perverse pleasure in contemplating modern theories about "the insignificance of man in the great lonely universe" (LG, 309). He saw "the good life" as the no-longer-possible compensation for that loneliness (LG, 330). His last words to his son were, "In the last analysis, you are alone" (LG, 331). He was, Will says, "a proud and solitary man" (LG, 385), and his pride in his solitude was some compensation for his lack of recognition. Perhaps his solitude as a dispossessed and abandoned aristocrat gave him insight into the truth of human contingency. An aristocrat without illusions sees what Tocqueville calls the democratic truth about the human condition.

So perhaps Ed was in some sense ironical at the end, taking proud pleasure in the absolutely futile gesture of his suicide. If a man cannot live reasonably, Marcus Aurelius said, he ought to commit suicide. For Percy, Ed's highly self-conscious suicide reveals the despair always at the bottom of the Stoic or aristocratic view of the world. He was insufficiently diverted by proud and effective political action and by the shared pleasures and self-understandings of a class. Would Tocqueville himself have shared Ed Barrett's despair had he been as certain that the mob had won? But for Tocqueville and especially Percy, Ed's apocalyptic despair was not wholly in accord with reality, with the facts.

Will, near his journey's end, is inclined at first to excuse his father's suicide by saying he lived at the wrong time. It was not his fault that he was a superfluous aristocrat in a democracy. But then Will thinks his father was "looking in the wrong place." He looked inside himself and to his code of honor for purpose. By this time in the novel, Will has become much less self-absorbed and more open to how strange, wonderful, and

"droll" nature and human nature really are, even or especially in democratic times (*LG*, 332). And so Will knows that the reality outside of himself is not nearly as bad as his father thought. He had even missed the
compensation of the love of his own son. At this point, the difference
between father and son, Percy says, is that "in terms of traditional metaphysics, he [Will] has caught a glimpse of the goodness and gratuitous-
ness of created being" (*SSL,* 221). That Being is somehow both good and
gratuitous is what sparks his wonder.

The Stoic character in *The Moviegoer*, Binx's Aunt Emily, speaks more
emphatically or at least at far greater length of what democracy has done
to her class and its human excellence. She tells her nephew that we live in
a time of national mediocrity. People both lack character and "are kinder
than ever." There's nothing new about "liars and thieves and adulterers,"
except that today they "wish to be congratulated and are congratulated by
the general public, if their confession is sufficiently psychological or strikes
a sufficiently heartfelt note of sincerity." We have become the most sincere
and least judgmental of people. We want to be judged, like President Clinton, by our therapeutic words and not by our shameful action, whereas
aristocrats, characteristically, are short on words and long on action.

Aunt Emily says that her class, now about gone, is the class with "class."
"You're damn right we're better," she asserts, because "we do not shirk our
obligations to ourselves and others." In addition, "We do not whine." She
is perfectly aware that their right action may in fact have no natural or
divine support: "Perhaps we are a biological sport. I am not sure." But she
is sure that "we live by our lights, die by our lights, and whoever the high
gods may be, we'll look them in the eyes with no apology." Her class defines
itself against our ignorance about nature and the gods. Certainty comes
through self-definition through action, and it may be out of nothing, if
not for nothing. That certainty, of course, allows for resistance to democratic public opinion, but it seems to have no foundation but "class" action. In this view, Being may be gratuitous but it probably isn't good.

Aunt Emily, of course, does actually whine that her class is no longer recognized. She has, in fact, become irrelevant and solitary. She admits that she had no idea that her nephew had absorbed nothing of her moral code. She realizes that she might have done all of the talking when they "listened to music together" and "read the *Crito*," Plato's dialogue about what human beings ought to do without natural guidance. She does not really think about "goodness and truth and beauty and nobility"; she accepts the conventions of her class rather than miserably and futilely searching for the truth herself. But they do not really show her how to act now. She is unable to help or even really talk with her nephew, who can search for the truth, in part, because he is freed from aristocracy by the anonymous mediocrity of democracy.[18]

Aristocratic Truth

Will Barrett and Binx Bolling are too self-conscious, too detached, to find authoritative guidance from their aristocratic inheritance. But that is not to say that they do not remain influenced by the aristocratic contempt for the secular, scientific humanism of today's American democracy. Binx inherited from his aunt a capacity to smell the "merde," the "great shithouse of scientific humanism," as well as an aversion to the "everydayness" or the thoughtless, mediocre impersonality of ordinary life.[19] His dissatisfaction with both aristocracy *and* democracy is what, in fact, led him in the direction of the truth, including the possible truth of Christianity.

Even after he distanced himself from his father and his father's way of life, Will still was able to criticize the nihilistic scientist Sutter Vaught for wasting his life in fornication and suicidal reveries, for not using his talents to make a contribution to the world, for action in some sense noble.[20] And he agrees with his father that the crisis in sexual morality is at least as important as the black struggle for civil rights (*LG*, 131). Will knew that life is for something more than democratic diversions—fornication, consumption, theory, meaningful relationships, and so forth—but it took him a long time to find out what. He figured out that "proud and solitary" was bad for human beings. But he could not surrender his inherited and natural concerns with virtue, love, and truth. He tried to lose himself in groups and to consciously engineer all his social relationships according to scientific principles. In these extreme and in some sense democratic efforts—Tocqueville's apathetic self-surrender and self-interest rightly understood—he failed. He could not be satisfied with activities that were merely diversions.

Natural Excellence and Its Limits

Tocqueville and Percy agree that the aristocratic way of life is a natural excellence, a permanent human possibility, and that insofar as possible democracy must recognize the greatness of natural aristocrats. Percy's most outstanding example of aristocratic excellence lived during his time, and he presents him as having qualities that transcend the limitations of time and place. After his father's suicide, Percy was raised by his cousin, William Alexander Percy, whom he called Uncle Will. Critics, I think, too readily identify Percy's Stoic characters, such as Aunt Emily and Ed Barrett, with Uncle Will.[21] They each have some of Walker's uncle's qualities, but not all. Uncle Will did not share their misanthropy.

William Alexander Percy was a well-known poet and author of a most thoughtful and neglected memoir, *Lanterns on the Levee: Recollections of a Planter's Son*. In this book he makes clear that, for him, Stoic philosophy and southern, aristocratic partisanship did not culminate in irresponsibility and despair, but in an understanding of life that was noble, tragic, profoundly appreciative of the flawed beauty of human accomplishment, loving, extremely self-conscious, philosophic, and finally serenely understanding in the face of solitude, ignorance, and death.[22] Will Percy never seems to have been tempted seriously by suicide (unlike almost every other Percy male, including Walker). He assumed responsibility for his relative's sons with seriousness of purpose and without complaint, slowly died of heart disease in love with life and others, again without complaint, and did not think that the end of the aristocratic South was the end of what makes life worth living for human beings.[23] Southern stoicism culminated in nostalgic nihilism in most cases, but not the best case. Will, Walker wrote, was a "unique human being, and when I say unique I mean it in the most literal sense, he was one of a kind. I never met anyone remotely like him."[24]

What immediately comes to mind is Tocqueville's "one of a kind": Pascal. Walker emphasizes that Will's excellence was not entirely tied to the South; he left Mississippi as often as he could for just about everywhere, including the South Seas. In truth, Will Percy's "own aristocracy was a meritocracy of character, talent, performance, courage, and quality of life."[25] So Walker causes us to wonder and doubt whether democracy could ever produce such a remarkable character. Will did not whine about his misery in Pascalian fashion, although he knew that our deepest longings go unfulfilled and in the most profound sense we live and die alone. It is remarkable how well he lived with his "terrible loneliness," the kind of loneliness, in Walker's view, described by Pascal.[26]

Walker encourages us to exempt the personal example of this exceptional man from most of his general criticism of aristocracy. The criticism he gives of his uncle's thought concerns his moral and political, and not personal, despair. Walker gladly admits he would have been no philosopher-novelist had he not learned how to love reading the best of books, particularly Shakespeare, from his uncle. Will was a "great teacher,"[27] with "this extraordinary capacity for communicating his enthusiasm for beauty."[28] In the way he shows us Will Percy, Walker actually criticizes the unrealistic extremism of Pascal. Genuine Christian realism recognizes natural excellence for what it is. Will was a strange, wonderful, and most admirable man, and his was "a complete, articulated view of the world as tragic as it was noble." [29]

In his introduction to a later edition of *Lanterns*, Walker Percy gives a balanced and Tocquevillian case for both the aristocratic and democratic views of life.[30] He rejects the "ideological" or dogmatically democratic critic of Will's aristocratic views as blind to the facts, while adding that even the best of the aristocrats is willfully naïve about the injustice and exploitation caused by any form of paternalism. Democracy, in truth, is full of both moral decay and evidence for moral progress.

Walker is aristocratic enough to know that words like *noblesse oblige* refer first of all not to privilege but to duty. Why was it wrong, Walker asks, for his uncle to have believed "that his position in society entails a certain responsibility to others? Or is it a bad thing for a man to care like a father for his servants, spend himself on the poor, the sick, the miserable, and the mad who come his way?" One opposite of responsibility is indifference, which is a characteristic vice of democracy. It is also the precondition of all forms of despotism (*DA*, vol. 2, pt. 2, ch. 4). And Will's real-life resolute and life-risking confrontation with the Klan has to be compared with an individual in a democratic city "watching a neighbor get murdered and closing the blinds to keep from 'getting involved.'"

Democratic relationships are more egalitarian, more just, but they are also more utilitarian, less caring, devoted, and personal. Percy provocatively adds that paternalism "might even beat welfare." Welfare might seem better because the recipient is not degraded by being treated like a child by a particular person. But it is really worse because it is so impersonal and unresponsive to a person's real needs. Certainly Will's sharecroppers felt more secure than the urban underclass, and their "father" held them to a higher standard of responsibility. An even better system, the Christian Percy suggests, would be both egalitarian and personal. But there is no denying that the democratic doctrine of consent and rights isolates real persons and allows for irresponsibility toward others.

Walker Percy also largely agrees with his uncle's "gloomy assessment of the spiritual health of Western civilization." That assessment "seems especially prescient when one considers that his book was written in the between-war age of optimism when Americans still believed that the right kind of war would set things right once and for all." That the cure for what ails peace and excessive prosperity is war makes some aristocratic sense, but that there could be a war that would provide the definitive and permanent cure for what ails human beings is typically foolish democratic thinking. Will's "indictment of modern life seemed to be confirmed by the holocaust of the 1940s and American social and political morality of the 1970s." Only the incredible dimensions of the Nazi holocaust and the postwar "moral bankruptcy" would have surprised Will, because unlike nearly all other Americans he had come to terms with the collapse of "Western values." So he was also right to identify the "so-called sexual revolution" with "alley-cat morality." Will Percy's is a deeper and wider, much less specifically southern, version of the aristocratic view of Ed Barrett and Aunt Emily that democratic Americans have no idea how to live as human beings because the classical and Christian defenses of human purpose and dignity have collapsed.

But predictions of "decline and fall," Walker cautions, are seductive. The apocalyptic view that the moral and political world collapses as it moves from aristocracy to democracy does not take into account all the available evidence. Will, in fact, was blind to the injustice of his own time. He did not see the connection between his magnanimity and his self-interest. He was certainly naïve about the way the sharecropping system was implemented—"naïve, even about his own managers." Magnanimity might almost replace justice if everyone were magnanimous. But that virtue is too rare. Its paternalism keeps people childlike who, in fact, need not be. Uncle Will had the moral and political shortcomings that Tocqueville finds characteristic of even the best of aristocrats. For Percy, like Tocqueville, there is "the sacred right which must be accorded the indi-

vidual, whether deemed insolent or not," and the origin of the understanding of the "intrinsically precious" individual is Christian (*SSL*, 86).

Did Will, Walker adds, predict the "very homely, yet surely unprecedented social gains that have come to pass" during the time of moral
collapse? Ours is also a time of important improvements in the conditions for the poor, for the "working man," for black working men and
women in particular. Honor and excellence have in many respects been
displaced by mediocrity and worse, but that is not the whole story: "for
the first time in history a poor boy, black or white, has a chance to get an
education, become what he wants to become, doctor, lawyer, even read
Lanterns on the Levee and write poetry on his own, and . . . not a few men,
black and white, have just done that." To some extent, excellence or at
least opportunities for excellence have been universalized and generalized. Democracy could not produce the author of *Lanterns*, but it could
give him a broad and somewhat appreciative audience.

So we have simultaneously witnessed a decline in excellence and
progress in justice and much of morality. And it is doubtful that Will's
view would have been expansive enough to see both. But for Walker, "it
appears that what is upon us is not a twilight of the gods but a very real
race between the powers of light and the powers of darkness, that time is
short and the issue very much in doubt." The Nietzschean view, here
attributed to Will, that "the gods" or idealism have disappeared from the
West is compared with the Christian confrontation between light and
darkness, good and evil, God and the devil. Like Tocqueville, Percy says
that catastrophe is not inevitable, and the reconciliation of moral nobility with justice—natural excellence with Christian psychology—is up to
us. There is "a glimmer of hope" in our social and political situation, but
only a Christian realist, one who owes more than a little to aristocratic
concerns and aristocratic philosophy but is neither a secular aristocrat
nor a secular democrat (for whom very little now is wrong), can see it
clearly. Percy chooses, for Christian reasons, justice over excellence. He,

like Tocqueville, chooses God's view, but with less reservation, because he chooses more clearly out of love. But he also chooses human distinctiveness and excellence against those who would, in the name of democracy, deny them. He affirms beings who are capable of wondering and wandering, and so living and dying well.

Will Percy saw in his time only irreversible moral and political decline and fall. And so he washed his hands of political life, believing nothing could be done to make America better. He wrongly thought that most human beings had become incapable of being loved as human beings. Walker Percy, the Christian who accepted, in love, the justice of democracy and who had some hope for human choice even in our time, continues to ask what can be done. For both the South in general and southern poets and novelists in particular, he wrote, "The challenge will simply be *what to do* in the face of the peculiar nature of the economic victory of the Sunbelt and the ongoing Los Angelization of the Southern community" (*SSL,* 166). Percy the Christian criticized the aristocrats for being too apolitical. Tocqueville, of course, criticized aristocrats for their unreasonable despair, but he also criticized the Christians for their apolitical hope.

But Percy did have hope, a hope that was based on his conviction that our true home lies elsewhere, and that this fact is the most reasonable explanation for our experiences of homelessness. But hope for Percy also meant the persistence of human nature in all its complexity, the being who is social, political, spiritual, and philosophical. Given human freedom and responsibility, Tocqueville and Percy agreed, the future is in "doubt"; we do not know so much not to believe that it is largely in our hands. For Percy, our hopes and fears in this world are rooted in "the strange human creature himself," "an admixture"—of good and evil, grace and the demonic, courage and cowardice—who is "now . . . perhaps stranger than ever" (*SSL,* 36). The truth is there are still aliens in America, and their inability to be more than ambiguously at home is the strange truth about our souls.

Introduction

1. David Brooks, *Bobos in Paradise: The New Upper Class and How They Got There* (New York: Simon and Schuster, 2000); Dinesh D'Souza, *The Virtue of Prosperity: Finding Values in an Age of Affluence* (New York: Free Press, 2000); Francis Fukuyama, *The Great Disruption: Human Nature and the Reconstitution of Social Order* (New York: Free Press, 1999); Alan Wolfe, *One Nation, After All* (New York: Viking, 1998) and *Moral Freedom: The Search for Virtue in a World of Choice* (New York: Viking, 2001); Tom Wolfe, *Hooking Up* (New York: Farrar, Straus, and Giroux, 2000). For the rest of this chapter, I am going to follow the example of these fine authors and dispense with notes.

Chapter 1

1. Francis Fukuyama, *The End of History and the Last Man* (New York: Free Press, 1992).
2. The most accessible, if incomplete, version of these lectures is Alexandre Kojève, *Introduction to the Reading of Hegel*, trans. James Nichols (New York: Basic Books, 1969). For a more detailed account of Kojève and his relation to Fukuyama, see chapter 1 of my *Postmodernism Rightly Understood: The Return to Realism in American Thought* (Lanham, Md.: Rowman & Littlefield, 1999).
3. See my "The Therapeutic Threat to Human Liberty: Pragmatism vs. Conserva-

tism on America and the West Today," in *Vital Remnants: America's Founding and the Western Tradition*, ed. Gary L. Gregg II (Wilmington, Del.: ISI Books, 1999), 305–29.

4. Alexis de Tocqueville, *Democracy in America*, vol. 2, pt. 1, ch. 8.

5. Richard Rorty, *Philosophy and Social Hope* (London: Penguin Books, 1999), especially ch.10.

6. For more on Rorty, see chapter 2 of my *Postmodernism Rightly Understood* and chapter 4 of this book.

7. Marx's clearest expression of this point is in his "On the Jewish Question."

8. See the Hegelian history of America presented in Rorty's *Achieving Our Country: Leftist Thought in Twentieth-Century America* (Cambridge, Mass.: Harvard University Press, 1998), especially his account of the sixties, with his remark on the disappearance of the illusion of the soul among intellectuals "around 1910" (*Philosophy and Social Hope*, 168).

9. Aleksandr Solzhenitsyn, "Address to the International Academy of Philosophy in Liechtenstein (September 14, 1993)," in *The Russian Question at the End of the Twentieth Century* (New York: Farrar, Straus, and Giroux, 1995), 112–28. This speech is clearly a post–Cold War update and modification of Solzhenitsyn's famous 1978 Harvard Address ("A World Split Apart," in *East and West* [New York: Harper Perennial, 1980], 39–71). This summary is of the 1993 address with the 1978 one in mind.

10. Consider how outdated my "The Dissident Criticism of America," in *The American Experiment*, ed. P. Lawler and R. Schaefer (Lanham, Md.: Rowman & Littlefield, 1994), seems now.

11. See my "Havel's Postmodern View of Man in the Cosmos," *Perspectives on Political Science* 26 (winter 1997).

12. Daniel J. Mahoney, "The Ascent from Modernity: Solzhenitsyn on 'Repentance and Self-Limitation in the Life of Nations,'" *Faith, Reason, and Political Life Today*, ed. P. Lawler and D. McConkey (Lanham, Md.: Lexington Books, 2001), ch. 7.

13. Here I am thinking of Leo Strauss, Eric Voegelin, and Hannah Arendt, in that order. And I am not forgetting their common indebtedness to Heidegger.

14. These thoughts inform all of Percy's work, both his novels and philosophical essays. See my *Postmodernism Rightly Understood*, chs. 3 and 4. For a quick and exciting entry into Percy's concerns, see the summary he wrote of his novel *The Last Gentleman*, quoted in Patrick H. Samway's *Walker Percy: A Life* (New York: Farrar, Straus, and Giroux, 1997), 241–42. The modern world has come to an end through some catastrophe, and "the strange new world," indefinitely called "post-modern," is still really "the as yet unnamed Time After."

15. See Rorty, *Philosophy and Social Hope*, 190–97. Heidegger's thought is useful to the extent that we can separate it from his political views and moral character!

16. Richard Rorty, *Truth and Progress* (Cambridge, Mass.: Cambridge University Press, 1998), ch. 12.

17. Tocqueville, Introduction to *Democracy in America*.

18. See my "Tocqueville on Pride, Interest, and Love," *Polity* 28 (winter 1995).

19. This is a general account of what is, in my view, the key argument of vol. 2 of *Democracy in America*.

20. Tocqueville, *Democracy in America*, vol. 2, pt. 2, chs. 2–5, 8–9, with vol. 2, pt. 4, chs. 6–7.

21. Tocqueville, *Democracy in America*, vol. 2, pt. 1, ch. 17 on poetry or the representation of the ideal.

22. Tocqueville, *Democracy in America*, vol. 2, pt. 2, chs. 13 and 16.

23. Allan Bloom, *The Closing of the American Mind* (New York: Simon and Schuster, 1987).

24. Wolfe, *One Nation, After All*.

25. My general view of the relationship between the sixties and eighties is indebted to Mark Lilla, "A Tale of Two Reactions," *The New York Review of Books* 45 (May 14, 1998).

26. Rorty, *Philosophy and Social Hope*, xii.

27. Harvey C. Mansfield, "A Nation of Consenting Adults," *The Weekly Standard*, (16 November 1998).

28. Jeremy Rabkin in "The Culture War That Isn't" (*Policy Review* [August/September 1999]), documents and criticizes this withdrawal. Rabkin says it is plain un-American not to pursue religious objectives through political means.

29. Brooks, *Bobos in Paradise*.

30. Alan Wolfe, "The Greening of America," *New Republic* (June 12, 2000): 40–41.

31. Waller R. Newell, *What Is a Man?* (New York: Regan Books, 2000). My discussion is of Newell's concluding reflections to this wonderful collection.

32. See especially Walker Percy, *Lost in the Cosmos: The Last Self-Help Book* (New York: Farrar, Straus, and Giroux, 1983).

33. Peter D. Kramer, *Listening to Prozac* (New York: Penguin, 1997), ch. 9: "The Message in the Capsule." This chapter is an extended response to Percy's philosophic *The Message in the Bottle* (New York: Farrar, Straus, and Giroux, 1975).

34. Peter D. Kramer, "The Valorization of Sadness: Alienation and the Melancholic Temperament," *Hastings Center Report* 30 (March/April 2000).

35. Fukuyama, *The Great Disruption*. In the next chapter, I criticize Fukuyama for not reconciling the naturalism of that book with what he says in "Second Thoughts" (*The National Interest*, no. 56 [summer 1999]) about the likely biotechnological destruction of human nature. That is what I try to do here, drawing on the valuable scientific information Fukuyama presents in that article.

Chapter 2

1. For the details supporting the comments on Rorty made in this article, see my "The Therapeutic Threat to Human Liberty" and *Postmodernism Rightly Understood*, ch. 2.

2. For the latest and a particularly eloquent and comprehensive statement concerning the danger to human liberty and dignity of the contemporary interdependence of biological rhetoric and biotechnology, see Leon R. Kass, "The Moral Meaning of Genetic Technology," *Commentary* 108 (September 1999), 32–38.

3. This summary of Percy's thought presented here is based primarily on his *Lost in the Cosmos* and *The Thanatos Syndrome* (New York: Farrar, Straus, and Giroux, 1987). For more details, see my *Postmodernism Rightly Understood*, chs. 3 and 4.

4. Fukuyama, *The End of History and the Last Man*.

5. Fukuyama, *The Great Disruption.*
6. For more on Fukuyama's confused debt to Kojève, see my *Postmodernism Rightly Understood*, ch. 1.
7. Fukuyama, "Second Thoughts."

Chapter 3

1. For a very clear and accessible account of the relationships among Plato, Socrates, and Aristophanes presented here, see Mary P. Nichols, *Socrates and the Political Community: An Ancient Debate* (Albany, N.Y.: State University of New York Press, 1987). The view of Percy given here is presented at much greater length in my *Postmodernism Rightly Understood*, chs. 3 and 4. Also see my "Walker Percy: Catholic Socratic?" *Modern Age* 40 (spring 1998), 226–31.
2. Carl Sagan, *Pale Blue Dot: A Vision of the Human Future in Space* (New York: Random House, 1994).
3. For this line of criticism of Sagan, see the work of the physicist Paul Davies, including *Are We Alone* (New York: Basic Books, 1995) and *The Fifth Miracle: The Search for the Origin and Meaning of Life* (New York: Simon and Schuster, 1999).
4. Carl Sagan, *The Demon-Haunted World* (New York: Random House, 1995), 396.
5. Carl Sagan, *Contact: A Novel* (New York: Simon and Schuster, 1985).
6. Sagan, *Cosmos* (New York: Ballantine Books, 1985; first published 1980), 255–58.
7. Sagan, *Cosmos*, 269.
8. Walker Percy, *The Moviegoer* (New York: Alfred A. Knopf, 1961).
9. On Percy's Thomistic realism, see my *Postmodernism Rightly Understood*, ch. 3.
10. Parts of this account of the second part of the space odyssey are borrowed from *Postmodernism Rightly Understood*, ch. 3.

Chapter 4

1. Richard Rorty, *Contingency, Irony, and Solidarity* (Cambridge: Cambridge University Press, 1989), xv.
2. For an account of Rorty's thought prior to his two most recent books, see my *Postmodernism Rightly Understood*, ch.2.
3. Nietzsche, "Maxims and Arrows" (no. 12), *The Twilight of the Idols*, as quoted by Rorty, *Truth and Progress*, 324 n41.
4. See Rorty's review of Bloom, "That Old-Time Philosophy," *The New Republic* (4 April 1988): 28–33.
5. Rorty, *Contingency, Irony, and Solidarity*, 196.
6. The phrase "intellectual probity" is not Rorty's. It is drawn from Leo Strauss's criticism of Nietzsche. I was reminded of its relevance for understanding the limits of rationalism by Peter Berkowitz, "The Reason of Revelation: The Jewish Thought of Leo Strauss," *The Weekly Standard* 3 (25 May 1998): 31–34.
7. The idea of connecting Rorty's and the Socratics' pragmatic concerns came to me from Patrick Glynn, *God: The Evidence* (Rocklin, Calif.: Prima Publishing, 1997), 144–45.

8. Rorty recommends that Americans admire Havel's deeds but ignore the words with which he explained them (*Truth and Progress,* 236–43). See my "The Dissident Criticism of America."

Chapter 5

1. Mansfield has written on Aristotle, Burke, Marx, Machiavelli, Locke, Tocqueville, Rawls, and many other thinkers and on all sorts of political issues. For an introduction to his thought, see his *America's Constitutional Soul* (Baltimore: Johns Hopkins University Press, 1991) and *Machiavelli's Virtue* (Chicago: University of Chicago Press, 1996). A quick search of the Internet will give you some sense of the controversy he has engendered.

2. James W. Ceaser, *Presidential Selection: Theory and Development* (Princeton, N.J.: Princeton University Press, 1979); *Reforming the Reforms* (New York: Harper and Row, 1982), and a variety of articles and chapters.

3. Harvey C. Mansfield Jr., *Taming the Prince: The Ambivalence of Modern Executive Power* (New York: Free Press, 1989).

4. James W. Ceaser, *Liberal Democracy and Political Science* (Baltimore: Johns Hopkins University Press, 1990).

5. James W. Ceaser, *Reconstructing America: The Symbol of America in Modern Thought* (New Haven, Conn.: Yale University Press, 1997). Hereinafter, my discussion of Ceaser is based on his *Liberal Democracy and Political Science* and *Reconstructing America.* I take a minimalist approach to notes throughout this chapter.

6. See Ceaser, *Reconstructing America,* 249.

7. All comments on Rorty here are supported in my *Postmodernism Rightly Understood,* ch. 2.

8. Ceaser, *Reconstructing America,* 230.

9. Ceaser, *Reconstructing America,* 231.

10. See James W. Ceaser, "Toward a New Public Philosophy," published on-line by the American Enterprise Institute (1999), 3 (www.aei.org/bradley/b1O30899.htm); and Ceaser, *Reconstructing America,* 229.

11. Ceaser, "Toward a New Public Philosophy," 3.

12. Richard Rorty, "Marxists, Straussians, and Pragmatists," *Raritan* 18 (fall 1998): 128–36. (Rorty seems to make clear his criticism of the Straussians' undemocratic imperialism by calling Ceaser "Caesar.")

13. Ceaser, "Toward a New Public Philosophy," 12–13.

14. See my "The Dissident Criticism of America."

15. See my *Postmodernism Rightly Understood.*

16. "No greater document exists in the annals of human freedom than the Declaration of Independence, which bears no trace of the influence of natural history" (Ceaser, *Reconstructing America,* 53). Surely it is strange that Ceaser's theoretical American chauvinism includes no analysis of this greatness.

17. "An ironic political science is needed for an ironic world" (Ceaser, *Reconstructing America,* 231).

18. Ceaser, *Reconstructing America,* 231.

19. Pierre Manent, *Modern Liberty and Its Discontents,* ed. D. Mahoney and P. Seaton

(Lanham, Md.: Rowman and Littlefield, 1998), 217–29.

20. Fukuyama, *The End of History and the Last Man*. In *Reconstructing America,* Ceaser comments: "Not even Kojève's most famous follower, Francis Fukuyama, was able to live up to Kojève's rigorous standard . . . Kojève . . . unflinchingly followed his philosophical premise to its conclusion" (220). See my *Postmodernism Rightly Understood,* ch. 1, for more on this difference between Kojève and Fukuyama.

21. Fukuyama, *The Great Disruption*. See ch. 2 of this book.

22. Fukuyama, "Second Thoughts."

23. Ceaser, *Liberal Democracy and Political Science,* 146.

24. Allan Bloom, *The Closing of the American Mind.* For what is said here about Bloom and the connection between Bloom and Rorty, see my *Postmodernism Rightly Understood,* ch. 2.

25. Rorty, *Philosophy and Social Hope,* 129. There is actually a good deal of discussion of Straussians in this book (see the index for references to Strauss and Bloom). And the attentive reader will discover that Rorty is not afraid to agree with Bloom on a crucial point.

26. Rorty, *Philosophy and Social Hope,* 218.

27. See Strauss's remarks on Kojève in Leo Strauss, *On Tyranny: Including the Strauss-Kojève Correspondence,* ed. V. Gourevitch and M. Roth (New York: Free Press, 1991).

28. Ceaser, "Toward a New Public Philosophy," 8–12.

29. Michael P. Zuckert, *The Natural Rights Republic: Studies in the Foundation of the American Political Tradition* (Notre Dame, Ind.: University of Notre Dame Press, 1997).

30. James W. Ceaser, "The Party of Constitutionalism," *The Weekly Standard* (22 February 1999).

31. See my *Postmodernism Rightly Understood,* chs. 3 and 4.

32. Tocqueville, *Democracy in America,* vol. 2, pt. 2, chs. 12–13.

33. Tocqueville, *Democracy in America,* vol. 2, pt. 1, ch, 7; vol. 2, pt. 4, ch. 6.

34. Ceaser, *Reconstructing America,* 212.

35. Ceaser, "Toward a New Public Philosophy," 13–14.

Chapter 6

1. William A. Galston, *Liberal Purposes: Goods, Virtues, and Diversity in the Liberal State* (Cambridge: Cambridge University Press, 1991). Most of this chapter consists of an analysis of the overarching arguments of this book.

2. William A. Galston, "Socratic Reason and Lockean Rights: The Place of the University in Liberal Democracy," in *Essays on the Closing of the American Mind,* ed. Robert Stone (Chicago: Chicago Review Press, 1989), 121.

3. William A. Galston, "Socratic Reason and Lockean Rights: The Place of the University in Liberal Democracy," in *Essays on the Closing of the American Mind,* 121.

4. William A. Galston, "What Is Living and What Is Dead in Kant's Practical Philosophy?" in *Kant and Political Philosophy,* ed. Ronald Beiner (New Haven, Conn.: Yale University Press, 1993), 208–9.

5. Galston, "Socratic Reason and Lockean Rights," 122–23.

6. William A. Galston, "Cosmopolitan Altruism," *Social Philosophy and Policy* 10

(winter 1993): 118–34.

7. William A. Galston, "False Universality: Infinite Personality and Finite Existence in Unger's *Politics*," *Northwestern Law Review* 81 (summer 1987), 759.

8. Galston, "What Is Living and What Is Dead in Kant's Practical Philosophy?" 219.

9. William A. Galston, "Equality of Opportunity and Liberal Theory," in *Justice, Equality, Here and Now*, ed. Frank Lucash (Ithaca, N.Y.: Cornell University Press, 1986), 93.

10. Tocqueville, *Democracy in America*, vol. 2, pt. 3, chs. 8–12.

11. Tocqueville, *Democracy in America*, vol. 2, pt. 2, ch. 12.

12. Galston, "False Universality," 763–64.

13. William A. Galston, "Tocqueville on Liberalism and Religion," *Social Research* 54 (autumn 1987), 517.

14. Galston, "What Is Living and What Is Dead in Kant's Practical Philosophy?" 225–32.

15. Galston, "What Is Living and What Is Dead in Kant's Practical Philosophy?" 225.

16. Tocqueville, *Democracy in America*, vol. 2, pt. 2, ch. 10.

17. Galston, "Cosmopolitan Altruism," 118–28.

18. Galston, "Cosmopolitan Altruism," 131–32.

Chapter 7

1. John Courtney Murray, *We Hold These Truths: Catholic Reflections on the American Proposition* (New York: Sheed & Ward, 1960).

2. The interpretation of Lincoln here follows that of Harry Jaffa in *Crisis of the House Divided* (Chicago: University of Chicago Press, 1982).

3. The phrase "political religion" comes from Lincoln's Address to Men's Lyceum (1838). For a criticism of Lincoln's reductionism, see John Gueguen, "Modernity in American Ideology," *Independent Journal of Philosophy* 4 (1980), 79–87.

4. For interpretations of the American founding that stress its rationalism, see Harry Jaffa, *How to Think about the American Revolution* (Durham, N.C.: Carolina Academic Press, 1978); Walter Berns, *The First Amendment and the Future of American Democracy* (New York: Basic Books, 1976); and Thomas Pangle, *The Spirit of Modern Republicanism* (Chicago: University of Chicago Press, 1987).

5. Our problem, then, was not communism at all: "I would here maintain that Communism is not the basic cause of our present confusions, uncertainties, insecurities, falterings and failures of purpose," says Murray. "I would go so far as to maintain that, if the Communist empire were to fall apart tomorrow, and if Communist ideology were to disintegrate with it, our problems would not be solved. In fact, they would be worse in many ways" (*We Hold These Truths,* 88). And, of course, he was right.

6. Murray, "Reversing the Secularist Drift," *Thought* 24 (March 1949), 37.

7. For a discussion of the nihilistic extremes of relativism and decisionism, see my essay "Relativism, American Education, and Democracy," *Southeastern Political Review* 16 (1989), 1–16. My categories of relativism and decisionism are the equivalent of Ernest Fortin's categories of relativism and fanaticism; see "Natural Law and Social Justice," *American Journal of Jurisprudence* 30 (1986), 20.

8. See Leo Strauss, *Natural Right and History* (Chicago: University of Chicago Press, 1953), 7-8.

9. See John Finnis, *Natural Law and Natural Rights* (New York: Oxford University Press, 1980) and Alasdair MacIntyre, *After Virtue* (Notre Dame, Ind.: University of Notre Dame Press, 1982). For a critique of the failure of these authors to deal with natural or metaphysical issues, see Russell Hittinger, "After MacIntyre: Natural Law Theory, Virtue Ethics, and Eudaimonia," *International Philosophical Quarterly* 29 (1989), 44-61.

10. Fortin, "Natural Law and Social Justice," 1.

11. Fortin, "Natural Law and Social Justice," 20.

12. Fortin, "Natural Law and Social Justice," 19.

13. Fortin, "Rational Theologians and Irrational Philosophers: A Straussian Perspective," *Interpretation* 12 (1984), 356.

14. Fortin says that, even for Thomas Aquinas, "the status of the natural law as a philosophical concept was at best problematic" ("The New Rights Theory and Natural Law," *Review of Politics* 44 [1982], 609).

15. Fortin, "Rational Theologians and Irrational Philosophers," 356.

16. On this, see Robert W. McElroy, *The Search for an American Public Theology: The Contribution of John Courtney Murray* (New York: Paulist Press, 1989), 156-57.

17. Murray, quoted by McElroy, 101.

18. Murray, "Leo XIII: Separation of Church and State," *Theological Studies* 14 (1953), 160.

19. See Gueguen, "Modernity in American Ideology" and my essay "The Limits of the 'Secular Humanist' Interpretation of the Constitution," *Journal of Political Science* 9 (1988), 49-58. And, for a critique of the pretentious, even tyrannical rationalism of the unamended Constitution's understanding of nature, see Aristocrotis, "The Government of Nature Delineated" in vol. 3 of *The Complete Anti-Federalist*, ed. Herbert J. Storing and Murray Dry (Chicago: University of Chicago Press, 1981), 196-213. Also worthy of note is E. A. Goerner's *Peter and Caesar* (New York: Herder & Herder, 1962); Goerner describes Murray's history as a "noble, Platonic tale" (182).

20. For an interpretation of the place of the God of the philosophers in the founding of America, see Paul H. Rahe, "Church and State," *The American Spectator* (January 1986) 18-21.

21. See Michael Zuckert, "Self-Evident Truth and the Declaration of Independence," *Review of Politics* 49 (1987), 319-39.

22. For Murray's criticism of Vatican II's Declaration, see Francis Canavan, "Murray on Vatican II's *Declaration of Religious Freedom,*" *Communio* 9 (1982), 404-5.

23. Murray, "The Declaration on Religious Freedom," in *Religious Liberty: An End and a Beginning*, ed. John Courtney Murray (New York: Macmillan, 1966), 37-42.

24. For historical confirmation of this point, see Gary Glenn, "Forgotten Purposes of the First Amendment Religion Clauses," *Review of Politics* 49 (summer 1987), 340-67.

25. John Courtney Murray, "Freedom of Religion: The Ethical Problem," *Theological Studies* 6 (1945), 256-57.

26. On the perennial relevance of the critical thrust of orthodox Christian theology,

see my essay "Thoughts on America's 'Catholic Moment,'" *Political Science Reviewer* 17 (1988), 206-8; and "Natural Law and the American Regime: Murray's *We Hold These Truths.*" *Communio* 9 (1982), 370-71.

27. On Brownson, see my "Brownson's American Republic," an introduction to a new edition of Orestes A. Brownson, *The American Republic* (Wilmington, Del.: ISI Books, forthcoming).

28. Strauss, *Natural Right and History*, 160.

29. Murray, "The Return to Tribalism," *Catholic Mind* 60 (January 1962), 8.

30. For a good treatment of Heidegger's thought on this point, see Harry Neumann, "What Is Bigotry?" *Modern Age* 31 (1987), 45-51.

31. One issue not addressed here is the significance of the disintegration of the natural-law consensus in the Catholic intellectual community since Murray wrote. The destruction of the consensus has, in fact, critically energized those who still defend natural law. According to Ronald Lawler, "These are good days to be Catholic scholars. . . .When I was a young student, almost all Catholic moralists taught what the Church authentically taught. But as I look over the moral texts I knew in those days, I am impressed by their poor quality. When the teachings of faith were assailed in the revolutions of our time, it became necessary for Catholic scholars to provide far better defenses for positions that were assailed on every side" ("The Catholic Vision of Higher Education," in *Catholic Higher Education*, ed. Paul Williams [Scranton, Pa.: Northeast Books, 1989], 72). According to Murray, crisis requires and hence brings forth radical thought. For evidence that these are good days to be natural law thinkers, see Hittinger, "After MacIntyre" and Fortin, "Natural Law and Social Justice" and "The New Rights Theory and Natural Law."

32. Kenneth R. Craycraft, Jr., *The American Myth of Religious Freedom* (Dallas: Spence Publishing, 1999).

33. Marc D. Guerra, "Christianity's Epicurean Temptation," *Faith, Reason, and Political Life Today*, ed. P. Lawler and D. McConkey (Lanham, Md.: Lexington Books, 2001).

34. Craycraft, *The American Myth of Religious Freedom*, 186, note 15.

35. Craycraft, *The American Myth of Religious Freedom*, 187, note 15.

36. See my *Postmodernism Rightly Understood*.

Chapter 8

1. Barry Alan Shain, *The Myth of American Individualism: The Protestant Origins of American Political Thought* (Princeton, N.J.: Princeton University Press, 1994).

2. Pangle, *The Spirit of Modern Republicanism*, 208.

3. Pangle, *The Spirit of Modern Republicanism*, 83.

4. For this view of Rorty, see my *Postmodernism Rightly Understood*, ch. 2.

5. Tocqueville, *Democracy in America*, vol. 2, pt. 2, chs. 8-13.

6. Tocqueville, *Democracy in America*, vol. 2, pt. 2, chs. 12-13.

7. Tocqueville, *Democracy in America*, vol. 2, pt. 1, chs. 1, 3-5, 7, 10, 16-17, 20.

8. Solzhenitsyn, "Address to the International Academy of Philosophy (14 September 1993," 120. See my *Postmodernism Rightly Understood*, chs. 3 and 4 on Percy.

9. Tocqueville, *Democracy in America*, volume 2, part 2, chapter 2 on individualism.

10. The text of Rousseau summarized here is, of course, the *Discourse on Inequality*. See my *Postmodernism Rightly Understood*, chapter 1, for the connection between Rousseau and the famous argument for the end of history of the Hegelian Alexandre Kojève.

11. Tocqueville, *Democracy in America*, vol. 2, pt. 1, ch. 5.

12. Tocqueville, *Democracy in America*, vol. 2, pt. 2, ch. 3.

13. Tocqueville, *Democracy in America*, vol. 2, pt. 2, ch. 15.

14. Tocqueville, *Democracy in America*, vol. 2, pt. 1, chs. 2 and 5.

15. Tocqueville, *Democracy in America*, vol. 1, pt. 2, ch. 9, "Religion, Considered as a Political Institution" with vol. 2, pt. 2, ch. 15.

16. Zuckert, *The Natural Rights Republic*, 87–89. Robert K. Faulkner, who also confidently presents Jefferson as simply a modern and largely Lockean liberal rationalist, says what Zuckert suggests: "the philosophic hedonism of Epicurus is not very important to Jefferson" ("Jefferson and the Enlightened Science of Liberty," *Reason and Republicanism: Thomas Jefferson's Legacy of Liberty*, ed. Gary L. McDowell and Sharon L. Noble [Lanham, Md.: Rowman and Littlefield, 1997], 43). But he really gives no argument for this position, and he asserts, quite implausibly, that Jefferson's Epicureanism is simply a rhetorical weapon against apolitical Christianity.

17. See Charles L. Griswold, Jr., "Rights and Wrongs: Jefferson, Slavery, and Philosophical Quandaries," *A Culture of Rights*, ed. Michael J. Lacey and Knud Haakenssen (New York, 1988), ch. 4.

18. The letters of Jefferson referred to in the text can be found in *The Life and Selected Writings of Thomas Jefferson*, ed. A. Koch and W. Peden (New York: The Modern Library, 1946). They can be also found in *Thomas Jefferson: Writings*, ed. M. Peterson (New York: Library of America, 1984). My earlier and unfocused account of Jefferson's mixture of Christianity and Epicureanism is "Classical Ethics, Jefferson's Christian Epicureanism, and American Morality," *Perspectives on Political Science* 20 (winter 1991): 17–22.

19. My remarks on Epicurus and Epicureanism are indebted throughout to Griswold, "Rights and Wrongs," 154–69.

20. See Griswold, "Rights and Wrongs," 156, note 33 for references to the many times Jefferson identified happiness with tranquility in his letters.

21. Eva Brann, *Paradoxes of Education in a Republic* (Chicago: University of Chicago Press, 1979), 86.

22. Griswold, "Rights and Wrongs," 161. On the basis of his Epicurean theory, Griswold remarks, "Jefferson's participation in public life becomes difficult to explain" (161, note 47). But the same can be said for his Lockean theory, which also holds that political life is not intrinsically fulfilling for human beings, that they are not political animals. Epicureanism, the theory of many Roman political leaders, seems a better way of articulating the tension between political ambition and personal tranquility. It gives a less abstract or more complete account of human hopes and fears.

23. See Griswold, "Rights and Wrongs," 167–68.

24. The best account of Jefferson's view of the moral sense is Jean M. Yarbrough, *Thomas Jefferson and the Formation of the American Character* (Lawrence, Kans.: Uni-

versity Press of Kansas, 1998), ch. 2.

25. See Thomas Jefferson, *Notes on the State of Virginia,* Query XIV on the reconciliation of black intellectual and physical inferiority with their moral equality to whites.

26. See Griswold, "Rights and Wrongs," 176.

27. See Frank Balog, "The Scottish Enlightenment and the Liberal Political Tradition," *Confronting the Constitution,* ed. A. Bloom (Washington, D.C.: AEI Press, 1990), 196–98.

28. See especially Thomas Aquinas, *Summa Theologiae,* II-II, question 56 with question 65.

29. Balog, "The Scottish Enlightenment and the Liberal Political Tradition," 198–99.

30. For this view of Rorty, see my *Postmodernism Rightly Understood,* ch. 2.

31. Brann, *Paradoxes of Education in a Republic,* 92.

32. Griswold, "Rights and Wrongs," 150–52.

33. For abundant evidence of Jefferson's hatred of Calvinism, see Griswold, "Rights and Wrongs," 187, note 106.

34. Jefferson, *Notes on Virginia,* Query XVIII, quoted by Zuckert, *The Natural Rights Republic,* 201.

35. See Thomas Pangle, *The Ennobling of Democracy* (Chicago: University of Chicago Press, 1992), 172.

36. Jaffa, *The Crisis of the House Divided,* 324.

37. Marvin Meyers, ed., *The Mind of the Founder: Sources of the Political Thought of James Madison,* revised edition (Hanover, N.H.: University Press of New England, 1981), 7.

38. Meyers, ed., *The Mind of the Founder,* 187.

39. George Anastaplo, "American Constitutionalism and the Virtue of Prudence," *Abraham Lincoln, The Gettysburg Address, and American Constitutionalism,* ed. Leo Paul S. de Alvarez (Dallas: University of Dallas Press, 1976), note 52.

40. Rorty, *Achieving Our Country.*

41. Manent, *Modern Liberty and Its Discontents,* 102–3.

42. Walker Percy, *Signposts in a Strange Land* (New York: Farrar, Straus, and Giroux, 1991), 228–29. See my *Postmodernism Rightly Understood,* ch. 3.

Chapter 9

1. This wholly Lockean view of the Declaration is best defended by Michael Zuckert in *The Natural Rights Republic.* See chapter 8 of this book.

2. Murray, *We Hold These Truths.*

3. See Zuckert, *The Natural Rights Republic,* ch. 6.

4. Shain, in *The Myth of American Individualism,* ably shows—and overstates—the Calvinism and communalism of American life at the time of the founding. An elegant summary of Shain's Christian, communal, and traditional understanding of the eighteenth-century American view of liberty is "Liberty and License: The American Founding and the Western Conception of Freedom," *Vital Remnants: America's Founding and the Western Tradition,* ed. G. Gregg II (Wilmington, Del.: ISI Books, 1999). All students of the Straussian view of the founding should read this article as a quick and maybe welcome reminder of their own partisanship.

5. See Pierre Manent, *The City and Man* (Princeton, N.J.: Princeton University Press, 1998), 200–203.

6. Here, of course, I am reading Madison's "Memorial and Remonstrance" with his "Property" (29 March 1792). Both of these are found in Meyers, ed., *The Mind of the Founder.*

7. Thomas Jefferson, *Notes on the State of Virginia*, Query 17. Every Jeffersonian text I mention can be found in *Thomas Jefferson: Writings.*

8. For an introduction to dissident thought, see my "The Dissident Criticism of America."

9. Fukuyama, *The End of History and the Last Man.*

10. Fukuyama, "Second Thoughts." See also chapter 2 of this book. In "Second Thoughts," Fukuyama sees the end of distinctively human nature as more or less inevitable. But in his "A Milestone in the Conquest of Nature," *Wall Street Journal* (June 27, 2000), he urges human resistance to emerging biotechnological advances.

11. See Percy, *Signposts in a Strange Land,* 228–29.

12. As Walker Percy often explains, but perhaps best in *Lost in the Cosmos.*

13. See my *Postmodernism Rightly Understood,* ch. 4, for a defense of this position, using Walker Percy's novel *The Thanatos Syndrome.*

14. This is the early and true interpretation of the relationship between the founding and Lincoln by Harry Jaffa in *Crisis of the House Divided.*

15. See my "Murray's Transformation of the American Proposition," *We Hold These Truths and More,* ed. D. D'Elia and S. Krason (Steubenville, Ohio: Franciscan University Press, 1991).

16. That Jefferson was an Epicurean is most ably demonstrated by Griswold in his "Rights and Wrongs." See also chapter 8 of this book. See the references to many of Jefferson's private letters in both places. Begin with his letter to Dr. Benjamin Rush (21 April 1803).

17. See Zuckert, *The Natural Rights Republic,* 63, for the neglected, Pascalian dimension of Jefferson's thought.

18. For support for the discussion of Rorty here, see my *Postmodernism Rightly Understood,* ch. 2.

19. On this point, see Rorty, *Truth and Progress,* ch. 12. See also chapter 4 of this book.

20. Zuckert, *The Natural Rights Republic,* 103.

21. Ibid., 255n.

22. See my "The Therapeutic Threat to Human Liberty."

23. Michael P. Zuckert, "Completing the Constitution: The Fourteenth Amendment and Constitutional Rights," *Publius* 22 (spring 1992).

24. Wilson Carey McWilliams, "Science and Freedom: America as the Technological Republic," *Technology in the Western Political Tradition,* ed. A. Melzer et al. (Ithaca, N.Y.: Cornell University Press, 1993), 105.

25. For Rorty's education based on the thought that there is no truth, see his *Philosophy and Social Hope,* ch. 7.

26. See Rorty, *Achieving Our Country.*

27. Thomas G. West, *Vindicating the Founders* (Lanham, Md.: Rowman & Littlefield, 1997).

28. Much, although not all, of my discussion of Galston here is explored in greater detail in chapter 6 of this book.

29. Galston, *Liberal Purposes*, 280–81.

30. Ibid., 293.

31. Ibid., 292.

32. William A. Galston, "Policies for the 21st Century: Reexamining the Idea of Community," *Current* (October, 1998): 3–11.

33. Alan Ehrenhalt, *The Lost City: Discovering the Forgotten Virtues of Community in the Chicago of the 1950s* (New York: Basic Books, 1995).

34. William A. Galston, "Home of the Tolerant," *Public Interest* (fall, 1998), 121.

35. Galston, *Liberal Purposes*, 265–66.

36. Rabkin, "The Culture War That Isn't," 3–19. It is worth noting that Rabkin's argument against the cultural despair of religious conservatives mirrors Rorty's (in *Achieving Our Country*) against the Heideggerian cultural Left.

37. Gary D. Glenn and John Sacks, "Is American Democracy Safe for Catholicism?" *Review of Politics* 62 (winter 2000).

38. James Davison Hunter, *The Death of Character: Moral Education in an Age Without Good or Evil* (New York: Basic Books, 2000).

39. Hunter, *The Death of Character*, ch. 7.

40. Hunter, *The Death of Character*, 155.

41. Hunter, *The Death of Character*, 228.

42. Wolfe, *One Nation, After All.*

43. Hunter, *The Death of Character*, xv. For the pervasiveness of New Age pantheism among today's American "establishment," see David Brooks's *Bobos in Paradise.*

44. The progressive-orthodox distinction was made famous by James Davison Hunter in *Culture Wars: The Struggle to Define America* (New York: Basic Books, 1991). But my understanding of what orthodoxy is owes more to Chesterton.

45. Gertrude Himmelfarb, *One Nation: Two Cultures* (New York: Knopf, 1999), 91–92.

46. Robert William Fogel, *The Fourth Great Awakening and the Future of Egalitarianism* (Chicago: University of Chicago Press, 2000).

47. Any full account of the persistence of genuinely Christian belief in America would also have to include an analysis of the effects of the waves of immigration and the peculiar nature of the South—its aristocracy, its slavery, and its humiliating defeat.

48. Hunter, *The Death of Character*, 228–31.

49. Glynn, *God: The Evidence.*

50. This ambivalence is what shines through more than anything else in the interviews of middle-class Americans today described in Wolfe, *One Nation, After All.*

51. Bloom, *The Closing of the American Mind*, 118–21.

52. Christopher Lasch, *The Revolt of the Elites and the Betrayal of Democracy* (New York: W.W. Norton, 1995). On Lasch's realistic moral populism, see my *Postmodernism Rightly Understood*, ch. 5.

53. Lasch, *The Revolt of the Elites*, 242.

54. Lasch, *The Revolt of the Elites*, 243.

55. Lasch, *The Revolt of the Elites*, 228.

56. Lasch, *The Revolt of the Elites*, 244.

57. Marion Montgomery, *The Truth of Things: Liberal Arts and the Recovery of Reality* (Dallas: Spence Publishing, 1999), 5. So Adriaan T. Peperzak is able to claim that there really is something called the philosophy of religion (*Reason in Faith: On the Relevance of Christian Spirituality for Philosophy* [Mahwah, N.J.: Paulist Press, 1999], chapter 7). Peperzak explains that "The indispensability of preflective thinking about religion refers to a complete theory of the relationships between rationality, thinking, reflection, and affectivity" (86–87). And "A phenomenology of radical gratitude, hope, trust, delight, wonderment, and inner peace discovers their basic and irreplaceable significance when it understands them as modes of contact with the truth of reality" (86).

58. Lasch, *The Revolt of the Elites*, 246.

59. See Solzhenitsyn, "Address to International Academy of Philosophy in Liechtenstein," (14 September 1993).

60. Lasch, *The Revolt of the Elites*, 92–116.

61. See my *The Restless Mind: Alexis de Tocqueville on the Origin and Perpetuation of Human Liberty* (Lanham, Md.: Rowman & Littlefield, 1993).

62. A good summary of Murray's strategy to counter liberal monism can be found in Craycraft, *The American Myth of Religious Freedom*, 102–20. Craycraft does go too far in presenting Murray as an anti-American. See 186–87, note 15, where Craycraft helpfully discusses the differences between his own and my interpretations of Murray. See also ch. 7 of this book.

Chapter 10

1. Tocqueville, *Democracy in America*, "Author's Introduction."

2. On the Pascalian dimension of Tocqueville's thought, see my *The Restless Mind*. For a compressed version, see my "The Human Condition: Tocqueville's Debt to Rousseau and Pascal," in *Liberty, Equality, Democracy*, ed. E. Nolla (New York: New York University Press, 1992).

3. Walker Percy, letter to Caroline Gordon (April 6, 1962), quoted in Samway, *Walker Percy*, 224–25: "Actually I do not consider myself a novelist but a moralist or a propagandist. My spiritual father is Pascal (and/or Kierkegaard). . . . What I really want to do is to tell people what they must do and what they must believe if they want to live. Using every guile and low-handed trick in the book of course."

4. For this general view of Percy, see my *Postmodernism Rightly Understood*. Also see my "Walker Percy's Thought and Life," *The University Bookman* 38 (fall, 1998). On Tocqueville's view that he does not know how restore the vigor of American and Western faith, see *Democracy in America*, vol. 1-2, ch. 9, "The Main Causes That Make Religion Powerful in America," last paragraph. And so all he can advise is how to retain the residue of aristocratic faith that remains.

5. Percy, *Signposts in a Strange Land*, 261.

6. See the questions on the first page of *Lost in the Cosmos* and keep reading.

7. The compatibility of modern science with unfettered romanticism is one theme of Percy's *The Moviegoer* and persists throughout his work, culminating in *The Thanatos Syndrome*. See my *Postmodernism Rightly Understood*, chapter 4.

8. Percy, *Lost in the Cosmos*, 139.

9. *Conversations with Walker Percy*, edited by Lewis A. Lawson and Victor A. Kramer (Jackson: University Press of Mississippi, 1985), 12.

10. Percy, quoted in Samway, *Walker Percy*, 187.

11. See, for example, Percy, *Signposts in a Strange Land*, 191–96.

12. Walker Percy, *The Last Gentleman* (New York: Farrar, Straus, and Giroux, 1966; page references are to the Picador USA/Farrar edition, 1999).

13. See the write-up Percy did of *The Last Gentleman* for publicity purposes, which the publisher did not use (Samway, *Walker Percy*, 241–42).

14. See Percy's *The Thanatos Syndrome* and my *Postmodernism Rightly Understood*, ch. 4.

15. See Percy, *Conversations with Walker Percy*, 280–81 for his view of the importance of Guardini for his understanding of our "post-modern" world: "So I think the normal state for a man to find himself in is a state of confusion, spiritual disorientation, drawn in a sense to Christendom, but also repelled by the cultural nature of Christendom."

16. See my "Tocqueville on Pride, Interest, and Love."

17. The interpretation of Tocqueville in this paragraph is developed in my *The Restless Mind*.

18. Percy, *The Moviegoer*, 222–26.

19. Percy, *The Moviegoer*, 199 and passim.

20. See *Conversations with Walker Percy*, 253, where Percy connects the aristocratic criticisms of the two Wills, Barrett and his uncle.

21. Consider, for example, the otherwise excellent essays by Lewis A. Lawson: "Walker Percy's Southern Stoic," in *Following Percy: Essays on Walker Percy's Work* (Troy, N.Y.: Whitson Publishing Company, 1988); and "William Alexander Percy, Walker Percy, and the Apocalypse" in *Another Generation: Southern Fiction Since World War II* (Jackson, Miss.: University Press of Mississippi, 1984).

22. William Alexander Percy, *Lanterns on the Levee: Recollections of a Planter's Son* (Baton Rouge, La.: LSU Press, 1973; originally published by Knopf, 1941). This edition has an introduction by Walker Percy. This summary of some of the key features of Will Percy's recollections is probably all I will ever say about this genuinely remarkable and philosophic book. I do not intend to become known as an expert on a book that is obviously racist, aristocratic, and homosexual in its orientation. That's no way to get ahead in political science.

23. Percy talks about Uncle Will several times in *Conversations with Walker Percy*.

24. Percy, introduction to *Lanterns on the Levee*, x.

25. Percy, introduction to *Lanterns on the Levee*, xviii.

26. *Conversations with Walker Percy*, 308.

27. Percy, introduction to *Lanterns on the Levee*, xi.

28. *Conversations with Walker Percy*, 258.

29. Percy, introduction to *Lanterns on the Levee*, x.

30. Because Percy's introduction is quite short, I'm going to let the reader follow along now without tedious references to page numbers.

INDEX